FOREST ECOLOGY AND AGRICULTURE IN MUGHAL NORTH INDIA

Forest Ecology and Agriculture in Mughal North India

MOHD KAMRAN KHAN

MANOHAR
2026

Cover illustration: An illustrated Mughal Imperial Manuscript from the Collection of *Baburnama*, commissioned in the late 16th-century Akbari period. It is catalogued under accession number 50.336, Manuscript Department, National Museum, Janpath, New Delhi. The original painting is attributed to artist Narsi (signed in red ink). It features black buck, female deer, trees, and architectural elements.

First published 2026
First eBook edition 2026

ISBN 978-93-6080-554-8 (hardbound)
ISBN 978-93-6080-021-5 (eBook)

Published by
Ajay Kumar Jain *for*
Manohar Publishers & Distributors
4753/23 Ansari Road, Daryaganj
New Delhi 110 002

Typeset by Digital Print Hut

Cover design by Manoj Kumar

Printed and bound in India

To
My Amma and Abba

Contents

Illustrations

FIGURES

MAPS

Tables

Acknowledgements

I thank *Al Raheem* for everything.

I thank Mr. Ajay Kumar Jain and his entire Manohar Publishers & Distributors team for agreeing to publish my work. Secondly, I am thankful for the financial support rendered by the Indian Council of Historical Research (ICHR), New Delhi. Of course, the responsibility for the facts stated, and opinions expressed in this book is entirely mine and not of the Council who have extended a generous grant to support this publication.

I am deeply indebted to Dr. Vinod Kumar, ICHR, New Delhi, who helped me to get the travel grant. His support facilitated my visit to Lisbon, Portugal in 2019 to attend the *II International Meeting Histories and Environment: Shaping Landscape*. That visit opened many windows of perspective in my mind. I am thankful to Mr. Faiz Habib, cartographer, (CAS, Department of History, AMU) whose priceless expertise is visible in all the maps in this monograph.

I would like to express my sincere gratitude to Mr. Khatibur Rehman, the Deputy Curator of Manuscripts Department, National Museum, Janpath, New Delhi for his kind assistance in facilitating the collection of the Mughal painting featured on the cover page of this book. I would also like to thank, Daniel Patridge, Digital Imager (Royal Collection Trust, London) for providing several Mughal paintings used in this book. I am also thankful to Dr. Saurav Kumar Rai and Mr. Harish, who helped me in the Nehru Memorial Museum and Library, also known as the Prime Minister Museum and Library, New Delhi.

All the scholars who have worked on themes related to the theme of this book have contributed in making my vision on the subject clearer and I will always be indebted to them. I owe a lot to every teacher who has taught me at any level or in any way; right from my school onwards. Amongst the long list of influencers who have driven my dream to be a researcher and a teacher, I would love to mention Professor J.R. McNeill, Professor Naimur Rahman Farooqi, Professor Heeraman Tiwari, Professor Preeti Sharma, Professor Tabir Kalam, Professor Nishat Manzar, Late Professor Rizwan Qaiser, Professor Samina Hasan Siddiqui, Dr. Mayank Kumar, Dr. B.N. Prasad, Dr. Mohit Bishnoi, Dr. Iliyas Hussain and Dr. Rais Khan. I am grateful for the guidance and encouragement which I received from my M.Phil and PhD supervisors; Professor V.M. Ravi Kumar and Professor Farhat Nasreen. The ink of their pens will always remain mixed with the ink of my pen.

Words are insufficient to express gratitude to my mother Gulnara Begum, and father Afzarul Haque. Without their love and affection, I could never think of coming this far in my academic life. I am equally indebted to my wife Dr. Sadaf Jawed for her support and patience. She has been instrumental in reading and correcting the language of the draft. Her comments and suggestions made the draft more appealing and illustrative.

Sharing my thoughts on the forest ecology and agriculture of North India has only been possible because of the support of many. I thank everyone who has wished well for me.

New Delhi MOHD KAMRAN KHAN
17 April 2025

Abbreviations

AIN	*Ain-i-Akbari*
FRI	Forest Research Institute
HS	Historical Section
ICHR	Indian Council of Historical Research
IHCP	Indian History Congress Proceeding
JASB	*Journal of Asiatic Society of Bengal*
JP	Jaipur Records
JPHS	Journal of Pakistan Historical Society
MM	Maunder Minimum
NAI	National Archives of India
NGSI	National Geographical Society of India
NMML	Nehru Memorial Museum & Library
NWP	North-Western Provinces
OBC	Oriental Books Corporation
OUP	Oxford University Press
NBT	National Book Trust
RORI	Rajasthan Oriental Research Institute
RSAB	Rajasthan State Archives Bikaner

CHAPTER 1

Introduction

OVER THE LAST two decades, scholars have made significant efforts to define the terms 'environment' and 'ecology'. However, 'environmental history' or 'the history of the environment' are often used interchangeably, despite a substantial difference between them. This confusion arises due to the limited scholarly works on 'environmental history' or even 'environment and history'. Before we venture into the details, we need to grasp this disjuncture between 'environmental history' and 'the history of the environment'. The history of the environment deals with the evolution of the earth, the history of the formation of the earth, the role of climate and the evolution of the weather and interrogating the evolution of human life. This is dealt with by specialists; for example, geologists take care of the earth's geological history, paleobotanists take care of the evolution of flora and fauna and then zoologists take care of the evolution of animals.

However, environmental historians primarily discuss human relationships with nature when we discuss environmental history. The rise of the Himalayan Mountains, for example, has a history, and geologists determine its formation. Environmental historians must investigate how the Himalayas have influenced human occupation or settlement. Rivers have formed, but rivers have been changing their course at one level; environmental historians study how that river course has affected human settlement. Thus, the core of environmental history in this process is a continual negotiation between humans and the environment.

When we talk about Indian history, we must keep in mind that historians divided it into three periods: ancient, medieval and modern. However, this classification is not entirely suitable for understanding environmental history. The environment disrupts this artificial historical classification, as ecological factors have been constant from time immemorial and continue to influence us to this day. While humans have interacted with the environment differently across these periods, we cannot categorize all of these interactions as ancient, medieval or modern.

Environmental historians writing on contemporary India have been concerned about the loss of natural flora and fauna as well as the reasons and impact behind it. Historians' concerns are further reflected in the dispute ignited by the revisionist school of historical writing and the subaltern's efforts to investigate the roles of peripheral groups within civilization, which are often overlooked in historical narratives.[1]

The scholarly works have characterized environmental history and revealed the difficulty faced by environmental historians presently. According to a closer assessment of the publications appearing under the rubric of 'Environmental History', the documentation of the ecological changes caused by colonialism has dominated the discourse. There are, however, some notable exceptions. Colonialism induced significant ecological disturbances in India, and persisted long after Independence. Beyond economic exploitation, contemporary historians have also looked into how colonial powers used India's natural resources to serve the interest of their home countries.

EXISTING HISTORIOGRAPHY

In recent years, the historiography of environmental history has expanded at such a rapid pace that keeping up with it has become impossible. Environmental history has become a distinct sub-discipline of history in many nations.[2] However, the ecological aspect has been epistemologically less explored in academic writings, particularly the nature and significance of environmental concerns and climatic factors in pre-colonial India. Most historians tend to focus on economic aspects, such as relations of production and distribution, often overlooking the ecological fabric that influences these relationships and undergoes transformations alongside them. To begin, historians have emphasized the importance of climate in the creation and demise of civilization, particularly in the Indus Valley civilization.[3] In the early historical times, scholars like Makhan Lal studied forest clearance and urbanization, suggesting that the role and impact of environmental factors might provide fresh insights into the historical process.[4] They combined archaeological findings with the ecological context. In ancient times, M.K.L. Murthy had documented nuances of the *Pastoral Cultures of Southern Deccan* and pointed out the gradual evolution in their relationship with the environmental conflicts that often vacillated between contest and cooperation.[5]

The environmental history of the ancient Indian past has gained reorganization largely from the ecological reading of texts. Francis Zimmermann believes that the term 'jungle' in ancient Indian texts cannot be equated with the term 'forest'. Zimmermann's book *The Jungle and the Aroma of Meats: Ecological Themes in Hindu Medicine,* has argued that ancient societies classified animals broadly into two groups, jungle (those of the dry lands) and *anupa* (those of the marshy lands) and advocates that a closer examination of such texts may offer us insight into the functioning of ancient ecology.[6] Similar trends are visible in Rogers Jeffery's (ed.) *The Social Construction of Indian Forests.*[7] Recently, Romila Thapar has lucidly worked out *the perception of forests in ancient times.* Writers and poets captured the multiple readings of social perception of forests, which were integrated with social life at various levels.[8]

Inhabitants of forests have also attracted historians. More conventionally, Aloka Parasher Sen has attempted to 'understand how the state perceived the forest dwellers and sought to subordinate and assimilate them' during the Mauryan era. The empire's limits were determined by geography and the perception of opposing tribes, which had to be subdued for the state to expand and integrate.[9]

Nandini Sinha, for the region of Mewar (*State Formations in Rajasthan: Mewar during the Seventh-Fifteenth Centuries*),[10] argues that forested and hill areas were incorporated into broader imperial systems of South Asia. The landscape of economic activities in any sub-region was far more diverse than what is often realized. It is almost impossible to decipher clear-cut stages or phases like hunter-gatherers, herders, settled cultivators, artisans and city dwellers. Extending the line of inquiry to megafauna, Thomas R. Trautmann's book *Elephants and the Maurya* is a seminal work documenting the complexities of social negotiations with wildlife.[11] Shibani Bose in the recent past has contributed a couple of articles on wildlife in the ancient period. Her paper 'From Eminence to Near Extinction: The Journey of the Greater One-Horned Rhino' solidly documents history.[12] The role of hydraulic management in the process of settlement in the ancient period as part of environmental history was explored by Ranbir Chakravarti.[13]

Another primary concern has been the study of social formations, and it has been influenced by the methodologies and tools deployed by anthropology and archaeology.[14] Ranbir Chakravarti has emphasized the importance of hydraulic management in the ancient settlement process.[15]

As far as environmental history in pre-colonial India is concerned, the focus is primarily on the socio-political and economic history of India and the inherent ecological diversity of medieval India is epistemologically unattended in academic writings. Despite the grievance about the inadequate space given to the medieval past in the scholarly works, it is pertinent to argue against the rigid periodization of history and promote its transcending to facilitate a smoother understanding of the developments and transitions in knowledge. This approach helps appreciate, as the scholars suggest, a millennia-long history of India's ecosystems and their interaction with human desires and ambitions, triumphs and failures. 'Highly artificial' and 'pervasive divides' between the natural and humanistic disciplines and, more significantly, the labels of ancient, medieval and modern periods prevent one from establishing the connections that are significant and indispensable. What is necessary is 'more than mere dialogue or synthesis' and 'a sense of wider perspective'.

The Annales School of Literature affects studies of the man-environment in medieval India. Environmental influences on social formations have long focused on historical research for the Annales. From the outset, Annales historians sought to explore new materials to better understand the role of the environment in historical processes.

They have tried to place the role of the environment in the broader settings of social formations. They also attempt to transcend the barrier between medieval and modern history. Supporters of the *longue-durée* approach; they felt comfortable with the full range of human activity, not just political narratives.[16]

Harbans Mukhia, in collaboration with Maurice Aymard, has popularized Annales in India.[17] Borrowing extensively from the works of historians like March Bloch and other Annales historians, a study by Harbans Mukhia titled *Was there Feudalism in Indian History?* explores the influences of environmental factors on human settlement and social formation as a sub-theme and not as the central subject.[18]

The impact of geographical factors on the historical process provided a starting point for research into historical environmental history. The roots of this mode of investigation can be traced back to the two initial chapters of the *Cambridge Economic History of India.* In studies on the periphery of environmental history, Irfan Habib and Burton Stein on *South India: Some General Consideration of the Region and its Early History*, respectively. In the same vein, drawing upon the conventional sources, Shireen Moosvi's paper titled 'Man and Nature in Mughal Era' has offered helpful research on the ecological history of medieval India.[19] However, before the symposium on 'Man and Environment in Indian History' held at Mysore in 1993, Shireen Moosvi's essay on 'Ecology, Population Distribution and Settlement Patterns in Mughal India' semed to be the first fascinating work towards an ecological study of the Mughal period.[20]

'Environment and Pollution in Mughal India', by Mohd. Afzal Khan, published in 2002, is arguably the first paper to draw medieval scholars' attention to the subject of environmental pollution in Mughal India. His sources for the study of environmental pollution are extracted from the Persian writings and the works of contemporary European travellers. Mohd. Afzal Khan highlights the complaints and experiments made by the Mughal emperors regarding poor air and water quality in India. For instance, during the twelfth and thirteenth regnal years of Emperor Jahangir in Ahmedabad, he found so much dust rising in its streets that people's faces were invisible. The emperor, therefore, nicknamed it *Gardabad* (abode of dust) and mockingly called it a *khakdam* (dustbin).

Jahangir 'did not see any logic in the choice of the site by its founder Sultan Ahmad Shah, for a city at a place whose air is *poisonous,* the soil has little water and is full of sand and dust…'.[21] Afzal Khan, in his article, also notes of the heat, dust and water pollution in Mughal India.[22]

Within the broader study of medieval India's environmental history, Sumit Guha has introduced a new avenue of investigation. He argued vehemently that historical studies of the Indian subcontinent's pre-colonial past should not take categories from works on the colonial and post-colonial eras of Indian history. Unfortunately, Madhav Gadgil and Ramchandra Guha's essential book on *India's Ecological History* presents the pre-colonial period as 'prudent resource usage' rather than as a time of exploiting natural resources under colonial practices. Sumit Guha challenged such broad generalizations:

> 'It must be obvious that Gadgil's model breaks at every turn; small endogamous groups did not stay in the same location for longer timeframes.' Even when they did, they lacked exclusive access to resources. For centuries, the human species has been to opportunities and versatile to be confined to specific niches.[23]

The basic argument that Sumit Guha makes is that one needs to revisit the categorization of different communities, which has unfortunately been done merely based on resource-use practices, often ignoring the complex connection with the broader social and ecological settings. He also pointed out that modern categorization, primarily in terms of resource use practices, negates the possibilities of a wider social role in these communities.

Given the breadth of pre-colonial writing concerns, it's not unexpected that just a few writers have looked into the relevance of pre-colonial water systems, which is especially true in north and north-west India.[24] Kathleen Morrison, as part of a large project to examine the water systems in and around Vijayanagara during the sixteenth and seventeenth centuries, has documented the extension of agriculture in the marginal areas. Monsoon rains were increasingly harnessed to develop the agricultural potential of even the sites on the fringes of the agrarian landscape. The lack of water had restricted agricultural production most of the time, and with the channelization of monsoon rains, the expansion of farming settlements became stable.[25] G.S.L. Devra has argued that one can decipher a gradual extension of the desert in northern Rajasthan towards Punjab. He has suggested that a gradual shift in the river courses led to changes in the climatic landscape of the region.[26] At times, he challenges the findings of Dhavalikar, who has argued that the Indian subcontinent witnessed climatic variability between the seventh and eleventh centuries. Along with shifts in the river courses, Dhavalikar suggests that perhaps this era changed the climatic patterns.[27] Extending this line of investigation, Elizabeth Whitcombe has argued that 'irrigation works were financed by loan capital. Hence, in sanctioning constructions, emphasis was placed on the prospect of their remunerativeness'.[28]

Some scholars have highlighted the role of traditional village communities in constructing and maintaining of irrigation systems. David Hardiman suggests that 'small-dam irrigation methods existed in the past and were sustained over a long period by community-based control.[29]

Recently, *Frontiers of Environment: Issues in Medieval and Early Modern India* features a compendium of eleven essays and an introduction by Meena Bhargava. The book's introduction presents the central idea of the essay and a fruitful discussion about medieval environmental history. The volume provides a comparative analysis of nature, pastoralism, irrigation, wildlife and tribes to assess human-environment interaction. From the interest in nature shown by the Mughals to how rivers and forests have shaped communities, this volume highlights the linkages between the environment and social structure.[30]

Meena Bhargava has discussed the process of social agreements to shift river courses in medieval India, which is another vital contribution to the environmental history of medieval India.[31] On a different trajectory, for the later period, Yogesh Sharma has documented the perceptions of European travellers concerning artificial water bodies in India.[32] Similarly, Mayank Kumar has also attempted to examine the interaction between environment and society in medieval Rajasthan and argued that negotiations with climatic variability are a hallmark of human adaptation. There is a greater need for documentation of local village-level negotiations. He has investigated the notion that the communities in traditional societies always practiced the methods aimed at a prudent use of natural resources and pointed out several cases of 'exploitation' of natural resources by conventional organizations in Rajasthan.[33]

The essay 'Exploring Pre-Colonial Rajasthan from an Ecological Perspective: A Study of Mughal Suba of Ajmer' recently came out; it reminds us how geography serves as a basis of history. Since the 1950s and 1960s, investigation and reporting have shifted focus to the localized and grassroots transformation, involving generations of prior ecological enhancement addressing challenges in the various regions. Indeed, the author recognizes the region's environmental diversity in terms of climate, landscape, hydrology, the built environment, soil, crops and farming, inter-regional livestock fairs and pastoral transhumance, as the author proposes would so enrich the historical record. Tracing back the origins and development of each in this array of adaptive characteristics would be worthy of a historical task.[34]

A new area of study has emerged: the changing history of human-animal interactions, mainly in changing elite taste and growing human-wildlife conflict. Gradual but regular expansion of the agrarian landscape[35] has resulted in ground-level conflicts and has threatened their coexistence. In this context, *The End of a Trail: The Cheetah in India*[36] stands out. The author, Divyabhanusinh, traces the history of the *cheetah* in India, exploring its origins, distribution across the subcontinent, human attitude towards the species, the gradual loss of habitat and ultimately its extinction. The work offers significant insight into understanding the complex relationship between fauna and society, particularly the process of extinction of animals. Extinctions occurred because of the extensive historical process rather than as a natural progression of species eliminating, as was the case for other 'big game'. Another monograph by Divyabhanusinh on lions carries the quest further to explore the fauna in their world.[37] Different interesting writing genres have examined princely states' interactions with colonial power as mediated by the flora-fauna of their respective regions. Barbara Ramusack has explored the British hunting practices and their appropriation and reinterpretations by Indian princes.[38] Locating the role of environmental settings in warfare and human negotiations with animals, Pratyay Nath's book *Climate of Conquest*

War, Environment and Empire in Mughal North India has suggested that Mughals reconsidered their reliance on cavalry as they moved towards the wetlands of the Gangetic delta. This change from dependence on the cavalry to elephants is reflected in the writings of Mughal court chronicles and Mughal paintings reflective of changing relations and perceptions towards environmental factors.[39]

Most of the environmental movements were attributed to the disruptions caused by the British. Some argued elsewhere that in pre-British times, 'there was little or no interference with the customary use of forest and forest produce'.[40] Guha and Gadgil thus portrayed a romanticized image of the human-environment interaction in the Indian context, imagery received with open hands by writers who doubled up as environmental activists. Early writers were primarily focused on protecting the environment, actively advocating for the conservation of natural resources. Thus, they sought evidence of widespread protests against the exploitation and often neglected the contrary evidence. In the initial decades, works on the environmental history of South Asia often focused on specific themes at the expense of others: the forest rather than agriculture, movements of Adivasi and marginal peasants rather than the changing response of urban dwellers, histories of irrigation as opposed to conflict over water-right, etc. Among the first few who focused on the impact of colonial forest policies on the Himalayan region and central Indian forests were Ramchandra Guha[41] and Mahesh Rangarajan,[42] respectively.

On the one hand, Sumit Guha has attempted to bridge the pre-colonial and British periods and on the other, he has also avoided the illusionary divide between forest and agriculture and notions of ethnicity in the broader context of the environment. His study area has been the region dominated by Marathas, and fortunately for the part, we have rich repositories of documents. He has questioned the presumed isolation of tribals from the cradle of civilization.[43] Sumit Guha has pointed out that the sizeable areas of the western plateau (Maharashtra) outside the rain-drenched Konkan coast were rendered treeless even during a hard time for Marathas.[44]

Making the pitch for future researchers exploring the environmental history of the Indian subcontinent, Guha argued it is essential to keep in mind that in the South Asian past, only a relatively small area was under permanent cultivation. A much more significant percentage of land was often in transition, at least in the pre-modern period. He also advised caution by suggesting that historians go beyond the state's perspective of land, forest, water bodies, etc., for a comprehensive understanding of human-nature interactions. Ranjit Guha also highlighted the problems of statism, noting that colonial historiography, along with its later proponents, providing focused on examining historical progression through an 'evolutionary' time scale. For them, societies evolved in succession from primitive to tribal to chieftaincy to state and this process is unidirectional and mutually contradictory.[45] Ajay Skaria gave serious consideration to the question and explored the idea of wild and wilderness, usually in opposition to civilized. The relationship between triable people and the ruling dispensation has also been found in the binary of civilized and primitive.[46]

Following that works on India's environmental history during the colonial and post-colonial periods challenged the widely held belief that British policy was similar across the Indian subcontinent. Recent researchers have highlighted the divergence of colonial administrative views and procedures related to forest, agricultural production and water resources.[47]

Another critical aspect of Indian environmental history is the endeavour to counter the unfavourable image of the British by claiming that it was the British who first implemented a systematic forest conservation plan in India. 'The initial "greens" in India were colonial officials', it was claimed. Colonial officials, who sought to understand the link between climate and health, established colonial forestry policy. This policy, initially focused on climate and health, quickly shifted towards botany and ecology, showcasing their enlightened understanding of environmental issues. They argued a close connection between deforestation and environmental desiccation and pressed firmly for state-led conservation of forests. Through their pressure, the earlier *laissez-faire* attitude towards forests was replaced from the mid-nineteenth century onwards by active management and control.[48]

The state-led conservation of forests was legitimized by imparting modern knowledge or banishing the forest-dwellers from their habitat for harming the forests. By identifying lands suited to agriculture and developing marginal land as forests, people could achieve a balance between agriculture and forests. The importance of agriculture was thus quite clear. Groundwater availability was also a related issue, often combined with soil erosion. Forest growth was harmful to groundwater as it sustained itself on the groundwater only.[49]

Colonial concerns about forests were primarily driven by economic motives, although they outwardly emphasized the goal of conservation. The debate over the preservation of the environment was traced to the literary traditions of romanticism, where nature in its pristine form was a source of inspiration. The environment was conserved to protect the environment in its natural conditions—similar to the primitive state of the domain.[50]

Analysis of various policies affecting environmental challenges has been another field of investigation. Vasant Saberwal has contributed significantly to this discipline. He argues that 'among the academic ecological community, there is growing acknowledgement of the intricacies of ecosystem functioning, and the limits to our predictive and explanatory capabilities' about large-scale ecological conservation grown over a long period along with the growth in the scientific knowledge about the environment. He has also highlighted the state's role in appropriating scientific knowledge supporting its goals. He writes: 'The essay examines the chronological progression of the desiccation debate. Our analysis is situated within the broader scientific context in which these ideas were articulated throughout the late nineteenth and early twentieth centuries.'[51]

Similarly, *An Environmental History of India: From Earlier Times to the Twenty-first Century*, by Michael H. Fisher, is a new, comprehensive addition to the subject of India's environmental history. According to the author, this book 'builds on the expanding number of sophisticated and discerning works that examine crucial facets of India's environmental history'.[52] As the title suggests, this work covers a broad span of India's environmental history, and along with other scholarly publications, it may thus serve as a guide for scholars studying India's ecological past.

Several other valuable works have been written on colonial and contemporary Rajasthan pastures, fields and forests. But except for passing references in studies of agricultural production, few have examined the dynamics of water management in Rajasthan before

1800.[53] Jodha's primary concern has been to discuss 'the changing state and utilization pattern of natural resources and the potential of stopping the negative trends accompanying these changes'. P.P.S. Kavoori[54] has investigated the problem of 'common property resources' by looking at the current conditions of pastoralists. Similarly, R. Thomas Rosin has discovered a scarcity of 'common grazing areas', and the stress of a sedentary lifestyle has restricted pastoralists' opportunities. It also reduces the options available to the peasantry in times of drought and famine. Conflicts over natural resource usage, such as forest protection and conservation versus an extension of settled cultivation, have also been intensively examined in the later period.[55] Several studies highlight the problem with British forest management policies, where mono-culture has been a significant issue. Natural resource exploitation for a small elite that is unconcerned about the societal consequences of such practices is a substantial concern.

Investigating the effects of tribes living on the outskirts of settled agriculture has been another strand in this research for the forested region. It was significant as the British could not confront the tribes because they were not practicing settled agriculture.[56] The resistance offered by these tribes to the British policies has been extensively examined. Some argue that the British could not comprehend the complex functioning of their social relationships. Most times, the issue stems from a mismatch between the British vision of the landscape shared and the reality of the Indian landscape. Colonial discourses on ethnicity, the environment and resource extraction are influenced by the form of governmental intervention.

THE FOCUS AREA OF THIS STUDY

This study focuses on the region that lies to the north of the Narmada River and the Vindhya hills—the traditional divides between the northern and southern parts of the Indian subcontinent. We call this entire landmass 'North India'. Technically, it comprises the various western, northern, and eastern federal states of the modern republic of India—Rajasthan, Haryana, Punjab, Uttarakhand, Uttar Pradesh and Bihar. These northern Indian plains continue to the west beyond the Punjab and Rajasthan and have coverage with the Indus Plain in

Pakistan. They measure about 6,50,000 sq. km. These are among the most extensive plains of the world and they account for one-fifth of the area of India. These are primarily level plains without interruption, except for a few outliers of the Aravalli Range. The outliers surrounding Delhi, often referred to as the Aravalli Range, are significant geographical features. They form isolated low hills or ridges and emerge out of the surrounding alluvium as islands. This region was formerly a deep trench, 6 to 8 km in-depth, formed as a foredeep (the thickest sedimentary zone) when the Himalayas rose as fold mountains. Uniformity the level of these plains is mainly due to two facts: (a) deposition took place in water, and (b) no earth movement disturbed their flatness later. In the drier parts of the water fringe of Haryana and neighbouring parts of Rajasthan, the creation of these plains is because of the deposition of windblown dust. The southern border of the Ganga Plain features numerous ravines that significantly affect the fertility of the alluvial soil, particularly between the Chambal and Son rivers.

The rivers in the north Indian plain create several meanders throughout their courses. In areas like Haryana and Uttar Pradesh, where rainfall is scarce, rivers have been harnessed for irrigation, crucial for preventing famines could not have been eliminated from this densely plain tract. Here, rivers are prone to sudden and disastrous floods during the rainy season. The flatness of the plains' and large loops of meanders, the rivers are sluggish and cannot carry away water quickly after heavy continuous rain, leading to several sudden floods. In some areas with a high-water table, the floodwaters may stand for a few months and thus prevent rabi crops from being planted. The rivers look oddly small and misplaced in winter due to the low water volume.

CHAPTERIZATION

This monograph is organized into four chapters, each of which focuses on a progressively narrower period in the ecological history of India. The first chapter outlines the ecological history of the Punjab, Rajasthan, Agra region, Allahabad and Bihar. Punjab features a different topography and it possesses a network of now-fed rivers, that play a crucial role in its ecology. Because of heavy rains in the hills and the submontane region of Punjab, there were plenty of natural forests. Thick jungles of *dhak* trees covered the country at the foot of the mountain. In a comprehensive description of Punjab, James Douie provides an account of sub-regional variations in Punjab's natural vegetation and wildlife.

Another critical state of north India is Rajasthan and the chief aim is to highlight the ecological diversity found within it. However, comprehending medieval Rajasthan ecologically through contemporary sources is difficult. However, while going through the modern literature of Rajasthan, the role of pastoralism in the agriculture of Rajasthan is epistemologically untenable in the larger domain of historical narratives. Therefore, it is essential to discuss pastoralism while analysing Rajasthan's ecology. Pastoralism has been widely practiced in arid and semi-arid tracts of the Thar desert. Forest nutrients as sheep and goat dung cycled through daily grazing in the forested hills are the primary sources of agricultural fertilizers.

The ecological shift in Agra is not well addressed in most historical discourses, even though it ought to be recognized. K.K. Trivedi's studies on the region's forest cover might be beneficial; however, his research did not reveal the negative consequences of deforestation in the area. Extensive forest areas had been destroyed under the Mughals in the seventeenth century, with them former hunting grounds west and south-west of Agra had disappeared by 1800. The wells silted up, leading to the abandonment of the residency in Fatehpur Sikri, further highlighting this deterioration. In the late eighteenth century, the British were not the only foreign rulers to bring ecological catastrophe to India; Agra was one of the most affected regions by this degradation.

This monograph will explore the ecology of Allahabad and Bihar. The climate of Allahabad is characterized by pleasant cold weather, a long and almost intolerably hot summer and a nourishing rainy season. The average annual rainfall in Allahabad from 1800 onwards was 37.54 inches. The annual precipitation in the Doab area is greater than average. In contrast, the *suba* of Bihar, particularly the Tirhut, Patna and Bhagalpur regions, received high rainfall, making the region chiefly rice-producing. Besides scattered shrubs, there were both regular and dense forests in the northern part of the *suba* along the northern banks of the Ghagra. Thick forests once covered the areas near Allahabad and Kantit. Elephants roamed a dense forest near Kara-Manikpur. The region was once covered with forests from Kalinjar to Chunar and the Kaimur Hills in the south. The fort of Kalinjar was surrounded by a dense forest, where elephants, hawks and other animals were found. Bihar, with its moderate rainfall and fertile soil, is a natural habitat of a dense forest covered with *sal* and other species like *shisham, jamun, mahua* and *ber*. Even into the remnants of 1840s, a large area of Saryupar was densely forested as were the banks of Rapti, Ghaghara and other rivers. There were sizable pockets in South Ganga Plain. The remnants of the once extensive *sal* forests are found in the northern Gorakhpur, Saharsa and Purnea districts.

In the third chapter, 'Fauna, Agriculture and Forest: A Sustainable Interdependency in Mughal North India', the Mughals perceived the hunting ground as a transitional zone between cultivated land and uncultivated forest, establishing a continuity between hunting practices and agriculture. In the Agra region, hunting took place in gardens such as Darhra Bagh. Many elements of the garden were integrated into the hunting ground, where the natural landscape was dramatically transformed by imperial hunters. The natural environment of the forest cover areas was appropriated and transformed through deforestation and the introduction of features such as irrigation, which enhanced agricultural production and created a more favourable setting for hunting.

Chapter 4 addresses the ecological history of Awadh, a region in an ecologically rich *suba*. While discussing the forest ecology of Awadh, it is essential to explore the forest cover. This section will also examine the various reasons for deforestation and its severe repercussions on the ecology of Awadh during the later Mughal period.

The fifth chapter, titled 'Ecological Change and the Calamitous Events of North India: A Historical Overview' will explore the evidence of climate and environmental change in India. It will also illuminate the potential effects of climate change in India. Floods, plagues, famines and earthquakes that struck Mughal India in the seventeenth century vividly illustrate the disastrous effects of climate change. Another key focus of this chapter is the impact of these climatic shifts on agriculture. Additionally, it will explore the measures taken by rulers to mitigate the destruction caused by such natural calamities. The conclusion will briefly raise several fundamental questions that need to be addressed in the final part of this study. First, when did environmental issues begin to gain prominence in historical writings? Second, when and where environmental history first emerged as a distinct discipline of study? Third, why talk about the details of India's environmental history during the medieval and early modern periods particularly in north India, which is the most significant area?

NOTES

1. M. William, 'The Relations of Environmental History and Historical Geography', *Journal of Historical Geography,* 1994, pp. 3-4; A. Baker, ed., *Geography and History: Bridging the Divide,* Cambridge: Cambridge University Press, 2003, p. 72.
2. Ranjan Chakrabarti (ed.), *Situating Environmental History,* p. 11.
3. F.R. Allchin, *The Archaeology of Early Historic South Asia: The Emergence of Cities and State,* New Delhi: Cambridge University Press, 1995; V.N. Misra, 'Climate, a Factor in the Rise and Fall of the Indus Civilization: Evidence from Rajasthan and Beyond', in *Frontiers of the Indus Civilization,* ed. B.B. Lal and S.P. Gupta, New Delhi: Books and Books, 1984, pp. 461-6, 473, 481; Gurdeep Singh, 'The Indus Valley Culture (seen in Post-Glacial Climate and Ecological Studies in North-West India)', *Archaeology and Physical Anthropology in Oceania 6,* no. 2, 1971, p. 177; D.P. Agrawal, *The Copper Bronze Age in India,* New Delhi: Munshiram Manoharlal, 1971.
4. Makhan Lal, 'Iron Tools, Forest Clearance and Urbanization in the Gangetic Plains', *Man and Environment,* 10, 1986, pp. 83-90.
5. M.K.L. Murthy, 'Sheep/Goat Pastoral Cultures in the Southern Deccan: The Narrative as a Metaphor', in *Indian Archaeology in Retrospect: Archaeology and Historiography,* vol. IV, ed. S. Settar and Ravi Korisettar, New Delhi: Manohar, 2002, p. 297. Also, see Shereen Ratnagar, 'Pastoralism as an Issue in Historical Research', *Studies in History,* no. 7, 1991, pp. 181-93.
6. Francis Zimmermann, *The Jungle and the Aroma of Meats: Ecological Themes in Hindu Medicine,* Berkeley and Los Angeles: University of California Press, 1987, p. 34.
7. Roger Jeffery, ed., *The Social Construction of Indian Forest,* New Delhi: Manohar, 1998, p. 67.
8. Romila Thapar, 'Perceiving the Forest: Early India', *Studies in History 17,* no. 1, 2001, pp. 1-16.

9. Aloka Parasher Sen, 'Of Tribes, Hunters and Barbarians: Forest Dwellers in the Mauryan Period', *Studies in History* 14, no. 2, 1988, p. 173; also, Shereen Ratnagar, 'Pastoralism as an Issue in Historical Research', *Studies in History,* 7, 2 n.s., 1991, pp. 181-93.
10. Nandini Sinha Kapur, *State Formation in Rajasthan: Mewar during the Seventeenth-fifteenth Centuries,* New Delhi: Manohar, 2002, p. 67.
11. Thomas R. Trautmann, 'Elephants and the Maurya', in *India: History and Thought: Essays in Honour of A.L. Basham,* ed. S.N. Mukherjee, Calcutta: Firma K. L. Mukhopadhyay and Co., 1982, pp. 54-73.
12. Mahesh Rangarajan and K. Sivaramakrishnan, eds., *Shifting Ground: People, Animals, and Mobility in India's Environment,* New Delhi: Oxford University Press, 2014, pp. 65-87; Shibani Bose, 'Human-Plants Interactions in the Middle Gangetic Plains (From the Mesolithic upto circa 3rd century BC): An Archaeobotanical Perspective', in *Ancient India: New Research,* ed. Upinder Singh and Nayanjot Lahiri, New Delhi: Oxford University Press, 2009, pp. 97-107.
13. Ranbir Chakravarti, 'The Creation and Expansion of Settlements and Management of Hydrauli Resources in Ancient India', in *Nature and the Environment,* ed. Richard Grove, Vinita Damodaran and Satpal Sangwan, New Delhi: Oxford University Press, 1988, pp. 87-105.
14. R. Ray, *Ancient Settlement Patterns in Eastern India,* New Delhi: Har-Anand, 1993, pp. 615-31.
15. 'The Development and Expansion of Settlements in Ancient India, as well as the Management of Hydraulic Resources', in Richard Grove, Vinita Damodaran and Satpal Sangwan, eds., *Nature and the Environment.* New Delhi: Oxford University Press, 1998, pp. 87-101.
16. Ravindra Kumar, 'Studying Ecological & Environments: An Introduction', *History of Ecology and Environment: India,* New Delhi: IGNOU, 2005.
17. Harbans Mukhia and Maurice Aymard, *French Studies in History,* vol. I, *The Inheritance,* New Delhi, 1988 and vol. II, *The Departure,* New Delhi: Sage, 1990.
18. Harbans Mukhia, 'Presidential Address, Medieval Indian Section', *Indian History Congress,* vol. 40, 1979, pp. 220-80.
19. Shireen Moosvi, 'Ecology, Population Distribution and Settlement Pattern in Mughal India in 1989', *Man and Environment XIV,* no. 1, 1989, pp. 109-16.
20. Shireen Moosvi, *People, Taxation and Trade in Mughal India,* New Delhi: Oxford University Press, 2008, pp. 89-102; her basic argument is that the ecological history of Mughal India cannot be addressed without considering agriculture. A basic shift in ecology occurs in ecology occurs in all agricultural societies whenever the plough makes inroads into the forest or grassland.
21. See, Jahangir, *Tuzuk-i-Jahangiri* (1624), ed. Syed Ahmad Khan, Ghazipur

and Aligarh, 1863-4, Sir Syed Academy (rpt. 2007), pp. 205, 210 and 231 cited in *Environment and Pollution in Mughal India,* pp. 102-3.

22. For more details see, *Environment and Pollution in Mughal India,* pp. 101-16.
23. Sumit Guha, *Environment and Ethnicity in India, 1200-1991,* Cambridge: Cambridge University Press, 1999, p. 43.
24. Tripti Wahi, 'Water Resources and Agricultural Landscape: Pre-colonial Punjab', in *Five Punjabi Centuries: Polity, Economy, Society and Culture, c. 1500-1900,* ed. Indu Banga, New Delhi: Manohar, 1997.
25. Kathleen D. Morrison, 'Production and Landscape in the Vijayanagara Metropolitan Region: Contribution of the Vijayanagara Metropolitan Survey', in *Vijayanagara: Archaeological Exploration 1990-2000: Papers in Memory of Channabasappa S. Patil,* eds. J.M. Fritz, T. Raczek and R. Brubaker, *Vijayanagara Research Project Monographs,* vol. 10, New Delhi: Manohar, 2005, p. 423.
26. G.S.L. Devra, 'Problem in the Delimitation of the Rajasthan Desert During the Medieval Period', in *Desert, Drought & Development: Studies in Resource Management and Sustainability,* ed. Rakesh Hooja and Rajendra Joshi, Jaipur: Rawat, 1999, pp. 371-82.
27. M.K. Dhavalikar, 'Green Imperialism: Monsoon in Antiquity and Human Response', *Man and Environment,* 26, no. 2, 2001, pp. 17-20.
28. Elizabeth Whitecombe, 'The Environmental Costs of Irrigation in British India: Waterlogging, Salinity, Malaria', in *Nature, Culture, Imperialism: Essays on the Environmental History of South Asia,* ed. David Arnold and Ramchandra Guha, New Delhi: Oxford University Press, 1995, pp. 237-40.
29. David Hardiman, 'Small Dam Systems of the Sahyadris', in *Nature, Culture, Imperialism: Essays on the Environmental History of South Asia,* ed. David Arnold and Ramchandra Guha, New Delhi: Oxford University Press, 1995, pp. 185-200.
30. Meena Bhargava, ed., *Frontiers of Environment: Issues in Medieval and Early Modern India,* New Delhi: Oriental BlackSwan, 2017, p. 10.
31. Meena Bhargava, 'Changing River Courses in North India: Calamities, Bounties, Strategies—Sixteenth to Early Nineteenth Centuries', *The Medieval History Journal 10,* nos. 1 & 2, 2007, pp. 183-90.
32. Yogesh Sharma, 'The Circuit of Life: Water and Water Reservoirs in Pre-modern India', *Studies in History* 25, no. 1 (January-June 2009), pp. 69-100.
33. Mayank Kumar, 'Claims on Natural Resources: Exploring the Role of Political Power in Pre-Colonial Rajasthan, India', *Conservation and Society* 3, no. 1 (June 2005), pp. 134-49.
34. Mohd Kamran Khan, 'Exploring Pre-Colonial Rajasthan from an Ecological Perspective: A Study of Mughal Suba of Ajmer', *Quarterly Journal*

of the Pakistan Historical Society, vol. LXX, no. 1 (January-March 2022), pp. 45-65.

35. Neeladri Bhattacharya, *The Great Agrarian Conquest: The Colonial Reshaping of a Rural World,* Hyderabad: Orient Black Swan, 2018, p. 56.
36. Divyabhanusinh, *The End of a Trail: The Cheetah in India,* New Delhi: Oxford University Press, 1999.
37. Divyabhanusinh, *The Story of Asia's Lion,* Mumbai: Marg Publications, 2005.
38. Barbara N. Ramusak, *The Indian Princes and Their States,* 1st Asian edn., New York: Cambridge University Press; Anand S. Pandianl, 'Predatory Care: The Imperial Hunt in the Mughal and British India', *Journal of Historical Sociology* 14, no. 1 (March 2001), p. 107; also see John M. Mackenzie, *The Empire of Nature: Hunting, Conservation and British Imperialism,* Manchester: Manchester University Press, 1988.
39. Pratyay Nath, *Climate of Conquest: War, Environment and Empire in Mughal North India,* New Delhi: Oxford University Press, 2019.
40. Ramchandra Guha, 'Forestry in British and Post-British India: A Historical Analysis', *Economic and Political Weekly* 20, 1985, pp. 1882-96.
41. Ramchandra Guha, *The Unquiet Woods: Ecological Change and Peasants Resistance in the Himalaya,* New Delhi: Oxford University Press, 1989.
42. Mahesh Rangarajan, *Fencing the Forest: Conservation and Ecological Change in India's Central Provinces: 1860-1914,* New Delhi: Oxford University Press, 1996.
43. Sumit Guha, 'Claim on the Commons: Political Power and Natural Resources in Pre-colonial India', *The Indian Economic and Social History Review* 39, nos. 2 & 3, 2002, pp. 181-96.
44. For more details see Sumit Guha's *Environment and Ethnicity,* Cambridge: Cambridge University Press, 1999.
45. Ranjit Guha, *History at the Limit of World History,* New Delhi: Oxford University Press, 2003.
46. Ajay Skaria, 'Being Jangli: The Politics of Wildness', *Studies in History* 14, no. 2, 1998, pp. 193-214.
47. K. Sivaramkrishnan, 'Conservation and Production in Private Forests: Bengali, 1864-1914', *Studies in History* 14, no. 2, 1998, pp. 237-50.
48. David Hardiman's review of *Nature & The Orient in Economic and Political Weekly,* issue dated 3-9 July 1999.
49. Rajan S. Ravi, 'Foresters and the Politics of Colonial Agro ecology', *Studies in History,* vol. 14, no. 2, 1998, pp. 217-36.
50. Archana Prasad, *Against Ecological Romanticism: Verrier Elwin and the Making of Anti-modern Tribal Identity,* New Delhi: Three Essays Collective, 2003.

51. Science and the Desiccations Discourses of the 20th Century', in *Environment and History,* vol. 4, no. 3, 1997, pp. 309-10.
52. Michael H. Fisher, *An Environmental History of India: From Earlier Times to the Twenty-First Century,* Cambridge: Cambridge University Press, 2018.
53. Ann Grodzins Gold and B.R. Gujjar, *In the Time of Trees and Sorrows: Natural, Power and Memory in Rajasthan,* Durham: Duke University Press, 2000; N.S. Jodha, *Life on the Edge: Sustaining Agriculture and Community Resources in Fragile Environments,* New Delhi: Oxford University Press, 2001.
54. P.S. Kavoori, *Pastoralism in Expansion: The Transhuming Herders of Western Rajasthan*, New Delhi: Oxford University Press, 1999.
55. Rajan S. Ravi, 'Foresters and The Politics of Colonial Agroecology: The Case of Shifting Cultivation and Soil Erosion, 1920-1950', *Studies in History,* vol. 14, no. 2, n.s. 1998, pp. 237-64.
56. Guha, op. cit., p. 78.

CHAPTER 2

An Ecological Study of the Mughal North India: Punjab, Rajasthan, Agra Region, Allahabad and Bihar

THE ECOLOGY OF north India has received little attention from writers. This has been because of a lack of readily available information. Several archival materials, British Statistical Accounts, State Gazetteers and Settlement Reports, which we have, were written in the late eighteenth and early nineteenth century. For the earlier period, Mughal documents and the works of European travellers like Francois Bernier, Francisco Pelsaert, Niccolo Manucci, John Marshal and J.B. Tavernier are our primary sources. In this context, an attempt has been made in the following pages to study the general ecological condition of north India.

TROPICAL LANDSCAPE OF PUNJAB

Punjab derives its name from a Persian compound of the words 'panj' and 'ab' (water), which translates as 'country of the five rivers', as the Jhelum, Chenab, Ravi, Beas and Sutlej all flow through it.[1] During the Mughal period, Punjab formed part of the Delhi *suba* and flourished.[2] The fruits of Iran and Turan flourished here and some places yielded three harvests per year.[3] But after Aurangzeb died in 1707, the empire declined fast and tempted foreign invaders to advance upon Delhi. In February 1739, Nadir Shah, the Durrani invader, descended upon the plains of Punjab and on the way, ransacked Thanesar, Karnal, Panipat, Sonipat and Narela.[4] The people of Delhi suffered most terribly from his general massacre and the invader returned with a rich booty, including the famous Peacock Throne and *Koh-i-Noor* diamond.[5]

Punjab is bounded on the north by the Himalayan and sub-Himalayan ranges, on the west by the Sufed Koh and Sulaiman mountains, on the east by the river Jumna and the Agra province, and the south by the Sind and Rajputana deserts, a large wedge of which stretches to the Sutlej.

The Submontane area, extending from the Jumna to the Jhelum River, is characterized by low hills reaching heights of 1,000 to 3,000 feet, valleys called doons, and a plain at the mountain's base. The region encompasses the districts of Ambala, Hoshiarpur, Kangra, Gurdaspur, Sialkot, Gujarat and Jhelum. It is a fertile area that gets a lot of rain and greenery throughout the year. The region's main farming products are rice, maize and mango while wild animals, mostly deer, graze in herds here. During the monsoon season, a vast network of streams transports a large volume of water from the hills to the plains, carving deep gorges in the land. This natural drainage system made it easy to access the plains of Punjab.[6]

The plain's eastern part, encompassing the area between the Ravi and the Jumna, was more fertile and rainier than the western part of Punjab, resulting in richer product and higher population. It included nearly all the prosperous towns of the time, like Delhi, Lahore and Sirhind—the seats of various governments. The southern part of this tract merged into the desert of Rajputana. Manjha and Malwa were further subdivisions of the northern and southern parts of the region. The Manjha is a high upland between the Ravi and Sutlej. It was protected in the north by Gurdaspur's forest tracts and in the south by Montgomery's barren landscape. To the north, it is broad and well-cultivated. It shrinks in the south, becoming more and more of a desert, with only low plants and long grass. This grass proved to be a highly valuable as pasture for grazing horses and cattle. This dry region, in the 'Bori Doab' centre, was surrounded by extensive forests of *palash* trees and prickly plants.[7]

Malwa refers to the region situated between the Sutlej and the Jumna rivers, forming a watershed. This plain has, from times immemorial, been the site of some of the most fiercely contested battles in Indian history. The foreign invader, having surmounted the mountains and the Indus River, found the Delhi monarch's territory easily passable, posing no challenge to their advance. If the foreigner triumphed, the northern Indian empire would fall into his hands like ripe fruit.

Another essential point of this plain is that it is sandy. It is watered by about a dozen streams[8] from the hills in massive volumes during the monsoon season, bringing down and spreading significant quantities of sand and silt over the plains. Narrow in the east, it gradually widens towards the west. This region was another abode of the Sikhs, who followed a distinct line of action from their Manjha brethren in independence. The sandy desert provided them with a remote territory where they quietly pursued their life course. Here, too, the Manjha Sikhs often took refuge when driven from their homes by their oppressors.

From the Ravi to the Indus, the plain western tract extends. But then, it was a dry, desert region with only thorny plants and long grass for company. The bulk of the cultivation took place along the courses of rivers. Thieves, robbers and outlaws sought refuge along the riverbanks, thickly covered with flora. Multan was the only significant city in this area.

RAJASTHAN'S ARID REGION

The description of the physical features of the Rajputana state during the Mughal period based on contemporary records is an arduous task, as there are no extant contemporary treaties that comprehensively deal with the geography of the entire region.[9] The earliest geographic reference to Rajasthan is in connection with its arid landscape. The word *maru* is found in the *Rigveda,* signifying a desert region.[10] However, Rajasthan cannot be summarized by this term as *Maru Desh* referred explicitly only to the desert area of Rajasthan. In this context, it is essential to keep in mind that as far as the Rajasthan desert is concerned, 'scientists agree that the northern boundary of the desert never remained in fixate; it is changing'.[11]

For a better understanding of Rajasthan's geography, it is helpful to divide the state into the areas to the north-west and south-east of the Aravali Range. Nearly two-thirds of the territory lies in the north-west of Aravalis. In the northwest Aravali region, the land had undulating topography; soils were sandy in texture, rainfall was scanty and precarious and with a shallow sub-soil layer. There is a large tract of excellent soil drained by several rivers in the south-east of Aravalis. There is a significant variation in the annual rainfall and distribution in the state's different regions. The south-eastern area is a higher plateau. In the south lies the hilly tract of Mewar.[12] The Thar desert is an important physical part of the Rajasthan state, along with the Pat and the Ghaggar areas. The Steppe desert comprises the physiographic divisions of the vast expanses of land, which have long been a *cul-de-sac*.

H.D. Sankalia argued the Thar was once fertile with a perennial river like the Saraswati. Perhaps an extreme stage of desiccation now

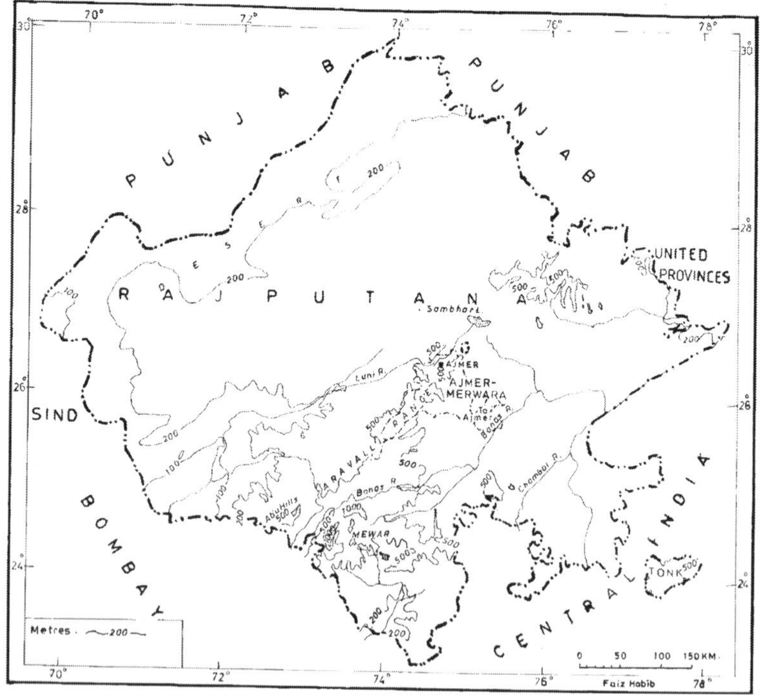

MAP 2.1: PHYSICAL MAP OF RAJPUTANA *c.* 1860. RIVERS AND MOUNTAINS ARE BASED ON IRFAN HABIB'S *AN ATLAS OF THE MUGHAL EMPIRE*, NEW DELHI: OXFORD UNIVERSITY PRESS, 1982, SHEET NO. 6B.

stretches with apparent indefiniteness over the heart of the Indo-Pakistan subcontinent. The main river of this part of Rajasthan is the Luni, with several tributaries like Lirli, Guhiya, Bandi, Sukri, Jawai, Jori, etc. The rivers have long dried up, rendering the area (Jaisalmer, Barmer, Bikaner, significant portion of Jodhpur and a part of Jaipur), a formidable barrier to overcome before the arrival of the machine age. However, it is pertinent to note that the desert is not a barren or lifeless land devoid of either flora or human activities. Like other organisms, livestock have learned to thrive in challenging conditions and make the best use of scarce resources.

Geological studies further curiously added that a considerable portion of this tract was initially covered by a body of water, with the presence of salt in the desert of Rajasthan. The water evaporated because of the rains and accumulated in the depression, as could be seen in lakes of Sambhar, Didwana and Pachapadra. Shell oysters and cowries are also primarily mixed with sand, which further supports this fact.[13]

Epigraphical sources and literary works of Rajasthan, like Nainsi's account, *Arshattas, Vir-Vinod* and *Twarikh-i-Jaisalmer* report only about the contemporary politico-administrative history of the region. Whatever information we find about the region's physical features was attributed to production purposes or agrarian production. Besides, Rajasthan is a portrait with the identity of a desert landscape. However, it may be wrong to portray Rajasthan solely as a desert. The construction of the Rajasthan image with a desert landscape seems to be a recent phenomenon.[14] Besides, a closer examination of the pre-colonial landscape amply substantiates our argument that large tracts of land are left uncultivated or covered by forests. The contemporary sources clarified that there were sparse habitations. Similarly, the extensive pervasiveness of diverse wildlife has been corroborated in many contemporary sources, which suggests a spare agricultural landscape.[15]

In the topography's line of Rajasthan, Ajmer is the part of south-eastern Rajasthan lying between $25^{0}24'$ and $26^{0}42'$ North latitude and $73^{0}47'$ East longitude. The province comprises two districts, Ajmer and Marwar, surrounded by the native states. Ajmer is located at the foothill of Taragarh, a high plateau with a rocky natural landscape. Despite this, it is a beautiful valley, picturesque and surrounded by Nagapahar or Serpent Hill, which is a part of the Aravali range. 'Ajai-merch', 'Ajai's hill', or 'invincible mountain', occupied an important strategic position in Rajasthan during the pre-colonial period.[16]

The Aravali range divide the whole Ajmer *suba* into two parts. On the western side, the ranges pass through the *sarkars* of Chittor, Kumbhakwer, Ajmer and Nagaur. Thus, the *sarkars* Jodhpur, Bikaner and a small part of *sarkar* Ajmer and Nagaur lay on the western side, largely a desert. On the eastern side lay the *sarkars* of Chittor and Ranthanmbor, and the remaining portion of *sarkars* were Ajmer and Nagaur.[17]

AGRA AND ALLAHABAD: A STUDY OF THE SEMI-ARID REGION

The *suba* of Agra was made by Akbar in 1580[18] when he superseded the earlier division of the empire into *sarkar,* inherited from the Lodi period.[19] The *sarkars* of the earlier period were made smaller, many of the old being divided up and many completely new *sarkars* being created. Thus, Agra *suba*, as a ewly-created province, extended over territory lying between the Indo-Gangetic Plain on the Yamuna (Jumna) River and formed a portion of the Jumna-Ganga Doab,[20] lying between 75^0 and 8^0 of East longitude and 24^0 and 29^0 of North latitude. It is bounded on the west by the Bharatpur state, to the south by Dholpur and Gwalior, with the Chambal River serving as the dividing line between Gwalior and this region, and the north, lay the British districts of Mathura and Etawah.[21]

The *suba* consisted of two distinct geographical blocks: first, the middle *doab* and the trans-Yamuna plains, north and south of the Chambal River, which are both wholly alluvial and form part of the Ganga plains;[22] and second, the rocky region extending in a rough area from Kowat to Erachh.[23] This region does not contain very high ranges or plateaus but mostly isolated hillocks and narrow alluvial valleys, which often break into ravines.

Rationally, the *suba* of Agra is close to the northern limits of the area of the Braj-speaking belt, separating it from the area of *Khari-boli.* Its western boundary runs along the lines where Rajasthani replaces Hindi. Similarly, the eastern border, in part, corresponds to the edge of the Awadhi dialect but correspondence with the language or dialect is not clear towards the south. We can say that the nuclear zone of the *suba* Agra was the Braj speaking areas, which extends into *doab* on the one side and the purse of the Aravalis on the other.

The Yamuna and Ganga rivers were the principal rivers of the *suba*. They have their sources in the Himalayas, while their major southern boundaries Chambal, Sind and Betwa rivers, rise in the Vindhya hills when they traverse the hilly terrain of Malwa and Bundelkhand. Towards the west, there is no large river.

In 1580, Akbar reorganized the territorial boundaries of the Mughal Empire and divided it into twelve *subas*. The Allahabad *suba* was a combination of three provinces: the province of Jaunpur, the region of Kara-Manikpur, and the territories of Bandhogarh and named the *suba* of Allahabad after its capital. This newly formed *suba* was again divided into ten *sarkars* for administrative purposes.[24] Allahabad *suba* extended up to the bank of the river Ghagra in the north, Chausa ferry in the east, and Ghatampur in the west. The topography of the Allahabad *suba* can be divided into two distinct parts—the entire northern portion, which lies between the river Ghagra in the north and Jumna in the south. Ballia in the east and Ghatampur in the west were famous for their fertility from the ancient period. The area was a vast plain except for a slight undulation, which the north-west of the valley might have caused to the south-east. This part of the region may be called the great alluvial plain. Its surface was composed of the deposits of the rivers flowing from the Himalayas. The area's soil was a mixture of *balua* (sand) and *matihar* (clay), commonly called *domant*.[25]

The second part was the southern area of the *suba,* which lay between the river Jumna in the north and the approaches of the Kaimur hills in the south. The northern portion of this area had alluvial soil. Still, this part of the *suba* presented a picture of the wilderness of hills and valleys, ravines and crags, with hills encircling the alluvial basins here and there. This southern region of the *suba* included Mahoba, Ajaigarh, Kalinjar, Khairagarh, Kantit and Chunar, along with the entire territory of Bandhogarh (Baghelkhand). Its soil contained *mar*[26] and *kankar*.[27] There were detached rocks or hills scattered all over the area. It was traversed by an east, enclosing steep valleys. Most of the area was covered with heavy forests.[28]

BIHAR'S TROPICAL HUMID REGION

Bihar may be divided into two broad natural zones, the middle Ganga Plain (the western part of the central Ganga Plain covered the districts of Uttar Pradesh) and the Chotanagpur Plateau. The more significant portion of the *suba* fell in the middle Ganga Plain. In contrast, almost

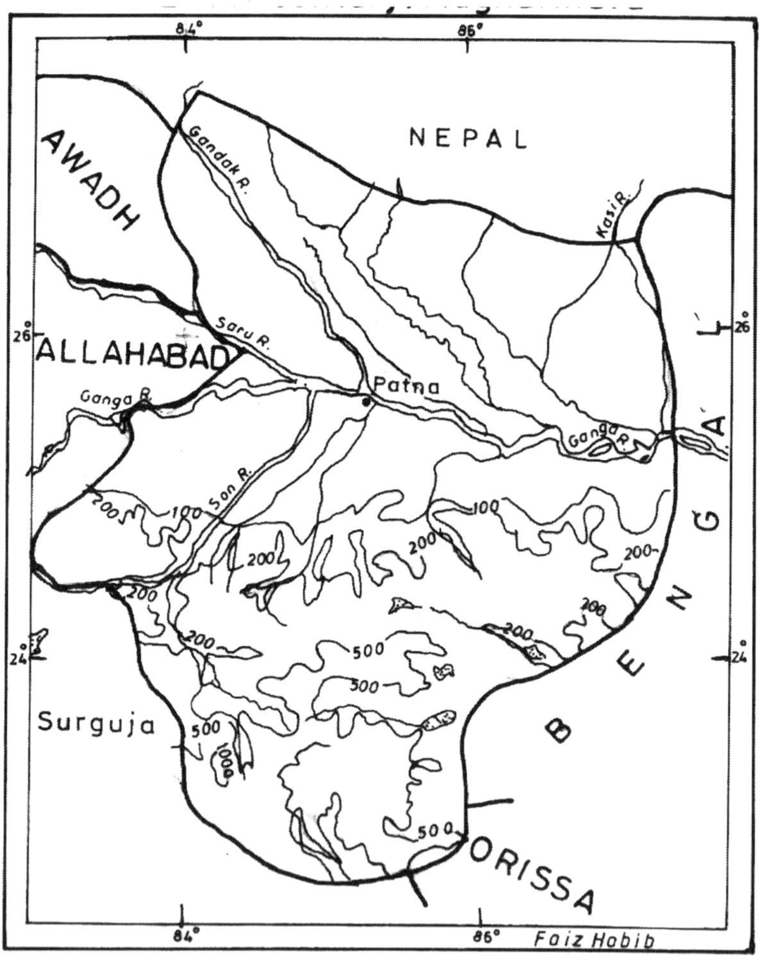

MAP 2.2: BOUNDARIES OF BIHAR *SUBA* DURING THE MUGHAL PERIOD. *COURTESY*: IRFAN HABIB'S *AN ATLAS OF THE MUGHAL EMPIRE,* NEW DELHI: OXFORD UNIVERSITY PRESS, 1982, SHEET NO. 8B.

95 per cent of the *parganas* mentioned in the *Ain-i-Akbari* were in this zone; the Chotanagpur plateau had only a few *parganas*.[29]

The eastern part of the Middle-Ganga Plain, which comprised the *suba* of Bihar, may be further divided into: The Middle-Ganga Plain (North) and the Middle-Ganga Plain (South), with Ganga forming the dividing line between the two.[30]

Except for a small portion of the Shivalik hills in the north, the Middle-Ganga Plain (North) is a level riverine plain. The region is made of fertile alluvial soil, having widespread vegetation and thick groves of fruits and other trees.[31] Bihar *suba* is predominantly an agricultural region.

(a) Ganga-Ghagra Doab (covers Eastern Uttar Pradesh)
(b) Saryupar Plain
  1. Terai (covers Eastern UP)
  2. Saryupar West (covers Eastern UP)
  3. Saryupar East (Saran Plain)
(c) Mithila Plain
  1. Himalayan Plain t
  2. Mithila Plain West
  3. Mithila Plain East
(d) Kosi Plain
  1. Kosi Plain West (Saharsa Plain)
  2. Kosi Plain East (Purnea Plain)
(e) Middle-Ganga Plain (South)

This region covered the *sarkar* of Rohtas and the northern part of the *sarkar* of Bihar of Akbar's area. The region has a fertile alluvial cover, having a considerable east-west extent, with wide variation in rainfall. The region may be divided in the following order:[32]

(a) The Ganga-Son Divide
  (i) The Ganga-Son Divide West (in Eastern UP)
  (ii) The Ganga-Son Divide East (Bhojpur Plain)
(b) The Magadh Anga Plain
  (i) The Magadh Plain
  (ii) The Anga Plain

The above region has good natural irrigation facilities from the tributaries of the Son and is favourable for paddy cultivation.

Most of this region was called Jharkhand or the jungle region. The portion in the extreme south was called Kokhra, also known as the Chotanagpur plateau. The region contained less than 5 per cent of the *Parganas* of Bihar *suba*. Chotanagpur has India's most crucial mineral belt, accounting for 40 per cent to about 100 per cent of the national production of minerals.[33] The annual rainfall in the plateau is 100-25; therefore, agriculture depends entirely on the monsoon. However, the region has a great belt of luxuriant forests.

NETWORKS OF RIVERS IN PUNJAB AND MID-GANGA BASIN

Punjab possesses a network of now-fed rivers, which have played the most crucial part in the country's history. These rivers have added to the agricultural prosperity of the province and have also been helpful in various other ways. They have served as boundaries of *suba, sarkars* and *doabs* since the time of Akbar. They were used as a means of defense because, in those days when the building of bridges and provision of boats was no simple task for the invader, they blocked him, especially when travel became nearly impossible during the rains. Because of this difficulty, the invaders followed a northern route to Delhi, just below the hills, where the river was narrow and the bridge-building work easier. For the same convenience, they invaded India initially. They departed at the end of winter, thus enjoying the best weather in this country while avoiding the worst season of their land. On the other hand, forts were built on the rivers' banks, particularly along the highway, to check the invaders' progress and defend the locals.

The inhabitants were drawn to the waterways because of the widespread sense of insecurity and several ferry towns coming into existence. The first ferry (Shah Guzr) on the Indus was at Attock, under Akbar's massive fort, in 1583. At this place, the famous Grand Trunk Road crossed the Indus. At Nilab, there was another fort,[34] situated 35 *kos* from Peshwar. The third ferry was near Kalabagh, and the route led to Multan after crossing the river.[35] The most famous ferry on the river Jhelum was just below the town of Jhelum. The Chenab had two well-known ferries at Wazirabad[36] and Akhnur. At Mirowal and just below the fort of Lahore, the Ravi was crossed.[37] The Beas is said to have thirty-two[38] ferries between Mandi and its confluence with the Sutlej, but only those at Wirowal, Goindwal, and Rohilla Ghat were famous.[39] The Sutlej had four ferries at Ropar, Machhiwara, Ludhiana and Hari-ka-Patan.

They were also helpful for trade, for country boats could travel up and down these rivers, transporting various items from one location to another within the province and Sind. Wood was also transported from the hills to the lowlands by waterways.[40]

The principal stream of Ajmer is the Banas, which rises from the Aravali range and enters the Ajmer *suba* at the extreme corner of the south-east. Besides Banas, other principal rivers of Ajmer are the Khari Nadi, the Sagarmati and the Saraswati. It came to light during the excavation and it has disappeared now.[41] All have appeared as mere rivulets during the hot weather, but become torrents in the rainy session; neither they nor the Banas are used to transport produce. In the Merwara area, the Khari Nadi rises in the hills near the settlement of Birjal. After forming a boundary between Mewar and Ajmer for a short distance, it merges into the Banas at the northern extremity of the Sawar *pargana*. 'The Dai Nadi, flowing from west to east across the Ajmer district, is intercepted in its early course near Nearan to Baghera, eventually discharging its waters into the Banas River. The Sagarmati River rises near the Bisla Tank in Ajmer and as it flows, it fertilizes the Ajmer valley It then takes a sweep towards the northwards side by Bhaonta and Pisangan to Govindgarh. Here, Sagarmati meets with the Saraswati, which carries the drainage of the Pushkar Valley and the united stream from this point until it falls into Rann of Kutch; the name knows them as Luni. This river is salty, and it is on this stream the Marwar fertility is dependent. The effluent of these streams is many, and some independent rivulets are running northwards into the Sambhar Lake. None of them has got a name as they are merely drainage running only in the rainy season.[42]

The rivers and streams of the Agra comprise the Jumna, its two large tributaries, the Chambal and Utangam along with several smaller streams. The latter is more prone to torrents that swell to a considerable size during the rains but shrink in the hot weather to nominal dimensions. In many cases, they become little more than a series of disconnected pools, with their depth and velocity depending on the intensity of the rainfall during the monsoon. The *doab* in the thirteenth century almost certainly contained pockets of jungle and forest, well connected to the submontane forests through ravines and wilderness that extended along the Yamuna and Ganga rivers. Similarly, elephants could only have roamed the Rajpipla forest of Gujarat in the seventeenth century if there was an unbroken belt of woodland extending to Malwa. But before 1761, the human settlement had cleared the intervening ground and barred elephants' entry.[43]

The total estimate of forest land is about 646 acres under grass, 2,023 acres of bush or tree jungle, and 2,936 acres occupied by scattered trees. The amount available as pasture is consequently tiny; the grasslands are mainly confined to the Agra, Khairagarh, and Bah tahsils, but they are supplemented to some small extent by the ravines and for a very brief portion of the year by the *usar* plains.

Another fact is that Agra was notably devoid of tree forests, which is one of its most distinguishing qualities when contrasted with the north-east districts. The shortage of trees is also confirmed by Pelsaert, who says that there was a significant shortage of firewood in the Agra region, and trees were scarce.[44] Two-thirds of the forest area in the Agra region, where there are a few patches of *babool* or *dhak*, as about *janaura*; the rest of forest cover is mainly in the trans-Jumna *parganas*, for instance, at Ibrahimpur in Itimadpur and Piluaand Karkauli in the south, and near Kotla in the north of Firozabad. There are small stretches of scrub about the hills of Khairagarh. A little is to be seen in the Chambal ravines of Bah, but elsewhere, the surface of the country is comparatively bare. The scattered trees are of the species common to the Gangetic plain. The kinds of mist commonly met with the figs known as *barged, pipal,* and *gular,* the *dhak* and *babool* already mentioned, and the *neem, siras, shisham, ber, tamarind, palms* and bamboos.

Several rivers, creeks, and streams flowed through the *suba* of Allahabad, with the mighty Ghagra River appearing to serve as its northern boundary. With the south-east course, it touched *pargana* Kharid,[45]—the eastern borders of the Jaunpur and Ghazipur *sarkars*, it was navigable for its length and caused significant damage due to flooding during the wet season.[46] The Sai River made its way through Manikpur *sarkar*. It touched the *mahals* of Salon and Rae Bareli[47] and near Jaunpur, joined the river Gomti, which flowed into the Ganges.

The Ganges, the most sacred river in Hinduism, entered the *suba* through Sarkar Kurrah; it passed through Jajmau, Kara, Allahabad, Singraur, Bhadoi and other *mahals* and flowed eastward. [48] towards Dalmau and Kantit.[49] The Ganges divided Kara and Manikpur. At Allahabad, the Jumna joined the Ganges.[50] It traversed Kantit and Chunar. The Gangas then passed through *sarkar* Benaras, touching the *mahal* Ghazipur, Chausa and Ballia before entering Bihar's *suba*.

Taking the Allahabad *suba*, the Jumna divided it horizontally into almost two equal parts. The most fertile plains were found north, up to the Ghagra River. Jaunpur was the name given to the area south of the Jumna. In the *sarkar* of Kara, the Jumna touched the *mahal* Karari.[51] The Ken, a river that originates in central India and flows through Kalinjar's *sarkar* before joining the Jumna, is another river in Allahabad. It passed through dense forests and separated the Kalinjar *sarkar* into two sections, with the *mahals* of Mahoba and Maudaha to the west. Ajajgarh and Kalinjar were to its east. The *mahal* Sihonda in Kalinjar's *sarkar* was touched by Ken.[52]

The Son rises near the Narmada at Amarkantak in the Maikal range. The hill on which its nominal sources are located is Sonbhadra, commonly Son-Munda. It passes through Phaphund.[53] Several tributaries such as Banwas, Gopat, Rihand and Kanhar, all rising from the Kaimur range, joined the Son before reaching the Rohtas region (in the Suba of Bihar).[54]

Bihar has an extensive river system that influences its urban-rural pattern and socio-economic life. The rivers in this region have traditionally been a source of prosperity, transporting mountain soils to the plains and providing commercial transportation. As the primary river in Bihar; the Ganges serves as the final destination for all the water flowing through the region. It divides Bihar into two parts, namely North and South Bihar. During our study, the Ganges was also the essential navigable river for Bihar, providing a water route from Allahabad to Bengal and connecting Allahabad to Agra through the Jumna. Tavernier, in 1665-6, travelled along the Ganges from Patna to Rajmahal in a boat and recorded the course of the river.[55]

In 1670, John Marshall took a ship from Rajmahal to Patna and back, documenting the course of the Ganges between these two points minutely.[56] A comparison of the accounts of Tavernier and Marshall with the present course of the river shows it has changed since then.

In addition, the Ganges entered the province of Bihar from the west near Chausa and left the *suba* to join Bengal near Garhi. Since Marshall's time, the Ganges have seen two significant changes – first; it used to take a more circuitous route between Surajgarh and Ghoraghat than now and second, between Kahalgaon and Garhi, it ran a somewhat straight course.[57]

The Ghaghra or Sarju River is another important river of Bihar that was joined by the Ganges in the *sarkar* of Saran, near the *pargana* of Cherand.[58] The Gandak was also a north-flowing river joining the Ganges near Hajipur.[59] The Burhi Gandak, coming from the north, joins the Ganges northeast of Munger; the Kosi had been the wildest and the most devastating of the Indian rivers for centuries. E. Ahmad calls it the 'Hwang Ho of Bihar'. It is tough to trace its course during the period of our study. However, it entered the Ganges near Cultery in the eighteenth century. According to E. Ahmad, 'its route has altered seventy-five miles in the last two hundred years, transforming nearly three thousand square miles of fertile lands into sandy fields and green marshes and gravely disrupting the rural economy'. A protective barrier was built from Bagha to its confluence with the Ganges to tame and train the river. The Kosi initiative has significantly enhanced the region's agriculture.

The Karamnasa was the first of the southern rivers to reach the Ganges near Chausa.[60] The Son, which merges with the Ganges near Maner, is an essential southern river. However, the river has been known to change its path in the past. The Pun-Pun also comes from south Bihar. According to the *Ain*, it joined the Ganges near Patna.[61] However, Marshall noticed it joined the Ganges near Fatwah. Rennel's *Bengal Atlas* enables the India map survey and shows it was joining the Ganges near Fatwah.[62]

The Chotanagapur plateau was an essential part of Bihar with multiple rivers and streams, the most notable of which were the South Koel, North Koel, Sabarkantha, Damodar and Barakar rivers. The southern rivers have vast shallow channels that run across a level plateau. However, the river courses are broken by waterfalls because of the region's relief. As a result, the plateau's rivers were notoriously unreliable, with continuous flow only during the rainy season and primarily dry riverbeds. The lack of habitation was due to the river pattern. The unearthing of mineral networks has developed a chain of developed communities on the plateau during the last one hundred and fifty years.[63]

THE DOAB OF PUNJAB AND AGRA REGION

Doab is a Persian word comprising 'do' (two) and 'ab' (water), and it means the land between two rivers that join. It is the peculiarity of Punjab that all its rivers join each other separately and then collectively. It's also worth noting that the names of the four *doab* comprise the first letters of the terms of the two rivers enclosed by it.

Punjab is essentially a land of the five *doabs*. The Bist Jullundur Doab between the Sutlej and the Beas, surpassed the rest in population and agricultural produce though the smallest of all. No part of it was a desert. Grain grew in such abundance here that it could meet the needs of the entire province, earning it the title of 'granar comprised'. It comprised 69 *mahals*. The crucial towns were Jullundur, Sultanpur, Kapurthala, Kartarpur and Alawalpur. The Bari Doab is the largest doab, located between the Beas and the Ravi. It included[57] *mahals* and several well-known cities and towns, including Lahore, Amritsar, and Multan.[64] The Rachna Doab, between the Ravi and the Chenab, consisted of 49 *mahals*.[65] It was a primarily an arid area that couldn't be farmed. Its lower level was known as the Sandal Bar.[66] The important places in this *doab* were Wazirababd, Sialkot, Eminabad and Jhang.[67] Between the Chenab and the Jhelum, the Chaj Doab has 22 *mahals*. There was no water in this area, and it was covered with thorny plants and bushes. Gujarat, Shahpur, Bhera, Miani, Sahiwal and Mian Daulah were significant places.[68]

Between the Jhelum and the Indus is the Sind Sagar Doab. It had 48 *mahals*, 42 of which were in the province of Lahore and the rest in Multan. The terrain was hilly in parts and desert in others. Water was limited, the population was sparse, and communities were few. The *Thal* was the name given to the arid area. Attock, Rohtas, Jhelum, Pind Dadan Khan and Hasa Abdal were the places of note.[69]

In 1580,[70] Akbar reorganized the administrative division of the empire; he placed different parts of the *doab* under three *subas*, namely, Delhi, Agra and Allahabad. This division remained unaltered throughout the seventeenth century. Agra Doab comprises Bulandshahr, Aligarh, Eta, Mainpuri, Etwah, Farrukhabad, and Kanpur districts.[71] The whole of the *doab* is a flat alluvial plain. Towards the Jumna on the south, deep and extensive ravines formed by the drainage of the country above break the level surface; they occupy a large area which they render uncultivable and also produce much poverty and infertility of soil in the lands above them. The ground is broken, uneven, and cut up by small channels leading to the slopes that have been so washed away as to leave scarcely enough mould for the seed to germinate; such soil as remains is hard, dry and full of *kankar*. The ravines affect almost one-fourth of the entire area, as the soil above them is sandy and un-irrigable; this belt is chiefly devoted to grazing and thinly covered with *babool* trees. Below the ravines, there are narrow strips of *khadi* land that occasionally widen out to a considerable breadth.

A STUDY OF CLIMATE ON REGIONAL BASIS

The climate of Punjab was moderate but still varied from the moderate cold and hot of Karnal and Panipat to the extremely dry, hot and cold conditions of Rewari and Hisar. As the tract lies within the confines of the Rajputana desert, there was an extreme dryness in the climate, which was salubrious and thus conducive to health.[72] Moreover, in winter, the weather is cool and can be even frosty at night. The heat in summer is intense and in many parts, oppressive.

All the plains heated up during April and May, and June saw intense dry heat and dust storms. The monsoons followed this from July to September. Punjab's temperature falls to over 20 °C in October and November, and by December, the winter had arrived, with temperatures dropping to 0 °C and occasional rain in January. The plains thus had an extreme climate, scorching summers and intensely cold winters. The submontane areas had an equable climate and good rainfall of 30-40 inches per annum. North-west regions experienced a longer, colder winter with less rainfall. In contrast, the central plains had a shorter winter and a heavier rainfall of 16-30 inches a year. The south-west and south-east parts were relatively dry, with only 5-15 inches of annual rain.[73]

Rajasthan's climate has been divided into two distinct climatic zones: western Rajasthan and eastern Rajasthan. A tropical desert, dry and scorching with a moderate winter season, characterized the state's western side. Western Rajasthan included the cities of Barmer, Bikaner, Churu, Jaisalmer, Jodhpur, and Nagaur. Eastern Rajasthan had a drought-prone environment and received less than 75 per cent of the annual rainfall. Ajmer, Alwar, Udaipur, and Jaipur were also part of this region. The climate of Rajasthan was marked by varying temperatures and aridity. Although it experienced seasonal fluctuations of the monsoon throughout the year and remained India's warmest area. The dunes of the desert resulted from a dry climate with very limited or no rainfall. As far as the general weather condition of Rajasthan was concerned, except for some hilly regions, almost the entire state was under the influence of scorching heat waves. Zahiruddin Muhammad Babur wrote about the weather of Agra and north-east Rajasthan, describing it as scorching hot in May and June.[74] Even Abdul Qadir Badauni offers a similar description of the weather in Rajasthan.[75] Mughal chronicler Abul Fazl and Emperor Jahangir[76] have placed Rajasthan in the second category out of the seven climatic zones. The entire world seemed to be divided into climatic categories, and Rajasthan was in second place in the overall climatic classification, which signified a region with extreme heat and cold winters.

In the case *suba* of Ajmer, the winter is comparatively temperate, and the summer is intensely hot, which is an essential description of Ajmer's climate. Further, Ajmer is placed in the second climatic zone as per the prevailing climatic condition of the region. The spring harvest in Ajmer is inconsiderable.[77] Ajmer is a physically a very distinct region from most of its area, either hilly or narrow plain. Evidence suggests that Ajmer was composed of a mixture of sandy soil and stiff yellow loam, in a proportion of one to two, which is ideally not suitable for agriculture. However, the nutrient-rich soil is found only in the Pushkar area, where sugar cane is a crop that could be quickly grown without irrigation.[78] Abul Fazl mentioned in *Ain-i-Akbari* that Ajmer depended primarily on rainfall for irrigation. The soil is sandy and water can be obtained only from a great depth.[79] Thus, the variability in monsoon, *jowar, lahdarah,* and *moth* is the most preferred agricultural crop in Ajmer.[80]

Mr. Wilder believes that though the land of Ajmer is sandy, yet fertile.[81] Ajmer is also considered a zone of dry land. Thus, millet cultivation was a predominant crop over the cereals crop in Ajmer.[82] The success of harvest depends on the rainfall, and in case of rainfall failure the peasants shifted to artificial irrigation from tanks and wells. In *Waqai Sarkar-i-Ajmer*, there was a reference to the *istisga* (rain prayers) during the drought time, where the people of the town gathered outside the city for *namaz-e-barish.*[83] Despite Ajmer being considered a zone of low rainfall, there were two important tanks of Malluser, near Taragarh Fort, Ana Sagar Lake, and the number of *Bagris Jhalras* that had met the irrigation requirement if rainfall was in deficit.[84] Some sources suggest that the rulers permanently extended their helping hand to the sufferers during natural calamities. The ruling class continuously aspired to make the landscape more cultivatable and fertile for agricultural production.

The climate of Agra is drier and hotter than that of any neighbouring British district. While the north experiences shorter hot spells, here the heat lingers longer. Additionally, rainfall is noticeably lower between April and August. While the temperature in Benaras is high, Agra could be the warmest station in the United Provinces. October marks the start of the cold weather. In January, frost is expected; in former days, it was customary to collect ice for the hot weather by filling shallow earthen saucers with water and scraping off the ice that formed upon it. Towards the end of March, the hot west winds from Rajputana's rocky hills and sandy desert blow and gradually increase in intensity during April and May. It varied only by occasional dust storms towards the end of June; a cool breeze comes up from the south-west at midday, presaging the monsoon. During the rains, the temperature is much lower, breaks are frequent and they render the heat extremely trying if protracted.

The climate of Allahabad *suba* is characterized by delightful cold weather, a long and almost intolerably hot summer, and the rainy season, which at its commencement,[85] at all events, is nearly as pleasant as that of Bundelkhand. From November to March, the weather is all that could be desired, the mean temperature approximately that of an English summer, but about the middle of March, the thermometer rises rapidly until May, and in the first half of June, Allahabad becomes one of the hottest stations in United Provinces,[86] if not in India. A marked feature of the climate is the extreme dryness of the atmosphere from November to the beginning of the rains, but when the monsoon bursts, the condition undergoes a remarkable change. The temperature immediately drops to 10 or 15 degrees and varies during the next three months. Still, there is negligible difference between the day and night temperatures because of excessive humidity. Little rain falls in October, but the heat is still oppressive until the humidity decreases with the dry westerly winds, which bring in the cold weather.

About Christmas, there is usually a little rain brought by the storms which pass over these provinces from Sindh and Rajputana. During the hottest parts of the year, the strong westerly winds which blow during the daytime over the Gangetic valley do not infrequently bring dust storms and thundershowers. These winds sweep across the rocky hills of Bara and Meja with incredible fury, and the extreme heat of those tahsils was mainly because of the radiation from the stony outcrops. The government has maintained an observatory at Allahabad since 1870. The mean barometrical pressure for twenty-two years is 29.479 inches, ranging from 29.753 in December to 29.205 in June and July. The temperature is lowest about the beginning of January, and on average, the coldest days are the 8th and 9th. Of that temperature on the grass often falls below freezing point and, in some years, hoar frost is frequently to be seen. The highest daily average temperature is 94.50^{0}, reached on the 4 June. The highest maximum recorded is $119.8^{0,}$ registered on 19 June 1878, but a maximum of 113^{0} or 114^{0} is reached almost every year at the end of May or the beginning of June. The extreme range of temperature during the year is astonishingly great, amounting to an average of 75.3^{0}, the maximum being 114^{0} and the minimum 39.6^{0}. Comparatively, the climate of Allahabad *suba* was healthy, moderate, and quite agreeable.[87] The eastern part of it was moist, except in cold weather.[88] The central part was delightful in winter but intolerable in summer; the southern region, a hilly tract, had an extreme climate.[89]

While describing the regional variations in climate of northern India, Abul Fazl also mentions the general climate of Bihar as intensely hot summers and moderate winters. He adds that the rainy season continues for six months and that warm clothes are not used for over two months in a year.[90] The climate of Bihar can best be described following the three seasons into which the year is divided; the hot season from March to May, rainy season from June to October, and the cold season from November to February.

RAINFALL PATTERNS

The rainfall varies widely in the hill, submontane, and plain tracts of Punjab, and the average rainfall ranges from 28 inches at Rupar to 61 at Kasauli.[91] Most of it occurs in July and August and a little in December and January. The submontane region receives the heaviest rainfall, the easter plain gets an adequate supply, while the western plain comprises of alluvial soil deposited by its rivers. It is naturally very fertile and yields good crops with little cultivation. Besides, a closer study of the pre-colonial landscape amply substantiates our argument that large tracts of land were left uncultivated or under forest cover. The contemporary sources have clarified that there were sparse habitations. Similarly, the extensive pervasiveness of diverse wildlife has been corroborated in many contemporary records, which suggests a sparse agricultural landscape.[92]

As per the *District Gazetteer* record, rainfall at Agra has been maintained since 1845 and at the various tahsil headquarters since 1862. According to the returns of the Meteorological department from 1862 to 1904, the mean average rainfall for the district is 26:53 inches. The rainfall distribution varies considerably; Bah was one of the wettest tahsils in Agra, lying between the two chief rivers. Next comes the trans-Jumna station of Itimadpur and Firozabad, with 27.47 and 27.22 inches, respectively. The wettest years on record are 1845, with a fall of 42.55 inches at Agra. On the other hand, some droughts have been remarkable in Agra. In 1840, the rainfall was a severe defect everywhere; Agra and Khairagarh obtained precipitation of less than 10 and Kiraoli less than 8 inches, while the district average was 11.63 inches,[93] the worst drought ever recorded in Agra.

The average annual rainfall in Allahabad from 1864 onwards was 37.54 inches. The annual precipitation in the Doab area is greater than the average. Of the trans-Ganga tahsils, Handi comes first with

37.34, followed by Phulpur with 36.27 and Soraon with 35.34. In the trans-Jumna tract, Karchana took the lead with 39.57 and the next to come to Mehja with 38.95 and Bara with 37.8 inches. This figure illustrates the influence of the Southern hills and forests and the principal rivers. In the Doab, conditions are similar to those of Fatehpur, north of the Ganges, and to those of southern Oudh. However, the comparatively heavy rainfall in Karchna seems to result from its location, which falls within the path of both the storms that follow the course of the rivers and those that sweep over the Vindhya Hills.[94]

The *suba* of Bihar, especially the Tirhut, Patna and Bhagalpur regions, received high rainfall, making the region chiefly rice-producing areas.[95] Of the total rainfall of the province, about 85-90 per cent is from the monsoon. In north Bihar, the annual rainfall is around 120 cm[96] while in the extreme north, it is 152 cm;[97] in the plateau region, too, it's above 150 cm An average amount of rain in Ranchi, Hazaribag and Dhanbad regions is 151 cm, 134 cm and 131 cm respectively.

VEGETATION: BUSHES, GRASS AND TREES

On account of heavy rains in the hills and the submontane region of Punjab, there were plenty of natural forests. Thick jungles of *dhak* trees covered the country at the foot of the hills. Besides, there were several forests of note. One of them was the Lakhi Jungle. It was in the Bathinda district, measuring about 24 *kos*[98] on each side. In the north, it was bounded by the country of Rai Kalha (Jagraon), on the coast by the government of Haryana, on the south by Bhatner and the west by the desert of Bikaner. It was noted for its fine pasture ground, admirable cattle and excellent horses, introduced during successive invasions of Nadir Shah and Ahmad Shah Durrani. The inhabitants of this place were given to thieving, cattle lifting, robbery and fighting and the imperial officers could not punish or check them.[99]

There was also a thick overgrowth of tall grass, reed and scrub stretching for miles along the riverbanks in the *doabs*. These afforded excellent shelter to the Sikhs and other predatory bands. The systematic collection of information on Punjab's natural vegetation and wildlife could be only after the rise of the modern sciences of botany and zoology. Therefore, it is not surprising that attempts at collecting and classifying such information were made only after the annexation of the kingdom of Lahore to the British Indian Empire in 1849. The *District Gazetteers* of the third quarter of the nineteenth century contained detailed information on flora, showing the change coming about. In a comprehensive description of Punjab, James Douie has recounted sub-regional variations in Punjab's natural vegetation and wildlife. However, this does not mean that the Punjabi writers or the early European travellers to Punjab did not take any interest in the natural environment. They did, and their information has its significance.

The earlier references to the flora of Punjab during the medieval period come from the creative writers of the region, who wrote in the language spoken by the common people. Sheikh Farid, for example, refers to flowers and fruits and trees, thorns and the jungle. He refers specifically to the flowers of *kasumbh* and *kaval.*[100] We know that Baba Farid lived mostly in Pakpattan on the bank of the Ravi and he was familiar with the flora around Pakpattan.

Similarly, Guru Nanak (d. 1539) refers selectively to the natural vegetation of Punjab: the trees blossoming in forests, the mango groves, the twigs draped in new colours, the gnats wailing in the forests, the lush green twigs, the water reeds in bloom, the twigs shorn of their leaves and the green grass. Guru Nanak's purpose was to underscore that all the twelve months are auspicious, and all the days and nights, every hour, minute and second, are happy if one is absorbed in the love of God.[101] Further, in his *Bara Maha*, Guru Arjan Dev (d. 1606) refers only to the twig that withers without water and to forest and grasses in bloom.[102]

Shah Husain, a contemporary of Guru Arjan, is concerned with flora and fauna. He talks of the jungle, *bela* and *jhall,* the trees and their branches, and the leaves of the *pipal* trees; he refers to *shisham, babul,* and thorns; he talks of *mehndi, chamba, aruna* and flowers, etc.[103] Shah Husain lived in Lahore, on the bank of the Ravi; he was primarily familiar with the flora of the country around Lahore.

The systematic information on the natural environment in the sixteenth century in Mughal documents seems unclear. It was the *Ain-i-Akbari,* which provided detailed information on several aspects of Indian life. The *Ain* refers to a forest near Khushab because of the interest of the Mughal emperors in hunting grounds.[104] That it was not the only forest in Punjab is clear from the *Atlas of the Mughal Empire,* which records the Lakhi Jungle below the confluence of the Sutlej and the Beas where *cheetahs* were hunted;[105] the *chhamb* of Kahnuwan where birds were shot, a jungle near Bhera and a forest between Samana and Bathinda, a hunt of the *cheetahs*. There was yet another area close to Hissar and Agroha, preserved as the imperial hunting grounds.[106] Though not shown in the *Atlas*..., there was a hunting ground near Sheikhupura where the Mughal emperor Jahangir constructed the Hiran Minar (Stag Tower).[107] The deer, like the tiger, was the preferred animal for hunting.

The European travellers of the Mughal times give little information about the flora and fauna of Punjab. William Finch, for example, refers to flowers of all sorts at Sirhind, which would not be wild.[108] Bernier refers to a peculiar grass used as fodder for horses.[109] In the Sikh works of the seventeenth and eighteenth centuries, there is more detail but without reference to specific areas: in the *Vars* (ballads) of Bhai Gurudas (d. 1638), for example, there are references to flowers and trees such as *chameli, dhatura, dhrek, kamal, kikar* and *painju.* He talks of the *simmal* trees with their red flowers and all trees and plants are becoming green in the rainy season when the *akk* winters are away.[110] See Appendix I on page 211 for more details about the trees of the Punjab plain.

Writing in the second half of the eighteenth century, Waris Shah refers to several items, of which we will highlight only a few. There is *chibarh,* a miniature melon that is usually not sweet but sour. Among the medicinal plants are *sit, bhakhra* and *kuar-gandal.* Among the grasses is *munj;* among the trees is *neem,* known for its bitter taste; among the bushes is *sar, sarkanda* or *kana.*[111]

The European travellers to Punjab in the time of Sikh rule were more curious about its flora than the travellers of the Mughal period. They noticed the domesticated animals referring to wild animals, birds and natural vegetation. Moorcroft, for example, refers to the mulberry tree, the fig, the *pipal,* the *shisham* and the *haldi.* He also refers to hemp and *dab* grass.[112] Alexander Burnes noticed the wild fruits *peelo, ber* and mango. Among the trees were cypresses, date trees, the weeping willow, and the *jand.* Apart from *dob* grass, there was the rose bush, the milk bush, and the *kari.*[113] The trees are *kikar/babul, cypresses,* date trees, pines and ziziphus.[114]

William Barr, who marched from Delhi to Kabul in 1839, gives more specific information in terms of location. Between Sonipat and Patiala, there was a jungle abounding with game and so was a *dhak* jungle near Nilokheri and Shahbad. There was another vast jungle beyond Rajpura, broken at places by patches of cultivation and groves of large trees. Near Khanna, a pretty grove of *babul* trees with yellow-scented blossoms. Beyond Sonipat was a banyan tree of significant dimensions. There was a jungle of *ber* trees beyond Hasan Abdal. Pretty groves of date trees were conspicuous near Gharaunda and in Lahore. Mango groves were extensive around Thanesar and Ambala. Mulberry trees were noticeable in Hasan Abdal and Naushahra across the Indus. There were handsome *pipal* trees near Karnal, Rajpura and Hasan Abdal. The brushwood and trees around Patti provided an 'agreeable change from the increasing barrenness' south of the Sutlej. The bushes were stunted on the hills around the Kuhan in the Sind Sagar Doab. Around Nilokheri and near Shahbad, there was long grass. In the swampy land beyond Lahore, the grasses were 10 feet tall. There was a long stretch of the jungle with grass between Gujranwala and Wazirabad. Wild shrubs and brushwood filled the ravine in Rohtas in the Sind Sagar Doab. There were wild and sweet-smelling dandelions across the Indus.[115]

The soil and climate conditions across the rest of the plain were suitable for drought-resistant scrub jungle, which once flourished across extensive areas between the Yamuna and Jhelum rivers. The most giant and truly indigenous trees of the Punjab plains, according to Douie, were the *farash* and the thorny *kikar,* which grew well in sandy soils and yielded wood for agricultural implements. Smaller thorny acacias like *nimbar* or *raunj, khair, pilchi* or *jhao* and the dwarf tamarisk were common. The scrub jungle comprised *jand, jal* or *van,* and the *karil* (*karir*) had long roots, small feathery leaves, and thorns. The *jand* was a proper tree; the *jal* gave a fruit called *peeloo,* popular in times of famine.[116] Among other plants, families were the *khip,*

Farid ki booti, jawasa or camel thorn, cleomes, orchid and three types of Mediterranean plants.[117] The sandier tracts had *akk, harmful,* and colocynth gourd growing abundantly. Several weeds were also prevalent.[118] Along the roads, the *shisham* or *tahli, kikar, sirsi, pipal* and *borh* were planted trees. A detailed list of shrubs, plants and weeds in the Punjab plain is given in Appendix II on page 213.

The north-west plains east of the Jhelum had a distinctly Mediterranean flora. Poppies, crucifers, diplotaxis, and moricandia were Italian species. Some Asiatic plants like *borange* and *paighambari phul* were also expected, along with the thorny *acacias, phalahi* and other xerophytes. The scrub forest in north-west Punjab was covered with bamboo and, in some parts, with the dwarf palm. A scanty growth of *phalahi* and wild olive was also prevalent along with *jand, jal, karil* and *farash*. Between the Sutlej and the Jhelum, much of the scrub had disappeared with the advance of canal irrigation by the early twentieth century.[119] This area had grasses, too, and in good seasons formed an extensive grazing area.

The submontane areas of the plain, abroad belt along the Shivaliks, had a solid Indo-Malayan element in their flora. The *dhak, chichru, palah* and *palas* extended all over and provided excellent firewood, good timber, valuable gums, dye and leaves as fodder for buffaloes. A tree commonly planted was the *dhekar* along with *bahera,* an enormous Indo-Malayan tree. Like Marwan, *bansa, bhekar* and Indo Malayan, shrubs were usual. A curious cactus-like Euphorbia Royleana also grew abundantly and was used as a hedge.

In the sub-Himalayan zone, a strong infusion of Indo-Malayan flora was noticeable as many flowering trees—the *simmal* or silk cotton tree, the *amalts* and *dhawi* with bright red flowers.[120] Flowering shrubs included *sanatha* or *mendru, garna, clematis, mimosa* and Mediterranean flora like oleander. The wild pear, olive, *khair, tum, khaman* and species of figs were 'valuable' products of the lower hills. Bamboos, impatiens, lilies, ipomoeas and gloriosa were found in the low hills.[121] Alpine flora of the Mediterranean type became more noticeable at higher altitudes.

Writing in the early twentieth century, James Douie presents a broad overview of the natural environment of Punjab plains and points out certain specific species found in particular areas. He also notices some changes in the flora with the passage of time and links these with the extension of colonial rule to the region in the mid-nineteenth century. Douie, thus, takes a comparatively keen interest in the natural world. However, he does not go into much detail or variations within each sub-region.

The gazetteers of the Punjab province and its districts add more information on its flora and fauna and enable us to appreciate the variation in the natural environment at the sub-regional level. The submontane areas were affluent in natural vegetation level. There was an abundance of *shisham* in the Shakargarh tahsil of Gurdaspur.[122] Common trees included *siris, phalahi, kikar, jaman, phagwara, pipal* and *ber*. The Pathankot area also had *simmal, the chilla, kar, kokoab, sufeda and bahera.* There were *neem, mohwa* and date palms in moist places. Though rarely, *mava, puna, chamror, dhaman, kamela, kaho, gun, amla, pansora* and *jand* could also be seen. Fruits trees like *amb* and *tut* grew everywhere and in some areas, *sangtara, mitha, khatta, nimby, chahotra, loquat, aru* and *anar* were found. *Tut, jaman* and *shisham* were primarily known in canal plantations. Mulberry was typical and considerably large but was not as satisfactory as timber. *Shisham* was the most valuable timber. It was safe from white ants and usually goats; *phalahi* and hill olive were not readily available; hard to work with. They were not as popular as timber. *Sirsi* was used for oil presses, but it was liable to be destroyed by goats, as were *phalahi, kikar* and *ber*. Camels depleted the *pipal.*[123]

The area of Gurdaspur was rich in grasses. The *dhub* or *dhubra* variety grew in fertile soils and the riverbanks were covered with the coarse *dab*; *khair* or *jhar* was found everywhere. *Dodh* and *mahva,* growing everywhere in the Shakargarh tahsil, were used as fodder. *Kaserla, bulrushes, reeds, kandiairi, leh* and *thatch* grew in swamps. The *bughat* or wild leek emerged in spring. *Benku* grass, poisonous to cattle, also sprang up in some places. *Bhang* grew freely. Bushes like *mendu* or *santha, basati* and *garna* were prominent as undergrowth. Cactus grew wild and was also used as hedges around fields. The Ambala district had a smaller variety of grasses. *Sarkanda* and *kahi* were valuable in protecting soil from erosion. They were useful for thatch and rope making, too.[124] The low slopes in the Hoshiarpur district were well covered with grass and brushwood, though not as luxuriantly as the Gurdaspur belt.[125]

In the submontane zone, we can notice that the eastern and western edges were somewhat barren, with scanty growth of trees, some shrubs and grasses. The central portion, Gurdaspur and Sialkot, had luxuriant flora of a wide variety—trees, shrubs and grasses of several types.[126]

The western plain formed an arid region with various soils that were not uniform in quality. Some were *maria,* a fertile loam and another saline. The quality of soil determined the kind and density of vegetation. With the slightest rain, the area got covered with various grasses and forms of *lana.*[127] The arid western flora was represented by the *van* or *pilu, jand, kari, ber* and *malha* as bushes. The *van* was of no use as fuel or for agriculture, *jand* was used as firewood and for making charcoal, while *kari* provided small rafters. The edible berry fruits of the *kari, ber* and *pilu* were used as medicine and food.[128] Some tracts away from the river valleys showed a startling transition to waste and jungle, where the decrease of plants and animal life was oblivious.[129]

In the *bar,* a barren region due to the absence of water, ample grasses sprang up after the rain, and it became a pasture ground for immense herds.[130] Tree vegetation was limited to hardy varieties like *karil* or wild *caper, jand* and *pilu.* In riverine tracts and near bungalows, *kikar* and *farash* were planted and sometimes, *shisham* and *sirus* could also be found. The British administrators tried to promote the growth of 'useful' trees but only with partial success. The few trees could be counted on the finger and were found only around villages.[131]

The Salt Range tract had somewhat different vegetation because of salt in the soil. The internal areas were well-wooded and green. With bushes of bog myrtle and *bahekar* and hardy kinds of trees—wild olive or *kau, phalahi* or Indian mulberry and *kunger.* The *shisham,* though shorter, also thrived here. The outer area of the Salt Range, especially the southern face was marked by stunted *phalahi* and *salsolas* as vegetation.[132]

Near the confluence of the rivers in the south-west corner of Punjab, the riverain areas had thick jungles of reeds, tall *sar* grass and low tamarisk. The river islands were often overgrown with dense *kanh* in Mianwali and *kan* and *munj.* The riverain tract had graves of date palms as well.[133] Scrub as *lana, phog, bui* and a sprinkling of *khaggal, kari* and *jand* and *sain* provided fodder for cattle after the rains.

The central part of the Punjab plains was an unbroken continuous-level plain, sparsely wooded, owing to extended cultivation in these fertile areas. The trees indigenous to the country and planted by cultivators near ponds and wells were *pipal, borh, dhrek, tut, bokain* and *acacia.* [134] The Kapurthala area had *shisham, kikar, tut, ber* trees and a palm in the Sultanpur.[135] The *pipal* was revered and hardly ever cut down, though lopped as fodder by camel drivers. The *ber* was valued for its fruit and roofing capacities. It was a favourite tree near Muslim shrines. The *kikar* was the principal timber tree and was found all over since it grew in all kinds of soils. The *jand* was rapidly disappearing with the extension of the cultivation. Other trees included the *karil, phula, ber, reru* and *dhak* or *chichna.* The *dhak* leaves were used as fodder for cattle and to wrap foodstuff; its scarlet flowers were used as a dye its juice was used as gum, and its wood was used as fuel. Although not indigenous to this tract, the *tahli* was a proper tree and was rarely planted by cultivators. The *pharwan* was planted for shade and the *sirinh* was a roadside tree that suffered from the ravages of camels and goats. Closer to towns were orchards of mango, *loquat, peach, pear,* limes and *jaman* grown for fruit. Ornamental trees like *tun, neem, sohanjana* and *amaltas* were rather rare. The double rows of trees planted along, and the roads were well cared for.[136]

The southernmost parts of this region were relatively rare in natural vegetation.[137] The *kikar* and *karil* were found near habitations, including bushes like *khep, pala* and *babul. Akk* and *sar* plants were also to be found at places. This zone bordering the desert area was barren.

On the whole, the picture of the natural vegetation of the plains that emerges from the gazetteers is one of the marked variations. The submontane belt was one of abundant vegetation of several varieties —trees, shrubs and grasses but in its central parts, this belt's eastern and western edges were somewhat lacking in greenery and had an arid type of vegetation, stunted bushes and scanty grasses. The central plains had a variety of trees—both evergreen and arid types, fruit trees and some shrubs and grasses. On the western plains, desert-type flora was limited, with only a few plantations of acacia and *shisham.* Grasses sprang up only after the rains and only a few dwarf bushes survived. The inner salt range area has broken this monotony with some greenery of the low hills kind. The south-western and southern boundaries of the Punjab plains were rather desolate concerning natural vegetation, having only a few date palms in the south-west corner and some grasses. Desert-type trees, plants and scanty, dry grasses were also found in the south-east tract. While the vegetation gradually diminished as one traveled further south and south-west. The entire region's most pressing need was water.

The vegetation was fragile and sparse, especially in the central and western parts of the Rajasthan. There were very few forests in the region. In such conditions, it was necessary to protect the existing ones. Lal Chand complained to the ruler of Amber about the tree falling in his *pargana* and he expected punishment from the ruler for the culprits. We also have a reference from Jaipur. It records about a cash punishment for such crimes.[138]

The attitude towards tree conservation is reiterated in the following anecdote written by Nainsi in *Khyat.* He informed us that Maldevji got the *babool* trees of Merta cut. In response to it, Viram Deo said that he would cut the mango trees of Jodhpur. People urged Viram Deo not to cut the trees, as they were considered sacred. In his anecdote, the chief is reiterated from cutting trees by his advisors and supports conservation. A significant example in this regard was the representation of the *khejari* tree in the official flag of the Bikaner kingdom. It is ascribed to the accordance of due recognition of the region's natural vegetation.

It is difficult to compare the above instance and environmental conservation practices with today. It is essential to keep in mind that the present-day environmental movement result from the emergence of industrialization and colonialism. However, in this context, Rajasthan in the pre-colonial period was part of an attempt made by state or religious sects to protect the natural resource base.

The attempt made by states cannot be separated from their concerns to protect and maximize revenue from natural resources. There is plenty of evidence that suggested punishment was awarded for cutting green trees. The punishment was always demanded in cash and its amount became the source of state revenue. In the village Saithal, *pargana* Bahatri, a person was punished for cutting down a *neem* tree.[139] *Neem* has excellent medicinal properties and, thus needs protection. It was inauspicious to cut *neem*. Therefore, doing so was punished. Similarly, cutting *peepal*[140] and *harmful*[141] trees was deemed to be inauspicious. It is essential to point out that *peepal* and *bad* had been worshipped; thus, religious consideration also led to punishment.

We also have instances of punishments for cutting *jamun* trees, etc., cutting *babool* trees was also a punishment. *Babool* had been part of the natural vegetation of Rajasthan, and it needed little or no care. In the arid part, *babool* was the dominant tree and provided food for the camels. Considering *babool's* economic and ecological value, punishing people who tried to cut it was necessary.

From the above discussion, we can say that the state was not protecting any tree. Instead, it was interested in extracting maximum revenue and safeguarding its economic interests. It is essential to point out that even cutting grass from forests or hills was a punishable offence. Reducing the practice of conservation to mere economic explanation shall be only a partial explanation. The preservation of trees has been an ancient practice and part of the culture.

In the Agra region, the trees found in artificial groves are usually mangoes, with a small admixture of *jamun, bel* and other indigenous species, while in the gardens of the well-to-do may be see limes and oranges, pomegranates, custard-apples, guavas and other well-known fruit trees cultivated in northern India. At a mere 0.4 per cent of the total, the grove's proportion is probably smaller than in numerous other districts. The average grove area in each tahsil is only 668 acres and this is only exceeded to any appreciable extent in Agra and Firozabad.[142]

The trans-Ganges tahsils of Allahabad contain no forest and very little jungle. There are patches of *dhak* or *chhiul*, the chief being between Phulpur and Sarai Mamrez. Along the Ganges, there are large areas with tamarisk, which is of some economic value. The banks of the Ganges are covered in places with a good growth of *babool* and *ber,* which in the lowlands of the river, *sarpat* grass grows in abundance.[143] In the south of Karchana, as also in the *mar* lands of the other *parganas*, the *gandar* grass grows in abundance, and this is utilized for thatching and making brooms, while its roots are well-known as *khas-khas*. The *babool* is very common in the same areas, but other trees are comparatively scarce. On the upland plateau of

Meja and Bara, grass and shrubs are interspersed with more or more miniature thick jungle comprising *ber, tendu, jamun, salai seoha* and *gular*, with a sprinkling of *mahua*, mango, *salai* and *gular* trees and clusters of bamboos. In some parts of Meja, *haldi*, *chhayan* and *sagon* or teak are found. The largest of these jungles are the Loni in Meja and the Gandhewa in Bara, both possessing fine clumps of bamboo and tree growth, the area, in either case, being 2 or 3 square miles.[144]

Besides scattered shrubs, there were regular and dense forests in the northern part of the *suba* along the north banks of the Ghagra.[145] The areas near Allahabad and Kantit were covered with thick forests.[146] In the vicinity of Kara-Manikpur was a dense forest in which elephants were found.[147] The region was covered with forests from Kalinjar to Chunar and Kaimur Hills in the south. The fort of Kalinjar[148] was covered with a dense forest, where elephants and hawks and other animals were trapped. Ebony was found there, and many kinds of fruit grew.[149] The ravines of the river *ken,* along with the hilly region of Bandhogarh, were covered with forests.[150]

The *mahal* of Bhadoi and Kantit in the *sarkars* of Allahabad and Chunar formed the central tableland. This part of the *suba* was covered with hills, valleys, and forests.[151] The area around Chunar was considerably backwards. Abul Fazl says, 'In its vicinity, there is a tribe of men who go naked, living in the wilds and subsist by their bows and arrows and the game they kill.'[152] Elephants were also found in these forests.

Bihar, with moderate rainfall and fertile soil the region was a natural habitat of a dense forest cover of *sal* and other species like *shisham, jamun, mahua, ber,* etc. Even up to the end of the 1840s, a large area of Saryupar was densely forested, and so also were the banks of the Rapti, the Ghaghara and other rivers. There were sizeable pockets in South Ganga Plain. The remnants of the once extensive *sal* forests are found in the northern Gorakhpur, Saharsa and Purnea districts. Elsewhere, the induced vegetation is seen as *savannah* with grasses and bushland dotted with trees of different sizes. Naturally growing trees like the *peepal* cover the village wastelands or vacant places. *Neem, babool, palmyra*, date-palm, *dhak,* etc., are found in the *diaras*, Tarai or other low-lying areas. The more omnipotent *dub, motha* and different less pervasive types are in cultivated fields, mounds or field boundaries, and left-over lands. The planted fruits orchards and groves of trees comprise mango, *jamun,* guava, *mahua,* jack fruit, plums, lemon, etc., timber like *shisham,* etc., while bamboo clumps grow around and within settlements. Also, such thorny-bushy plants as the *senhur,* plum bushes, etc., grow on waste or neglected lands but the former is sometimes planted for fencing farms or orchards.

The Champaran forests are classified as (1) Siwalik *sal,* (2) Moist (Gangetic) high alluvial *sal* and (3) Gangetic moist deciduous riverain forest.

There is some difference in vegetal cover north of the Ghaghara and the Ganga on the one hand and to their south on the other. The groves, orchards, marshy vegetation, etc., are more frequent, particularly in the northern Bihar plains. There is more open parkland vegetation in the south, the frequency of groves decreases, and isolated trees are more common. *Sabai* is the most important grass in the region, mainly north.[153]

AGRICULTURE

Agriculture was the mainstay of Indian economic life. Agriculture means the science of practice, farming, which includes cultivating the soil to grow crops and rearing animals to provide food, wool, cotton and other products.[154] The most encompassing use of the term agriculture includes the distribution, processing, and service industries, for instance, food manufacturing. The study of agrarian life and agriculture included, among other things, geographical features form, soil fertility, climate and production. In short, the study of agriculture is ascribed to the human-nature interaction as a general term—agriculture includes most of the activities associated with farming, exploitation, and breeding of plants and farm animals and the scientific and technological study of agricultural processes and the means of increasing production.[155]

The great-cultivated expanse of India's plains, valleys, and hill-slopes has been created in a stubborn struggle against nature, which the Indian peasant has carried on for thousands of years. Forest and waste have been treated, recovered and retreated in an endless cycle before his hoe and plough. Therefore, every period in Indian history has had its forest line and desert frontier, besides its political and military boundaries. For the study of Indian history in any aspect, this boundary line between man's domain and nature's is essential. A necessary feature of Indian agriculture has been the large number of crops raised by the peasants. In *Ain-i-Akbari,* Abul Fazl gives an exhaustive list of the sixteen crops of the *rabi* harvest.[156]

(A) Cropping Patterns

The importance of agriculture in the economy of the Punjab region can be visualized by the fact that more than 70 per cent of its people reside in rural areas. There are two main crop seasons: the *kharif* and *rabi*. The major *kharif* crops are *bajra*, maize, *jowar*, cotton, rice and sugar cane. Among the *rabi* crops, wheat, gram, barley and mustard are notable in Punjab. The most important crop from the standpoint of the area occupied is wheat. It is the dominant crop in the irrigated areas of the Malwa Plain. The following important cereal is *bajra* which is almost entirely grown in the dry and sandy district of south Punjab. Among other cereals are barley mainly grown in the drier parts, and rice is becoming important in the wetter and water-logged and some of the canal-irrigated districts of the region. Karnal has the largest area of rice in the rice-growing district of Punjab (now Haryana).

Jowar and maize are both cereal and fodder crops that attain importance—grown in the drier and the latter in the comparatively wet parts. The cultivation of *jowar* is predominately on the north-east side of Punjab. Cotton is the most important among the traditional cash crops, though the acreage under sugar cane is also increasing. After the Partition, the central cotton-producing regions of the West Punjab and Sind went with Pakistan. Only the districts south of the Sutlej are Punjab's central cotton producers region.

An essential concern for agrarian society has been water availability in the arid and semi-arid regions. The state of Rajasthan is an exception. Where did an unequal annual distribution of rainfall and a low water table that was often saline? Continuous water availability was a primary concern, which requires scholarly examination at the social and political levels. This will bring out the role of responses of social elites in water politics.[157] The general geographical features of the region suggest that there were inadequate water resources, thus, leading to limited possibilities for human settlement and agriculture in

Rajasthan.[158] However, the fact is that various indigenous methods of water conservation were prevalent in the pre-colonial period; some of these still exist today. Wherever feasible, the essential way to secure water was through wells.

The very nature of the monsoon in Rajasthan can also be seen in the effect on agriculture production. The crops to be sown depended on the timing of the rains. If the rains got delayed, they would plant coarser crops like a *moth*. Crops like *bajra* and *jowar* require watering, whereas *moths* can only sustain themselves on two to three watering.[159]

However, the fact is that most of the south-eastern region of Rajasthan have two crops productions in one session. *Kharif* cultivation depended almost entirely on the rains; the availability of irrigation facilities primarily determined intensive cultivation during the *rabi* and a variety of lucrative crops. The diversity of crops was an essential feature of the agriculture of the eastern region. In the *kharif* harvest, the dominant crops were *bajra, moth, mung, urad, jowar,* etc., as such, *bajra* cultivation dominated the region. Apart from food crops, cash crops like cotton, sugar cane, indigo, etc., were also grown. The range of crops grown during the *rabi* harvest was limited. Wheat, barley and gram dominated the *rabi* harvest. The aridest western and north-western part of Rajasthan has generally sustained a single crop a year because of minimal rainfall. However, with the help of irrigation facilities, possibility of two crops was always a reality. Like the eastern part, the cultivation of *bajra* dominated the crop in *kharif* and wheat in *rabi*.

The practice of inter-mixing of crops was another characteristic feature of Rajasthan farming. Many minor millets were grown along with cereals to replenish the productivity of the soil,[160] the most crucial being *kangri, kodra, kuri, malicha* and *sama*. The creeping pulses *moong, urad* and *moth* was sown sometimes with *jowar*. The winter pulses *masur* and *tur* were grown to perform the same function.[161] Similarly, crops were rotated to conserve the productivity of the land. The system of crop rotation was based on the result of local experience.[162] For example, a cotton field was left fallow in the next harvest when it was sown with maize in the fall, barely in the following spring, maize follow during the spring before cotton was again planted in the fall.

The remarkable feature of Agra that impressed contemporary observers was that harvesting two or three crops in some areas was a reasonable possibility of an available irrigation facility.[163] As far as information given in *Akbarnama* gives revenue rates for sixteen crops of the *rabi* harvest cultivated in all the revenue circles of the Agra province. Further, the seventeenth century saw the introduction and expansion of two major crops, tobacco and maize; both were immigrants from the New World. Initially, tobacco was cultivated on the western coast; soon after 1600, it was grown in almost all parts of the Mughal empire.[164] Shireen Moosvi, who had made a detailed comparison of the yield table in the *Ain* with the date on yields of various crops in the Delhi *doab* region during the latter half of the nineteenth century, argued that there was little change in the yield of food crops in Agra circle. This accords with Moreland's earlier finding, based on the *Ain*'s prices and assessment rates of different crops in the provinces of Awadh, Agra, and Delhi, that the value of produce per acre of one food crop in terms of another did not change substantially between 1600 and 1910, an exception being offered by *bajra* which appears to have been undervalued in the earlier period.[165]

With cash crops, it is identical to what in Mughal records are termed *jins-i-kamil* or *jins-i-ala,* 'high-grade crops' chiefly grown for the market. The best quality of indigo grew in the Bayana tract near Agra.[166] a lower rate of indigo was produced in the *doab* around Khurja and Kol (Aligarh).[167]

Apart from that, the fruit plants were always important in the mind of the royal family; they aspired to grow almost every variety of fruit in their gardens. The attempt to cultivate Central Asian fruit plants had begun with Babur,[168] and it was claimed during the reign of his grandson (Akbar) that melons and vines as good as those of Turan and Iran were being grown in the plains around Agra.[169]

Based on the *District Gazetteer of Agra*, the agricultural development of Agra attained a high level, and the proportion of the land cultivated was very significant during the British period, despite the comparative absence of natural advantages. The usual harvest is the *kharif* or autumn, the *rabi* or spring, and *zaid* or additional yield. The crops grown in the *zaid* harvest are chiefly melons and vegetables, while occasionally a little *chana*. In terms of area sown, the *kharif* harvest stands out as the most important of the main harvests. The total area the *kharif* harvest covered was 61.6 per cent against 43 per cent occupied by the *rabi*. The crucial crops planted under the *kharif* harvest were *bajra*, *juar* and cotton; these three, sown either by themselves or with *arhar*, occupy more than 87 per cent of cultivable land. The other *kharif* crops were maize, sugar cane, *moth*, *urad* and *moong*. The crops sown under *rabi* were wheat, gram, peas and *bajra*. A little *Masur* was also grown in the area.[170] Apart from it, other fruit plants were also grown in the Agra region; during Jahangir's reign, thousands of pineapples were gathered every year in the imperial gardens of Agra.[171]

Akbar divided Allahabad *suba* into 15 *dasturs*. That division of *suba* into *dasturs* was based on agricultural efficiency of land, cropping pattern, nature of the harvest, and quality of the soils. This *dastur* helps us study the relative position of agricultural efficiency of different areas of the *suba*. The rate of land revenue demand can also be treated as an index of soil fertility. Referring to *Ain-i-Akbari*, Abul Fazl mentioned forty-one crops were cultivated in Allahabad *suba*. Out of which ten were food grains, and the remaining crops were either cash crops or crops of other minor nature. A close study of the *Ain-i-Akbari* reveals all crops did not grow equally well in all *dasturs*.[172]

Refering to *Ain*, Abul Fazal has given the rates of government demand per *biga* for various crops of the *suba*. Regarding determining rates in the 'ten-year settlement', he stated, 'From the beginning of the 15th year of the Divine era to the 24th year, an aggregate of the collection rates was formed and a tenth of the total was fixed as the annual assessment.' One-third was the government's demand. He further adds, '... The best crops were considered each year.'[173]

It is evident from the statement of Abul Fazal that the figures of the government demand per *bigha*, described in various *dasturs*, were determined based on the average produce of ten years. Therefore, it can be said that the rate of demand and the productivity of the land were co-related. The demand rate can also be treated as an index of soil fertility in a limited sense. 'Even if the *dastur* rates appear to be exaggerated, they at least help us study the relative position of the agricultural efficiency of the different areas of the *suba*. It is on this presumption that the data of the *Ain-i-Akbari* have been utilized and worked out. An analysis of the figures of various *dasturs* of the *suba* reveals exciting results compared with the relevant District Gazetteers. The study may be divided into separate heads (a) crops, (b) crop patterns, and (c) average agricultural efficiency of the *suba*.

In the reign of Akbar, forty-one[174] crops were cultivated in the *suba* of Allahabad, out of which about ten were food grains, and the remaining thirty-one were cash crops or crops of other minor nature. A comparative study of principal crops mentioned in the *Ain* and the District Gazetteer concerned shows a continuity of crop cultivation up to the early years of the twentieth century. Such crop continuity is found with wheat, barley, peas, linseed and poppy among the *rabi* crops and cotton, rice, *kodon*, sugar cane etc., among the *kharif* crops.[175]

In the early seventeenth century, Bernier recorded the area around Benares as 'extremely rich and fine' for agriculture.[176] Even Manucci has also discussed many kinds of vegetables and cereals grown near Benares, rich in fruits.[177] The extensive cultivation of sugar cane and poppy at Benares had been a source of great attention to the English agents during the later period.

As far as the southern part of the *suba* of Allahabad (i.e. the Baghela territory) is concerned, contemporary sources do not provide information about the rate of government demand or details about agricultural produce. The only source that gives some information about the matter is the *Rewa Gazetteer*. However, the information supplied by it was from a much later period, and it was not considerable.

Agriculture in the northern portion between the rivers Ghagra and Jumna was flourishing.[178] The primary and essential crops of the north part of the *suba* were wheat, poppy, Persian muskmelon, sugar cane, indigo, *pan,* and *singara.* It produced a variety of fruits and flowers and had melons and grapes in abundance.[179]

In the southern part of the *suba*, especially south of the Jumna, the main crops of *sarkar* Bhatghora were coarse, primarily grains such as *chana* (gram), *sawan*, *kodon* (a type of coarse rice), *moth*, *kapas* (cotton), *matar* (peas), *masuri, jau, bajra, urad* and wheat.[180] Among the vegetables grown in this part were cabbage, carrot, garlic and onion. The best-known fruits were mango and melon.[181]

The region of Bihar is perhaps somewhat less diversified agriculturally than is the Upper Ganges Plain, although most of the drier crops of the west continue into Bihar and in the east, a new one, jute, has appeared since Partition.

The broad change from west to east can be best seen by comparing the six divisions wholly or mainly within the region: Benares, Faizabad, and Gorakhpur in UP, Tirhut, Patna and Bhagalpur in Bihar. Rice is easily dominant in all of them; in Faizabad, wheat acreage is over half that of rice, but it has fallen to 12-15 per cent in the east. Except in Benares and Faizabad, *jowar* and *bajra* were negligible and in these two divisions, oilseeds are of little importance. With its heavy demand for moisture, sugar is a crop of the north; gram is most potent in Patna. Unfortunately, it is impossible to directly compare the role of irrigation in Bihar appears to mean something quite different from those at UP. The increase in irrigated rice might refer to the double paddy harvest, but the decrease in irrigated wheat is not so easily answerable. In Bihar, some 25 per cent of the net sown area is irrigated, against 31 per cent UP; but the former figure is swollen by primitive irrigation on the plateaus in southern Bihar, and in the central lowland north of the Ganges, the figure is under 20 per cent falling to under 5 per cent in Purnea.

The appearance of a three-harvest year marks a further stage in the transition to the humid delta; the *kharif* of the west is replaced by a *bhadai* (fall) and *agahni* (winter) harvest. The *bhadai* crops-quick growing rice, maize, millets, jute are sown in May-July and harvested August-September; they are most important in north-east, approximately in Bengal conditions. In the west, the *rabi* acreage exceeds *kharif*, *bhadai* and *agahni* combined but in central Tirhut, *agahni* predominates; some 90 per cent of it is rice sown at the beginning of the rains and harvested in November-December. The *rabi* crops are much more varied than those of the rains-sown harvest but contribute comparatively little to the local food supply, essentially cheap cash crops such as pulses or cash crops such as oilseed, tobacco and wheat. 'Good *bhadai* and good *rabi* go hand in hand', but *agahni* rice stays too long on the ground to leave time for the better *rabi* crops; the *bhadai-rabi* combination also offers better security against the mischance of the seasons.[182]

There is a notable intra-regional variation in Bihar's agricultural land distribution. It varies from 64 to 67 per cent of the total area in the western part of the south Bihar plain to over 70 per cent in its eastern counterpart and more than 80 per cent in the north Bihar plain.

The sown percentage of the total agricultural land is higher in east UP plain than Bihar plain. The net planted area percentage increase from west to east, coinciding with rainfall incidence and in accordance with the same, there is a north-to-south decreasing trend. The cropping pattern is typical of an underdeveloped agriculture economy, with most of the cultivated area (about 90 per cent) devoted to subsistence food crops. Cash crops and industrial raw materials, such as sugar cane (4.8 per cent) and oilseeds (1.4 per cent), have minimal coverage. With the increasing use of the HYV seeds and modern techniques of production and growing facilities for irrigation, storage, marketing, and transportation, some traditional substance crops such as rice and wheat may have become 'money' crops, at least for well-to-do farmers, and are competing with sugar cane, jute, etc. Jute has been recently introduced in parts of the humid zone, particularly in the Tarai and Purnea districts. Rice claims about 9 million acres in Bihar plains or 45 per cent of the total cropped area.

Wheat's most crucial *rabi* crop is concentrated in the north Bihar plain's rich, moisture-retentive loam silt. Maize is the third major crop concentrated in the well-drained, fertile sandy loam tracts south and west of the Burhi Gandak (Saran, South Champaran, Muzaffarpur, Darbhanga) and parts of Saharsa, Purnea and Monghyr (Munger). Next to wheat among *rabi* crops, barley covers new Saran, Champaran and Muzaffarpur in the North Bihar Plain. It is variably mixed with gram. Pulses are essential as the main and cash crops and stand second to rice. Gram aline covers 1/5th of all pulses or about 5 per cent of the total cropped area of the Bihar plain. It thrives in inadequately aerated and drained sandy and loamy soils of south Bihar plain and North Monghyr and South Saran, Shahabad, Ganga, Patna and Monghyr together account for 70.9 per cent of the pulses in the Bihar plain.

(B) Irrigation Patterns

Punjab is at the far end of the monsoonal currents. The state of Punjab is characterized by insufficient and erratic rainfall, and the agricultural prosperity of a large section of its area was dependent on the mercy of nature or artificial irrigation. Wells were, however, the most important indigenous means of irrigation. Apart from medieval times, the use of the canal emerged as the most effective means of irrigation not only in Punjab but also in all rainfed areas. Writing in the fourteenth century, Isami comprehensively discussed canal irrigation in his work *Futuh-al-Salatin;* it is one of the primary sources for studying the development of the canal in north India.

About the irrigation of Rajasthan, Nainsi, the seventeenth-century court chronicler of Marwar, has described several types of wells, such as chance, *kosita, dhimra, dhibra, kohar, kuwa* and *bera.*[183] These could be distinguished based on their function and utility for irrigation and portable purposes. The character of the sub-soil, especially in the desert and mountainous parts of Rajasthan, renders the construction of wells or tanks labour intensive and requires a large number of resources for its construction. Thus, it is an expensive task to dig well in that region. The limited prevalence of brick-lined wells suggests a high cost of construction.[184]

Tapping rainwater through artificial methods, on the other hand, emerged as a viable alternative to irrigation in certain parts of Rajasthan. People maximized the use of rainwater by evolving several indigenous water harvesting methods for irrigation purposes like *khareen, rela, sewanj* and *nahla.* These systems were adapted to manage the run-off rainwater by directing it to the cultivation fields. For example, village Motisaro in *pargana* Seewano could produce 200 mm of rainwater for Sewanj wheat with the full use of the *bahla* in the village.[185]

The contemporary record suggested that the state extended financial and material support for the construction and maintenance of the above water systems. The ruling elites continuously aspired to make the landscape more congenial and cultivatable. With the emergence and consolidation of Mughal power in north India, we witness a definite step forward. The *Ain-i-Akbari,* the administrative manual compiled during Akbar's reign, made a beginning in this direction.

Besides, tanks and reservoirs also played a crucial role in irrigation. Their reference is mentioned in the *Akbarnama,* which describes the use of tanks and reservoirs for irrigation. When Akbar was at Merta, he ordered reservoirs previously used for irrigation to be cleaned.[186]

The environmental feature of Rajasthan caused the use of tank irrigation. Whereas in the neighbouring region of Mewat lakes and dams also played an important role as sources of irrigation.[187]

Agra is somewhat backward in the case of irrigation and depends too mainly on the rainfall to be secure against the variation of the season. During the Mughal period, many canals were cut from rivers to counter the irrigation problem in the Agra region. Shahjahan's *Nahr-i-Faiz* was an impressive example of canal construction; it was miles, taking off water from Yamuna River when it leaves the hills, then running first south-west and then south-east to the parent river at Delhi.[188] The change that has taken place in the relative importance of canals can also be judged from the fact that the *Ain-i-Akbari* describes agriculture in the Lahore *suba* and cultivated area of western Punjab, which the modern government irrigated. Related to the Agra region, the first irrigation statistics were compiled during the survey of 1837-9. It was then found out that out of a total cultivated area, 51.4 per cent were watered only.

Referring to the irrigation method prevalent in the *suba* of Allahabad, Josep Tiffenthalar writes the people irrigated their fields using canals made by them. They also used lakes for irrigation purposes. The early irrigation records seem unreliable because they show the area classified as irrigable rather than the actual area irrigated each year. Wells were the primary source of water supply in the district. Additionally, tanks, *jhils*, and natural or artificial reservoirs were other modes of irrigation. The canal only serves the southern portion of the *doab* in the Atharban, Karari and Chail *parganas*, though there is minimal irrigation from this source in the extreme south of Kara.[189]

Bihar *suba* is one of the crucial parts of this chapter because it lies east of the middle Ganga Plain and is the last *suba* for the writing. Seasonal concentration and ill-distribution of rainfall in Bihar, both in space and time, and other monsoon vagaries cause supplemental irrigation for annual crops like sugar cane or *zaid* crops, which are grown in the pre-carious summer but also for higher yields of the *kharif* and *rabi* crops.[190] Of the net sown area, about 33 per cent in Bihar is irrigated but there is wide sub-regional and local variation in the irrigation's distribution patterns depending on the irrigation needs.

(C) An Analysis of Soil Taxonomy on Regional Basis

The high fertility of Indian soil has been an essential characteristic of agriculture. While talking about the fertility of soil Amir Khusrau has given references to the fertility and fruitfulness of the Indian soil and the temperate nature of their climate.[191] Refereeing to *Arthashastra* of Kautilya, they have also left essential descriptions of three kinds of soils, wet crops (*kedara*), winter crops (*haimana*) and summer crops (*graishmika*).[192] In the early fourteenth century, Ibn Battuta says that the Indian soil was so fertile that it enabled the farmers to produce two crops every year; fall crops and spring crops.[193] The revenue rates of Akbar's reign have also reflected the pattern of two crops—fall crops and spring crops each year.[194] There was, of course, some considerable variation. Abul Fazl recorded, 'there are yielding of three crops in the Delhi *suba* a year, while other regions, for instance, Ajmer *suba* was not so fertile and yielded one crop or an insignificant second'.[195]

Punjab was endowed with abundant natural resources with its geographic and strategic location. First, the region, barring the mountainous zone and parts of the sub-mountainous tracts, was a vast level plan of alluvial origin. The soil was sandy, deficient in humus but well supplied with essential minerals. Second, only crucial to the geographical position in its effect on the economic potentialities of the Panjab was the fact that a significant portion of the province contained deep alluvial soil. Excluding the Himalayan and other hill tracts and the ravines of Rawalpindi, Attock and Jhelum districts, the broad valleys of its rivers broke the vast alluvial plain only. Stones were rare in the plains, except at the immediate foot of the hills. Micaceous river sand was found everywhere at varying depths and the only mineral was popular accretions of limestone (*kankar*), which was produced in situ. The soil was a singularly uniform loam, actual clay was almost unknown, and the quality was determined chiefly by the more significant or smaller proportion of sand present. In the local hollows and drainage lines, the constant deposit of argillaceous particles had produced a stiff tenacious soil, singularly adapted to rice cultivation. Pure sand was commonly found in the beds of the great rivers and the wind-fretted waste sheds.

The more significant portions of Punjab which lay between the Jhelum-Chenab and the Indus rivers, were bordered on the south by the Rajputana desert. This area consisted of a series rolling sand hills formed by the wind, running parallel to the great breakwater of the Salt Range and separated by valleys where the original surface was exposed. In parts and significantly where local conditions raised the water table level, the salts natural to the soil had been concentrated on the surface by continuous evaporation. They had covered the ground with saline efflorescence known as *reh*,[196] often fatal to vegetable life for miles together. Although it was beyond doubt that an extension or further deterioration of these areas resulted from excessive irrigation, there was also evidence that such lands were not always unsuitable for irrigation and that they were, sometimes, improved or reclaimed by it. Where neither *reh* nor sand was present, the soil was uniformly fertile if only the rainfall was sufficient or means of irrigation were available. However, throughout the more significant part of the western plains of Punjab, neither of these conditions was satisfied and vast steppes of bars were applicable only as grazing grounds for camels and cattle. The soils of the Himalayan and lower ranges resembled those of the plains but both sand and clay were rare and the stony area was considerable.

The plain of Punjab may be described as vast expanses of alluvial clay and loam.[197] The Alluvial soil possesses excellent fertility. It requires minimal artificial drainage unless excessive irrigation have altered its natural condition. Therefore, it involves the expenditure of very little capital to bring it under cultivation and maintain its crop-bearing capacity. In these respects, the people of Punjab were far more fortunate than agriculturists in many other countries.

The most prevalent soil in Agra *suba* was the ordinary *dumat* or loam,[198] which covered about 75.3 per cent of the cultivated area. In the low-lying portion of Khairagarh tahsil, *dumat* is called *tarai,* very similar to *piliya.* It is a name derived from its yellow colour, but the dividing line between light loam and stiff *piliya.* The genuine sandy soil is known as *bhur,* which amounts to 3 per cent of the total cultivable land.

There are four kinds of clay soils in Agra which are altogether about 5.5 per cent of the cultivated area. The alluvial soil known as *kachhar* is essential only where it amounts to 9 and 11 per cent of cultivation, respectively. The thin deposit of silt found on the sandy bed of the Utangan is known as *khitri* and is chiefly confined to Kiraoli and Khairagarh. These alluvial soils all account for 3.6 per cent of the cultivated area.

The *suba* of Allahabad presented a picture of contrast so far as some of its natural features and products were concerned. The soil in the region between the Ghagra and Jumna rivers was alluvial and extremely fertile, in contrast to the southern part, which was predominantly a plateau characterized by black soil. The result was that the northern region was prosperous, while the southern portion where the arable land was still covered with forests was comparatively poor and economically backward. The southern tableland gently sloped upwards, reaching a height of approximately 3,000 feet above sea level in the south.

The situation of the *suba* was fairly crucial for any ambitious ruler who wanted to establish his hold on northern India. Its alluvial soil and a climate productive of rich harvests all the year-round was sufficient attraction for any political power. Several powerful fortresses in the south-west, situated and famous, were a further inducement.

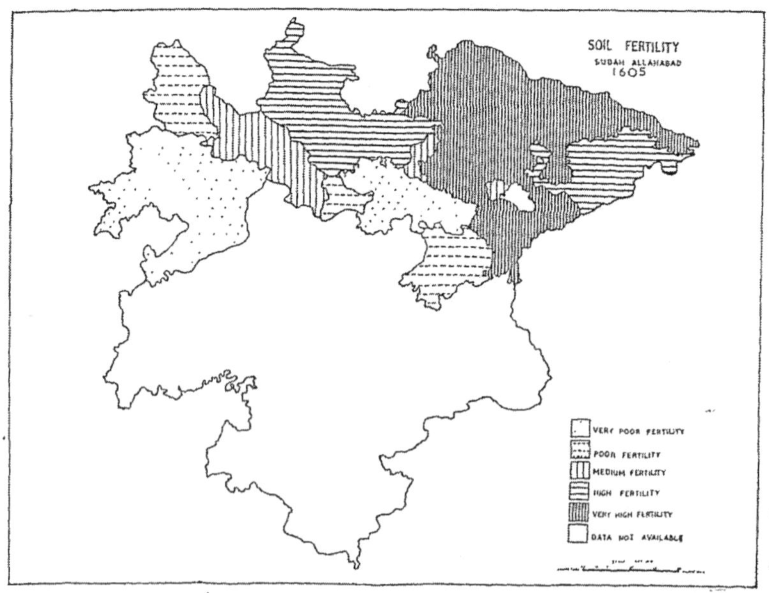

MAP 2.3: *SUBA* OF ALLAHABAD UNDER THE GREAT MUGHALS. TAXONOMY OF SOILS IS BASED ON S.N. SINHA

Mithila Sharan Pandey, in his book *The Historical Geography and Topography of Bihar*, has tried to analyse the modern state of Bihar, which comprises four administrative divisions—Trihut, Patna, Bhagalpur and Chhotanagpur. Still, physically, the state is divided into two broad divisions by the river Ganga. He argued that the land on the left bank of the Ganga is fertile and soft, while that on the right bank is full of rocks and is shallow and unproductive land. The land to the south of the Ganga may again be divided into two parts. The Patna division and part of the Bhagalpur division have plain and fertile land with a few ranges of hills here and there. While north Bihar has basic lands with fertile soil, and it comprises alluvial soil. Hence, the land is soft.[199] This is the reason we find the rivers quickly changing their courses. The most notorious for this is the river Kosi, which renders thousands of people homeless and washes away lakhs of property every year.

Thus, Bihar has an extensive network of rivers which affect its urban-rural pattern and the socio-economic life of Mughal India. The rivers in this region have always been sources of prosperity by bringing the soil of the mountains to make the land of the plain fertile and also means for commercial transport. The climate of Bihar was comparatively moderate and played a vital role in its ecology. Abul Fazl and Tavernier both mentioned the long ranges of hills that they encountered during their journeys in Bihar and Bengal.

NOTES

1. Hari Ram Gupta, *Studies in Later Mughal History of the Punjab 1707-1793,* Lahore: The Minerva Book Shop, 1944, p. 1.
2. The Mughal emperor Akbar gave the name 'Punjab' to the province of Lahore and gave names to its *doab* by joining the first letters of the rivers for each interfluve.
3. Abul Fazl, *Ain-i-Akbari,* vol. II, translated by Colonel H.S. Jarret, corrected and annotated by J.N. Sarkar, 2nd edn., Calcutta, 1949, p. 283.
4. James Fraser, *The History of Nadir Shah,* London: A. Millar, 1742, pp. 153-9.
5. Ibid., pp. 153-9.
6. When the people of the plains were threatened by invaders or repressed by the government, this location served as the best hiding place, offering safety, as well as a supply of food and game to the refugees.
7. Indu Banga, 'Ahmad Shah Abdali's Designs over the Punjab', *Proceeding of the Indian History Congress,* 29th Session, 1967, p. 188.

8. Tangri Ghaggar, Markhanda, Saraswati and Kosla are important, *Tarikh-i-Makhzan-i-Panjab*, p. 79.
9. Mayank Kumar, *Monsoon Ecologies: Irrigation, Agriculture and Settlement Patterns in Rajasthan during the Pre-Colonial Period,* New Delhi: Manohar, 2013, p. 59.
10. Dashrath Sharma, *Rajasthan through the Ages,* Bikaner: Rajasthan State Archives 1966, p. 11.
11. G.S.L. Devra, 'Desertification and Problem of Delimitation of Rajputana Desert during the Medieval Period', *Human Ecology,* special issue no. 7, 1999, p. 7.
12. *Rajasthan State Gazetteer,* vol. I, *Land and People,* 1995, p. 2.
13. H.D. Sankalia, *Indian Archaeology Today,* Bombay: Asia Publishing House, 1962, p. 68.
14. Dirk H.A. Kolff, *Naukars, Rajputs and Sepoy: The Ethno-history of the Military Labour Market of Hindustan, 1450-1850,* Cambridge: Cambridge University Press, 1990, p. 224.
15. Irfan Habib, *An Atlas of the Mughal Empire,* vol. 6, New Delhi: Oxford University Press, 1982, Sheet No. 6-B and 16-20.
16. Edward Thornto, *A Gazetteer of Territories under the Government of the East-India Company and of the Native States on the Colonial of India,* London: Wm. H. Allen & Company, 1858, p. 54.
17. V.C. Misra, *Geography of Rajasthan,* New Delhi: National Book Trust, 1967, pp. 23-4.
18. Abul Fazl, *Akbarnam* III, tr. by H. Beveridge, Calcutta Text, 1977, p. 202
19. For more detail, see the list of *sarkar* in *Baburnama,* tr. A.S. Beveridge, 1992, rpt. 1970, p. 581.
20. *District Gazetteer of United Provinces: Agra and Oudh Division,* vol. III, 1905, p. 1.
21. Ibid., p. 2.
22. O.H.K. Spate, *India and Pakistan: A General and Regional Geography,* London: Methuen & Co., 1964, pp. 415-16.
23. Ibid., pp. 415-16.
24. Abul Fazl, *Ain-i-Akbari,* II, S.H. Jarrett, ed. J.N. Sarkar, Calcutta: Royal Asiatic Society of Bengal, 1949, p. 129. These twelve provinces were Allahabad, Agra, Awadh, Ajmer, Ahmadabad, Bihar, Bengal, Delhi, Kabul, Lahore, Multan and Malwa.
25. *Domat* is a sand and clay combination.
26. *Mar* is a rich, darkand friable soil easily recognized from the large number of minutes '*kankar*' nodules. In its texture, it contains a high proportion of organic matter which enables it to be cropped continuously without manure, *Banad Gazetteer,* p. 6.

27. *Kankar* is stuffed tenacious soil with a large percentage of clay and deficiency of sand, *Banda Gazetteer*, p. 5.
28. Captain C.E. Luard, *Rewa State Gazetteer*, Lucknow: Newal Kishore Steam Printing Press, 1907, p. 1.
29. Mohd Kamran Khan, 'Environment in European Traveller Accounts during the 17th Century in Mughal India', unpublished M.Phil. dissertation, Lucknow, 2018, p. 16.
30. For more detail see R.L. Singh, 'Middle Ganga Plain', in *India: A Regional Geography*, ed. R.L. Singh, Varanasi, 1971, p. 246.
31. Ibid., p. 246, Abul Fazl also recorded a number of fruits in this region (*sarkars* of Champaran, Saran, Tirhut and Hajipur). For Tirhut, he specifically mentioned that the groves orange trees extended to 30 *kos*, *Ain*, p. 417.
32. R.L. Singh, ed., *India: A Regional Geography, National Geographical Society of India*, 1971, pp. 746-8.
33. J. Singh and Deepa Thapan, 'Chotanagarpur Region, India', ed. R.L. Singh, *India: A Regional Geography*, Varanasi: National Geographical Society of India, 1997, pp. 656-7.
34. *Nilab* refers to 'blue water', a term derived from the deep blue colour of the Indus at this location. It is a bit distance below Attock on the left side of the Indus.
35. Tarikh Amin, *Tarikh-i-Ahmad Shahi: The First History of Afghanistan*, New York: Oxford University Press, 2016, p. 42.
36. Akhnur is a small town in Jammu at the foot of the mountains.
37. *Tarikh-i-Ahmad*, op. cit., p. 42.
38. Fauja Singh, ed. *Sair-i-Panjab*, tr. Giani Lal Singh, Patiala: Punjabi University, 1971, pp. 1, 7.
39. Sujan Rai, *Khulasat-ut-Tawarik*, ed. Zafar Hasan and Maulana Abrar Hasan, Delhi: J. & Sons Press, 1918, p. 76.
40. Alexander Burnes's *Travels into Bukhara*, vol. I, p. 50.
41. C.C. Watson, *Rajputana District Gazetteers*, vol. 1-A, Ajmer: Scottish Mission Industries Co., p. 2.
42. Ibid., p. 3.
43. Tapan Raychaudhari and Irfan Habib, eds., *The Cambridge Economic History of India 1200-1750*, vol. 1, Delhi: Orient Longman and Cambridge University Press, p. 6.
44. Francisco Pelsaert, *Jahangir's India*, tr. W.H. Moreland and O. Geye, Cambridge: Cambridge University Press, 1925, p. 48.
45. *Ain-i-Akbari*, vol. II, op. cit., p. 174.
46. *Azamgarh District Gazetteer*, p. 6.
47. Salon, a *pargana* in the district of Rae Bareli is situated $26^0$2'N and $81^0$28'E, *Rae Bareli Gazetteer*, p. 214.
48. *Ain-i-Akbari*, vol. II, op. cit., pp. 172, 176, 178.

49. Kanti, a *mahal* in the *sarkar* of Allahabad situated on 25^{0}' N and 82^{0} 25'E.
50. *Ain-i-Akbari*, vol. II, op. cit., pp. 169, 170.
51. Ibid., p. 169.
52. Ibid., p. 177.
53. This Phaphund is not the same as the one between Kanpur and Etawah on the railway route.
54. *Rewa Gazetteer*, op. cit., p. 3.
55. J.B. Tavernier, *Travels in India, 1640-67*, vol. I, tr. V. Ball, London: Macmillan, 1889, pp. 123-5.
56. John Marshal, *John Marshall in India: Notes and Observations in Bengal, 1668-72*, ed. S.A. Khan, London: Oxford University Press, 1927, pp. 71-9, 95-7.
57. Irfan Habib, *Atlas*, Sheet No. 10B; also see J. Rennel, *A Bengal Atlas*, London: W. Faden 1781, river change from Patna to Surdah, map no. 15.
58. Abdul Latif, *Travel in Bihar 1680 A.D*, tr. J.N. Sarkar, *Journal of the Bihar and Orissa Research Society* (*JBORS*), vol. V, Patna: Bihar and Orissa Research Society, 1919, pt. III, p. 598.
59. *Ain-i-Akbari*, vol. II, op. cit., Calcutta: Asiatic Society of Bengal, p. 416.
60. Ibid., p. 416.
61. Ibid., p. 416.
62. Rennel, map. 15; Survey of India, quarter inch sheet, 72 G, 2nd edn., 1950.
63. Latif, op. cit., p. 598.
64. In this *doab*, the two major cities in Punjab. Lahore and Multan gave it a status that no other *doab* held, and it also piques Sikh interest in having the Manjha tract, the Sikhs' true home, inside its borders.
65. Bute Shah, *Tarikh-i-Panjab*, MS, SHR 1288 (Daftars 1-IV) & SHR 2289 (Daftar V), Amritsar: Khalsa College, p. 6a.
66. This 'Chenab Colony' area is rich in smiling agricultural fields and large communities.
67. *Tarikh-i-Ahmad*, 42, Bute Shah, 38a.
68. Ibid., pp. 42, 38a.
69. Ibid., pp. 42, 38a; Chahar Chaman, 194a.
70. *Ain-i-Akbari*, vol. II, op. cit., p. 67.
71. K.K. Trivedi, 'Historical Geography of Ganga-Yamuna Doab (13th-17th Centuries)', *Proceeding Indian History Congress*, vol. 42, 1982, pp. 303-9.
72. William Francklin, *Military Memoirs of George Thomas*, London: John Stockdale, 1803, p. 88.
73. James Douie, *The Punjab Northwest Frontier Province and Kashmir*, New Delhi: Low Price Publication (1916), rpt. Delhi, 1994, p. 3.
74. Zahuruddin Muhammad Babur, *Baburnama*, tr. A.S. Beveridge, New Delhi: Oriental Books Reprint Corporation, 1970, p. 577.
75. Abdul Qadir Badauni, *Muntakhab-ul-Twarikh*, vol. II, tr. W.H. Lowe, Patna: Academic Asiatic, 1973, p. 239.

76. Mayank Kumar, 'Situating the Environment: Settlement, Irrigation and Agriculture in Pre-colonial Rajasthan', *Studies in History*, 24, 2, (2008), p. 213
77. *Ain-i-Akbari*. Vol. II, op. cit.; p. 138.
78. Abul Fazl, *Ain-i-Akbari*, vol. II, p. 138.
79. Ibid., p. 273.
80. Ibid., p. 273.
81. F. Wilder's Letter to David Ouchterlony, dated 27 September 1818. RSAB
82. *Ain-i-Akbari,* vol. I, op. cit., p. 505.
83. *Waqai Sarkar-i-Ajmer*, JR, RSAB, pp. 14, 15, 16, 25.
84. Hari Bilas Sarda, *Ajmer Historical and Descriptive,* Ajmer: Scottish Mission Industries Company, 1911, p. 134.
85. Sinha, op. cit., p. 9.
86. *District Gazetteer of Allahabad*, p. 8.
87. *Ain-i-Akbari,* vol. II, op. cit., p. 169.
88. *District Gazetteer, Uttar Pradesh: Benares,* XXVI, 2909, p. 21.
89. *District Gazetteer, Uttar Pradesh: Allahabad,* XXIII, 1911, p. 23.
90. *Ain-i-Akbari,* vol. II, op. cit., p. 416.
91. *Imperial Gazetteer of India: Provincial Series Punjab*, vol. I, *The Province; Mountains Rivers and Historical Areas and the Delhi and Jullundur Divisions,* Calcutta, 1908, p. 248.
92. *An Atlas of the Mughal Empire,* op. cit., Sheet No. 6-B and 16-2.
93. *District Gazetteer of the United Provinces: Agra and Oudh Division,* vol. III, 1905, pp. 21-2.
94. *A Gazetteer of Allahabad*, vol. XXIII of the *District Gazetteer of the United Provinces of Agra and Oudh,* the Superintendent, Government Press, United Provinces, Allahabad, 1928, p. 24.
95. O.H.K. Spate, *India & Pakistan,* London: Routledge Library Editions: British India, 2017, vol. 12, p. 566.
96. Singh, op. cit., p. 198.
97. Spate, op. cit., p. 564.
98. The *kos* was roughly speaking equal to 2.05 English miles in the eighteenth century, as is clear the series of pillers extended along the Grand Trunk Road, the distance between each to being a *kos.*
99 Sujan Rai, *Khulasat-ut-Tawarik*, ed. Zafar Hasan and Maulvi Abrar Hasan, Muradabadi, 1918, p. 63.
100. *Slok te Shabad Farid ji Steek,* ed. Sahib Singh, Amritsar: Singh Brothers, 1905, p. 11.
101. Gurubachan Singh Talib, *Sri Guru Granth Sahib in English Translation.* Patial: Punjabi University, vol. IV, 2001 (3rd edn.), pp. 2251-7.
102. Ibid., vol. I, 1997, pp. 269-71.

103. Jit Singh Seetal, *Shah Husain: Jiwan te Rachna,* Patiala: Punjabi University, 1995, p. 56.
104. *Ain-i-Akbari,* op. cit., vol. II, p. 326.
105. Divyabhanusinh Sinha, *The End of a Trail: The Cheetah in India,* New Delhi: Oxford University Press, 1999, pp. 70-8.
106. *An Atlas of the Mughal Empire,* op. cit., Map No. 4B.
107. Ganesh Das Vadera, *Char Bagh-i-Punjab,* ed. Kirpal Singh, Amritsar: Khalsa College, 1965, p. 273. Jahangir gave the name of Jahangirabad to Sheikhupura and made it the headquarter of a *pargana.* Its Qanungos constructed a fort for the emperor, around which developed a town; a tank and the Hiran Minar was raised at 2 *kos* from the town in the *shikargah,* the imperial hunting ground.
108. William Finch, *In Early Travels in India 1583-1619,* ed. William Foster, New Delhi: S. Chand & Company, rpt, Delhi, 1986, pp. 57, 58, 59, 63, 65.
109. Francois Bernier (tr.), *Travels in the Mogul Empire, 1656-1668,* Westminister: A. Constable, 1842, pp. 381-2.
110. Varan Bhai Gurudas, ed. Sahib Singh, Amritsar: Khalsa Samachar, 1951 (6th edn.), p. 18.
111. Hir Waris, ed. Jit Singh Seetal, New Delhi: Navyug Press, 1973 (rpt.), pp. 11, 21.
112. William Moorcroft and George Trebeck, *Travels in the Himalaya Provinces and the Punjab,* London, 1837, pp. 1, 12, 30.
113. Alexander Burnes, *Travels into Bokhara,* London: John Murray, 1835, pp. 83, 105.
114. Hugel, Charles Baron, *Travels in Kashmir and the Punjab,* Patiala: Punjab Language Department (rpt.), 1970, pp. 37, 50.
115. William Barr, *March from Delhi to Peshawar and from thence to Cabul,* Patiala: Punjab Language Department (rpt.), 1970, pp. 5, 8.
116. Ibid., p. 74.
117. These plants are noted as tribulus, zygophyllum, fagonia, solanus and withania.
118. The names of the weeds are mentioned by Douie, as fumania parviflora, silence coroidea, spergulas and argemone Mexicana.
119. Ibid., p. 87.
120. Ibid., p. 79.
121. Other plants like nerium oleander, rhum cotinus, herbs such as viola patrinii, polygala, abyssinica, and plant like vigna vexillata, Trichodesma indicum and evolvulus alsinoides, were also found.
122. *District Gazetteer Gurudaspur,* 1914, vol. XXI A, Lahore: Government Press, 1915, p. 2.
123. *District Gazetteer Gurudapur,* op. cit., p. 9-11.

124. *District Gazetteer Ambala 1923-24*, vol. VII, Part A, Lahore: Lahore Government Press, 1926, p. 5.
125. *District Gazetteer Hoshiapur, 1904*, vol. XIII-A, Lahore: Lahore Government Press, 1905, p. 5.
126. *District Gazetteer Sialkot, 1920*, vol. XXIII-A, Lahore: Lahore Government Press, 1921, p. 8.
127. *District Gazetteer Chanab Colony. 1904*, Lahore: Civil and Military Gazetteer Press, 1905, p. 6.
128. *District Gazetteer Gujranwala*, p. 4.
129. *District Gazetteer Shahpur*, p. 2.
130. Ibid., p. 3.
131. *District Gazetteer Shahpur*, vol. XXI, Lahore: Government Press, 1929, p. 4.
132. *District Gazetteer Shahpur*, vol. XXX, Lahore: Government Press, 1918, p. 5.
133. *District Gazetteer Muzaffargarh 1929*, vol. XXXIV-A, Lahore: Government Press, 1930, p. 4.
134. *District Gazetteer Amritsar 1914*, vol. XIV-A, Lahore: Civil and Military Gazette Press, 1914, p. 6.
135. *State Gazetteer Kapurthala, 1904*, vol. XIV-A, Lahore: Civil and Military Gazette Press, 1914, p. 3.
136. *District Gazetteer Amritsar*, 1922, pp. 6, 7.
137. *State Gazetteer Dujana* 1904, vol. VII-A, Lahore: Civil and Military Gazette Press, 1908, p. 2; *District Gazetteer Delhi 1912*, vol. V-A, Lahore: Civil and Military Gazette Press, 1913, p. 2.
138. *Arhsatta, Pargana, Sawai Jaipur*, 1798, Historical Section, Jaipur Records, Bikaner: Rajasthan State Archives.
139. *Arhsatta*, Village, Kundal, *pargana* Bahatri, 1745 vs; Village Bilhata, *pargana* Bahatri, 1774 vs; Qasba Jaipur, 1798 vs; Village Deewara, *pargana* Malpura, Jaipur Records, Bikaner: Rajasthan State Archives.
140. *Arhsatta*, Chandpur, *pargana* Bahatri, 1775 vs; Village Mahin Nala Khurd, *pargana* Bahatri, 1781 vs; Village Brahmanvas, HS, JR, RSAB.
141. *Arhsatta*, Village Chauroti, *pargana* Hindaun, 1785 vs; Village Shivpur *pargana* Tonk, 1777 vs; Village Nuka Kivas, *pargana* Lalsot, 1820 vs, HS, JR, RSAB.
142. *District Gazetteer of Agra and Oudh*, op. cit., p. 56.
143. *District Gazetteer of Agra and Oudh*, Allahabad Division, op. cit., p. 18
144. *Allahabad: A Gazetteer*, vol. XXIII, of the *District Gazetteer of the United Provinces of Agra and Oudh*, 1928, p. 17.
145. *Ain-i-Akbari*, vol. II, op. cit., p. 396.
146. Ibid., *Ain*-II, p. 169; Ralph Fitch, p. 103.

147. *Baburnama*, op. cit., p. 488.
148. Its elevation is 1,230 ft. above the sea level. Also see *Ain,* II, p. 170.
149. Ibid., p. 172.
150. *Rewa Gazetteer,* op. cit., p. 1.
151. Ibid., p. 31.
152. *Ain-i-Akbari*, vol. II, op. cit., p. 170.
153. Singh, op. cit., *India: A Regional Geography,* pp. 204-5.
154. Oxford Learners Dictionary, London, 1962, p. 25.
155. *The New Cambridge Encyclopedia,* New York: Galahad Books Publication, 1978, p. 53.
156. Irfan Habib, *The Agrarian System of Mughal India 1556-1767* (2nd revd. edn.), New Delhi: Oxford University Press, 1999, p. 39.
157. David Mosse, *The Rule of Water: Statecraft Ecology and Collective Action in South India,* Oxford University Press, 2003; has examined extensively the functioning of the tank system of irrigation as practiced in the coastal regions of Tamil Nadu.
158. *India at the Death of Akbar: An Economic Study,* New Delhi: W.H. Moreland, 1962, p. 211.
159. *Arzdasht,* Asoj Vadi 11, 1756, Historical Section, Jaipur Records, Bikaner: Rajasthan State Archives.
160. *Arzdasht,* Swan Sudi 1, 1674 vs, HS, JR, RSAB.
161. S.P. Malhotra, 'Man and the Desert', in Rakesh Hooja and Rajendra Joshi, eds., *Desert Drought and Development,* Jaipur: Rawat, 1999, p. 27.
162. *Imperial Gazetteer of India,* vol. V, p. 50.
163. *Ain-i-Akbari*, vol. II, see Irfan Habib's book *Agrarian System*, p. 48.
164. Ibid., p. 218.
165. See Irfan Habib's *Agrarian System of the Mughal Empire* for more information, p. 43.
166. *Ain-i-Akbari*, vol. II, op. cit., p. 442; Finch, *Early Travels*, pp. 51-2.
167. Francisco Pelsaert, *Jahangir's India,* tr. W.H. Moreland and P. Geye, Cambridge, 1925, p. 15; Peter Mundy, *Travels of Peter Mundy in India in Europe and Asia (1608-1667),* vol. II, London: MDC, p. 96.
168. *Baburnama*, op. cit., for more detail see Irfan Habib book, *Agrarian System*, p. 56.
169. *Ain-i-Akbari,* vol. I, op. cit., p. 345.
170. *District Gazetteer of the United Provinces: Agra and Oudh Division*, vol. III, 1905, p. 5.
171. Habib, *Agrarian System*, op. cit., p. 55.
172. *Ain-i-Akbari*, vol. II, op. cit., pp. 98, 99; to find out the position of the various crops in the different areas of *suba*.
173. Ibid., pp. 94, 95.
174. Ibid., pp. 98, 99.

175. Compare relevant district gazetteer, see details under 'Principal Crops', *Rewa Gazetteer*, p. 29 and *Ain-i-Akbari*, II, pp. 98, 99.
176. Bernier, op. cit., p. 334.
177. Niccola Manucci, *Storia do Mogor or Mogul India (1653-1708)*, vol. II, tr. William Irvine, London, 1907, p. 428; *Ain-i-Akbari*, vol. II, pp. 169; Fitch, p. 103.
178. K.K. Trivedi, 'Historical Geography of Ganga Yamuna Doab', Proceedgins of Indian History Congress, vol. 42, 1981, p. 303.
179. *Ain-i-Akbari*, vol. II, op. cit., pp. 98, 99.
180. *Rewa Gazetteer*, op. cit., p. 29.
181. Ibid., p. 29.
182. Singh, op. cit., p. 518.
183. Munhot Nainsi, *Marwar ra Pargana ri Vigat*, vol. III, ed. Narain Singh Bhatt, Jodhpur: Rajasthan Oriental Research Institute, 1974, pp. 129-31.
184 P.W. Powlett, *Gazetteer of Bikaner*, Calcutta, 1874, p. 90.
185. Nainsi, *Marwar ra Pargana ri Vigat*, vol. II, p. 239.
186. Abul Fazl, *Akbarnama*, vol. III, tr. H. Beveridge, New Delhi: Rare Books, 1973, pp. 308-9.
187. *Babaurnama*, p. 52 .
188. Ibid., p. 217.
189. *District Gazetteer of the United Provinces*, vol. A, *Allahabad District*, 1928, sp. 41.
190. Singh, op. cit., p. 335.
191. Yusuf Husain, *Glimpses of Medieval Indian Culture*, Bombay: Asian Publication House, 1957, p. 122.
192. Kautilya, *Arthashastra*, Eng. translation R. Shamasastry, 9th edn., Mysore: Padam, 1988, pp. 131-2.
193. Ibn Battuta, *Rehala*, Eng. Mahdi Husain, Baroda: Oriental Institute, 1953, p. 18.
194. Abul Fazl, *Ain-i-Akbari*, tr. H.S. Jarrett, 2nd edn., vol. II, New Delhi: New Taj Office, p. 76.
195. Ibid., pp. 273-83.
196. Baden, H. Powell, *Handbook of Economic Products in the Punjab*, vol. I, Roorkee: Thomason Civil Engineering College Press, 1868, p. 145.
197. Ibid., p. 198.
198. *Agra District Gazetteer*, 1905, p. 4; *Ain-i-Akbar*, II, op. cit., p. 255.
199. Mithila Sharan Pandey, *The Historical Geography and Topography of Bihar*, Department of Ancient Indian History and Archaeology, Patna: Patna University, 1963, p. 55.

CHAPTER 3

Fauna, Agriculture and Forest: A Sustainable Interdependency in Mughal North India

So long as the earth bears woods and a forest full of wild animals will it continue to support the progeny of man.

– MADHAV GADGIL

THE MUGHALS ALWAYS had a deep interest in nature, first expressed by the dynasty's founder, Babur (ruled 1526-30), in his autobiography, the *Baburnama*, which offers a detailed description of the flora and fauna of Hindustan.[1] What stands out in his accounts is their remarkable truthfulness and accuracy.

Jahangir, driven by dynastic ambitions, commissioned his artists to create artworks inspired by European styles, alongside nature studies of flowers, birds, and animals, including his hunting spoils.[2] Dara-Shikoh furthered these interests and his patronage of paintings includes an album dated 1641-2 that is well known for its natural compositions.[3]

In the subsequent British period, the Mughal way of life highly inspired the British officials and rulers and they began to embrace the local customs and mores of the Mughals.[4] Hunting was one such Mughal practice that British officials emulated. These facts reveal the deep integration of wild animals into the socio-cultural practices of Indian people.

The common name for wilderness in India is jungle, which was adopted into English. The word has also been made famous in *The Jungle Book* by Rudyard Kipling. Almost all of us have heard the stories of wild animals during our childhood. Children love to listen to the tales of birds and animals, offering them significant inspiration for building their character. Wildlife in India has been the subject of many stories, such as the *Panchatantra, Hitopadesh* and *Jatak* tales. Varieties of wild animals and birds such as lions, tigers, bulls, jackals, tortoise, cows, monkeys, camels, elephants and sparrows have been characterized in these books. British rule in India led to different phases in the history of wildlife. British officials made hunting a symbol of masculine identities. British officials also realized that wildlife could also be exploited for economic benefit. This led to the commodification of wild animals under the British Empire, which resulted in the killing of many wild animals. This commodification brought some species, rhinoceros, lion, and *cheetah*, to the verge of extinction. Other species, such as elephants and leopards, were completely eradicated from regions where they once thrived abundantly.

LANDSCAPE

The Mughal Empire stretched from Herat in western Afghanistan to Bengal and beyond in the east covering a vast area from Kashmir in the north to the Deccan in south India.[5] According to estimates, the population during the Mughal Empire was 116 million, which increased to 285 million by 1901 in the same region. According to another explanation, the population in 1605 was recorded between 150 to 170 million, which later grew to 250 million around 1850, a rise of about 100 million over a 250-year period.[6] Calculations show that the population density of the Indian subcontinent in 1650 was 35 per sq. km.[7] At the heart of the Mughal Empire, the *suba* of Agra had only 27.5 per cent of the cultivatable land in 1608 and most of the places in Hindustan had even less land under agriculture. Consequently, vast areas served as pastures for cattle, with an abundant supply of firewood across most of the kingdom. It is possible that the extent of forest and *savanah* land was greater than initially thought.[8]

Francois Bernier was a French physician who travelled in Mughal India between 1656 and 1668 during the late Jahangir reign and the early years of the Aurangzeb period. Bernier has given a magnificent graphic description of the landscape between Agra, Delhi and Lahore, the three great Mughal capitals:

> In the neighbourhoods of Agra and Delhi along the course of the Gemna (*Jumna*) reaching to the mountain (Himalayas) and even on both sides of the road reaching to Lahore, there is a large quantity of uncultivated land covered either with copsewood or with grasses six feet high.[9]

Sir Thomas Roe, the Ambassador of King James I of England, had estimated that moving Mughal capital took 12 hours to pass one spot, and when the tents were put up, the circumference was less than 20 English miles.[10] Even Jahangir himself estimated it would take 100,000 *banjara* cattle to feed a sizeable Mughal army on its march from Multan to Kandahar, since there was little vegetation on the way.[11]

THE DISTRIBUTION OF FAUNA ON GEOGRAPHICAL BASIS

The following eight regions can be used to divide the Indian sub-continent:

1. Punjab and the adjoining semi-arid and desert regions
2. The alluvial plains of the Ganges and lower Brahmaputra
3. The western peninsular tract, excluding the Western Ghats
4. The eastern peninsular tract
5. The Western Ghats or Sahyadris
6. Ladakh and adjacent regions
7. The forested hill-slopes of the Himalayas
8. Assam and adjacent hill-tracts

Punjab

The region comprised Baluchistan, Sind, and Punjab, west of Delhi, along with the desert of western Rajasthan, the foothills of the Aravalli range, and the Cutch Peninsula.[12] Annual rainfall ranged between 100 and 600 mm, and the tract was largely desert or semi-desert except along the river courses.[13] This region was considered part of the Palearctic realm. Its fauna is relatively poor and lacking in the most prominent Indo-Malayan elements in the peninsular fauna, such as langurs, loris, and elephants. The notable species, including the ovid, urial, the wild goat, the wild ass, the chinkara, the hyaena and wild hog, were becoming scarce as cultivation advanced.[14] The region also harbours the great breeding colonies of the two species of flamingoes in the Rann of Cutch. The Indus River fauna is related to the Ganges and includes the mugger and the gharial.

Gangetic Plain

This region includes the Gangetic plain and delta from Delhi to the Bay of Bengal and the plain of Brahmaputra as far as Goalpara and all lower Bengal. The annual precipitation ranges from 600 mm in the west to 2,000 mm in the east. The natural climax vegetation of this tract was probably like the tall grass jungles of Terai interspersed with deciduous forest. It must have been the optimal habitat for the elephant and the rhinoceros. The tract is now almost completely cleared and has been under cultivation for centuries. The Brahmaputra valley, however, still retains some natural vegetation.[15]

This great plain dividing the peninsula from the Himalayas has a fauna mainly belonging to the former. Thus, characteristic peninsular forms such as hyena, ratel, blackbuck and nilgai occur in suitable localities. The most characteristic animals of the Gangetic plain are the hog deer and the hispid hare or Assam rabbit, although both extend into Assam.[16] This hispid hare is probably extinct now, and the hog deer is almost gone from the plains. The most extensive natural habitat still left in this region is the Sundarbans, a swampy mangrove forest at the mouth of the river Ganges. Most of the Sundarbans are now in Bangladesh, while the Indian section has shrunk considerably. However, they still possess some exciting wildlife, including the tiger. Notable freshwater animals of the Ganges include the gharial and the Gangetic dolphin; both are threatened species.[17]

Although most of the wildlife has thus been nearly wiped out of this thickly settled region, there remain substantial populations of the two monkeys, the rhesus macaque and the human langur, still live in rural and urban areas.[18] These monkeys, unmolested by man because of religious taboos, live in great troops throughout the tract. Of these, the rhesus has acquired a key position in biomedical trapping and export.

Western Peninsula

This region lies roughly to the west of 80^0 east longitude, to the south of Aravalli Hills[19] and Gangetic plain and the east of the Western Ghats. It is an undulating region with hilly outcrops and annual precipitation ranging from 400 to 1,500 mm. The region's natural vegetation consists of scrubs or deciduous forest. Most of this region has been cleared for cultivation and is fairly thickly settled, although farmers and residents have left tracts of thin forest, brushwood, and grass in the hillier terrain.

The fauna includes the typical forms restricted to India, such as blackbuck, nilgai, chinkara and sloth bear. This region also harbours the last surviving population of the Asiatic lion in the Gir forest. The Indian lion is one of the rarest and most important of the wild animals of India, and yet it is one of the least known. It used to range over most of north India except in the easternmost part and as far south as the Narmada River.[20] The open scrub used to support vast herds of antelopes preyed on the wolf and the cheetah. Compared to forest wildlife, scrub jungle wildlife has suffered far more at the hands of man over the past fifty years. Humans have driven the antelopes, chinkara and blackbuck to the brink of extinction, the wolf is threatened with extinction, and the cheetah has now been extinct for the past quarter-century. The tree shrew and the *slender loris* also occur in this region.

Eastern Peninsula

This region lies between the Gangetic plain to the north and the river Krishna to the south and extends from the Bay of Bengal to the longitude 80^0 East. It is a hilly country with an average yearly rainfall of 1,250 mm. Although relatively sparsely populated, the region still retains much forest cover. The natural climax vegetation is a deciduous forest dominated by *sal* over much of the region (*Shorea robusta*).

This tract has many forest species with Indo-Malayan affinities, such as the elephant, the gaur and the sambar and typical peninsular forms, such as the blackbuck, nilgai and sloth bear. Several tigers still survive in this region, as does the small population of two other threatened species, namely wild buffalo and the hard-ground race of *barasinga*. The giant squirrel occurs here, as in the Western Ghats. Several bird genera inhabit both the eastern peninsula, the Western Ghats and the Himalayas.[21] This suggests that there was once a continuous distribution of many forest forms from the Himalayas to the Western Ghats. Forest clearance likely exterminated them from the intervening areas.

FAUNA

The fauna that drew the emperor's attention, court chronicles and court artists can be classified into three categories: (1) those animals that were hunted; (2) those that were required for imperial; (3) those animals that were presented at court as rarities such as Burchell's zebra (*Equus quagga burchellii*), the standard turkey (*Meleagris gallavo*), the dodo (*Raphus cucullatus*), the blue-crowned hanging parrot (*Loriculus galgulus*) and the African elephants (*Loxodonta africana*). Interestingly, these animals and birds were not of the Indian landscape. There were other birds and animals such as the Barbary falcon (*Falco peregrunus babylonicus*), the Siberian crane (*Grus leucogerenus*, which are seen no longer in India since 2002), the Sarus crane (*Grus Antigone*), the western tragopan (*Tragopan melanocephalus*), the four-horned antelope (*Tetracerus qudricornis*), which were either migrants to or resident of India. They, however, do not give us any information about their landscape or their behavioural ecology. Therefore, we will limit our discussion to two examples in the first two categories only.

The Lion

Lion evolved in Europe, then moved down to Asia Minor due to climate changes. Africa and the Asiatic lion separated about fifty-five thousand years ago, and then they became two different subspecies. A thousand years ago, the Asiatic lion was found in North Africa along with Mediterranean Asia Minor, India and perhaps a part of Europe. Till the nineteenth century, it survived in a part of Asian Minor-Iran, Iraq and India. Still, it became extinct from all distribution ranges at the beginning of the twentieth century, except the Gir forest.[22]

In his fauna of Hindustan,[23] Abul Fazl mentions that lions as being numerous. Jahangir describes a lion hunt of his father, Emperor Akbar, in a jungle in the neighbourhood of Lahore, 'which was so infested by ferocious quadrupeds to the number of twenty, male and female'. Under the Mughal rule, the lion had become a royal game and their hunt was reserved so far only for the emperor and his favoured relatives, courtiers and guests could hunt it. Sir Thomas Roe was at Mandu in 1617 with Jahangir's encampment. He was much harassed by a lion who raided his camp. He had to seek special permission to tackle the menace 'for no man may meddle with lions but the king'.[24] Bernier records that during the reign of Aurangzeb, large tracts on the route of the three great capitals were 'guarded with utmost vigilance; and except partridges, quails and hares which natives catch with nets, no person, be he who may, is permitted to disturb the game, which is consequently very abundant' and of all the diversions of the field the hunting of the lion is not only the most precious but is peculiarly royal; for except by special permission, the king and the princes are the only ones who engage in the sport.[25]

Jahangir maintained records of his hunts. In the eleventh year of his reign, that is, in thirty-nine years during which he kept records of his *shikar,* he writes that he had either shot or was present at shoots when 28,532 game animals and game birds were hunted, which included 86 lions.[26]

The Tiger

Mughal records provide few details about tigers. Its rare appearance is not surprising at all. Wild animals like tigers always preferred tick cover; their solitary nature and their absence from grassland and scrub jungle somewhat made them very elusive. Moreover, tigers were unlikely to encounter each other frequently in the path of the royal cavalcade. The lion was a royal game, and the tiger was not; it was an object of *shikar* when it met with imperial peregrination. So, this could be a reason for their sparseness in the Mughal records. However, the fact is that two paintings explicitly show tiger encounters during the Mughal period.[27] Akbar's cavalcade was attacked near Narwar in Gwalior in 1561 by a tigress and five young cubs. The tigress was slained by Akbar himself, who then ordered the five sub-adult cubs to be dispatched.

The other painting is titled 'A Royal Hunting Scene' from the National Museum of Pakistan, Karachi. Its copy was also made at Lucknow between 1780 and 1790 from an earlier mid-seventeenth-century version. The painting shows Shah Jahan on an elephant's back with imperial cavalcades facing two tigers with a thick forest behind them. The artist depicted the tigers being driven out of the jungle into the open for the shoot. Tigers do appear as part of the animal world in the various paintings in the *Anwar-i-Suhaili;* the tigers also occur along with *cheetahs*, the blackbuck, the caracal and other animals in the *Razmnana,* the illustrated Persian translation of the *Mahabharata*, the great Indian epic which Akbar commissioned.[28]

Jahangir describes an instance of the most unusual behaviour by a tiger at Agra in the year 1609. He says: 'They brought a tiger from my private menagerie to fight with a bull. Many people gathered to see the show and a band of *jogis* (religious mendicants) were with them. One of the *jogis* was naked, and the tiger approached him playfully rather than with aggression. It threw him to the ground and behaved toward him as it would toward a female. The following day, and on several other occasions, the same thing occurred. As such things had been seen before and was exceeding strange.' This is recorded in the *Iqbalnama*.[29]

The same story is also related to the *Iqbalnama* (p.137). It stated that this tiger was one brought by a *kalendar* (mendicant) as a present to the monarch. It had the name 'Lal Khan' and was very tame. It is added that the tiger did not injure the jogi with his claws or teeth.

The *Cheetah*

India is at the vanguard of this march towards disaster with its exploding human, cattle, sheep and goat populations, and one little-known victim is the cheetah. This graceful, swift and unique cat family member remained in most Indians minds who often confuse it with the leopard. According to some, *cheetahs* were not native to India, but Indian princes introduced them from Africa for the sport of hunting antelope. The information about cheetah in historical records seem to have been a blur; even the absence of the cheetah from the chronicles of Babur and Humayun appears strange indeed. However, a painting by Ganga Sen and Narsingh shows Humayun and Shah Tahmasp hunting near *Takht-i-Sulaiman* and *Hauz-i-Sulaiman* in Persia, where a cheetah is visible. Young Akbar was introduced to a cheetah for the first time in 1555 when Wali Beg, father of leading courtier Khan Jahan, brought a cheetah to Akbar.

Akbar personally caught the cheetah (Fig. 3.1), and the *Akbarnama* records his doing so at Hisar Firuza in 1560 and near Gwalior in 1569.[30] A miniature of the *Padshahnama* showing the royal entourage on the move from Lahore to Agra in the 8th regnal year offers a cheetah being carried on the bullock cart.[31]

An elaborate organization was developed to keep the empire supplied with *cheetahs* and specific areas were earmarked for catching *cheetahs* in the wilds. They were the environs of Patna, Bhatnair, Bathinda and Hisar in Punjab and Haryana; Jodhpur, Nagaur, Merta and Dholpur in Rajasthan.[32] From these locations, it becomes evident that *cheetahs* were possibly the most numerous in western India's grasslands, scrublands and semi-arid regions.

According to the National Tiger Conservation Authority (NTCA), the *cheetahs* were completely wiped out India, mainly due to overhunting and habitat loss. The chronology of their extinction is given in Appendix III on page 215.

The Leopard or Panthers

The leopard (*Panthera pardus*) is the most widely distributed and persecuted cat among large cat species. In India, it largely coexists with other feline species like the tiger (*Panthera tigris*) across much of its distribution range and with a lion (*Panthera leo*) and clouded leopard in some regions of its distribution range. Due to its very high adaptability for surviving in various habitats and opportunistic feeding behaviour, it is often at the centre of the human-wildlife conflict. Retaliatory persecution, poaching, habitat loss and declining natural

FIGURE 3.1: AKBAR CATCHING HIS FIRST *CHEETAH*, HISSAR FIRUZA *SHIKARGAH* IN 1560. PAINTING BY TULSI AND NARAYAN, *c.* 1590-5, FROM AN *AKBARNAMA* MANUSCRIPT, IS. 2:2-1896. (*COURTESY:* VICTORIA AND ALBERT MUSEUM, LONDON).

prey lead to population decline.[33] Abul Fazl mentions this animal occurring in the *sarkar* of Kashmir, tracked.[34]

The White *Cheetah*

Jahangir notes, 'Raja Bir Sing Deo brought a white cheetah to show me. Although other creatures, both birds and beaters, have white verities called tugyhan, I had never seen a white cheetah. Its spots, which are (usually) black, were blue, and the body's whiteness was also inclined to bluishness.[35] Furthermore, of the albino animals that I have seen, there are falcons, sparrowhawks and hawks that they call *bigu* in the Persian language: sparrows, crows, partridges, florican and peacocks. Many hawks in aviaries are albinos. I have also seen white flying mice and some people with albinism among the black antelope, a species found only in Hindustan. Among the *chikara* (gazelle), which they call *said* in Persian, I have frequently seen people with albinism.'[36]

Wild Boar

Wild boar, thought to have been domesticated over thousands of years are the progenitors of the domestic pig we know today. They can be fearsome animal to encounter, possessing a robust body shape, snorting loudly and often bearing sharp tusks. The information about them in the Mughal records appears to be unclear. However, the painting made by Husayn Kashifi (a preacher and scholar at the Timurid court in Herat) in 1504-5 shows their presence and the painting inscribed Makra, Agra region in 1595-1600. See Fig. 3.2 for more information about wild boar, which appeals that the monkey throws figs down to the wild boar. In this tale, a wild boar sees a monkey in a fig tree and asks him to throw down some fruits, which the monkey continues to refuse and the greedy boar becomes impatient.[37]

Asian Elephant

Elephants and their deployment during the battle time have fascinated history. Chandragupta Maurya, the great king of the Mauryan Empire,

FIGURE 3.2. WILD BOAR PAINTING MADE BY HUSAYN KASHIFI IN 1504-5, PAINTING INSCRIBED, MAKRA, AGRA REGION IN 1595-1600 (*COURTESY:* CHESTER BEATTY LIBRARY, DUBLIN).

possessed a considerable number of elephants and used them extensively in war. It is estimated that there were between 750 and 1,000 war elephants in the *pilkhana* (elephant stables) of the Delhi Sultanate. However, the elephants' number had fallen to a little below 500 after 1,350 at the height of their power in the early fourteenth century during Firoz Shah Tughlaq's reign.[38]

Babur thus describes the animal: 'As for the animals peculiar to Hindustan, one is the elephant. The Hindustan calls it *Hathi*, which inhabits the district of Kalpi[39] and the higher you advance thence towards the east, the more do the wild plants in number. That is the tract in which the elephant is primarily found. There may be thirty to forty villages in Karran[40] and Manikpur[41] that are occupied solely for the employment of taking elephants. Irfan Habib's *Atlas*, which is distilled from contemporary sources of the Mughal Empire, notes such locations. From Harwar to the Gandak River and beyond, right up to Assam along the Shivalik, the terai and the foothills of the Himalayas to Murshidabad in Bengal and the Sunderbans in Bengal were their habitats. In western India, they were found at Dohad, on Gujarat and Madhya Pradesh border and from the west of the Malwa plateau to Sarguja in Chhattisgarh.

Abu Fazl has given information about the elephant in *Ain-i-Akbari*. He notes different types of an elephant and records their habits, diet, mating and gestation period. According to him, elephants were not bred in captivity because their breeding was unlucky. However, on Akbar's orders, elephant breeding was being started. As a result, only good-quality elephants were bred. The imperial stables carefully classified elephants into seven classes, with food, care and servants provided to them according to the needs of the animals in each category. They were regularly mustered for Akbar's inspection, and *khasa* elephants were specially earmarked for his use alone.[42]

Akbar himself took part in an elephant-catching foray at Sipri between Mandu and Agra, where he was impressed by a wild male from a herd of 70 elephants that were caught. The male broke the fort wall and ran off but was caught again and became a khasa elephant named *Gajapati,* king of elephants, see Figs. 3.3 & 3.4.[43]

At the beginning of the seventeenth century, it is estimated that there were 40,000 elephants in the Mughal Empire. According to R.

FIGURE 3.3. AKBAR'S ELEPHANT CATCHING FORAY AT SIPRI BETWEEN MANDU AND AGRA. (COURTESY: VICTORIA AND ALBERT MUSEUM, LONDON).

FIGURE 3.4. GAJ RATAN IS STANDING UNDER A CANOPY, PAINTING ON CLOTH (*COURTESY:* S.P. GUPTA INTERPRETING MUGHAL PAINTING).

Sukumar, the distribution of wild elephants at the end of the Mughal Empire's zenith remained unchanged until the British opened up the country in the nineteenth century. G.P. Sanderson, a renowned hunter and chronicler of British Indian sport, wrote as late as 1896 that the wild elephant 'abounds' in most of the extensive forests from the foothills of the Himalayas throughout the peninsula to the extreme south.[44] Currently, the situation is critical. R. Sukumar calculated India's elephant population between 26,390 and 30,770. The figure, according to him, for north-west and central India is between 3,150 and 3,700,[45] which approximates the Mughal Empire's heartland. However, some north-east and south Indian areas, either under Mughal control or were sources of supply, are left out. According to *Alamgirnama* of Muhammad Kazim, a record of Aurangzeb's rule, Assam had four or five places to supply 500 to 600 elephants every year.[46] On the other hand, *Mirat-i-Ahmedi* laments that elephants were no longer found at Dohad as their migration routes were now under human habitation, starting changes between the reigns of Jahangir and Aurangzeb.

The One-horned Rhinoceros

Babur, as we know, frequently hunted (Fig. 3.5) this animal, which he describes as follows:

> The rhinoceros is a huge animal. Its bulk is equal to that of three buffaloes. The opinion prevalent in our countries that a rhinoceros can lift an elephant on its horn is probably a mistake. It has a single horn over its nose, upwards of a span in length, but I never saw one of two spans. Out of one of the largest of these horns, I had a drinking vessel made and a dice-box and about 3 or 4 fingers' bulk of it might be left.[47]

Regarding the rhinoceros' distribution, Babur says, 'There are numbers of them in the jungles of Peshawar and Hashnagar and between the rivers Sind and Behreh in the jungles. In Hindustan, too, they abound on the banks of the Saru'. Towards the end of Humayun's reign, around 1556, a Turkish admiral, Sidi Ali Reis, travelled overland from Surat to Lahore; where he encountered two rhinoceros near Peshawar.

Contrary to the distribution of rhinoceros, their numbers are drastically decreased due to diminished territories of the animals,

FIGURE 3.5. BABUR HUNTING RHINOCEROS IN THE JUNGLE NEAR BIGRAM, *c.* 1525, SHIVDAS, *VAKIAT-I-BABURI, THE MEMOIRS OF BABUR* TRANSLATED FROM THE TURKI ORIGINALLY BY MIRZA ABD-AL-RAHIM KHAN-I-KHANA, 143 MINIATURE (*COURTESY:* ALMY STOCK PHOTOGRAPHY COMPANY, LONDON).

which are Burma, Assam and the Nepal Terai, nowhere of can be said to be plentiful in the last name.

Writing during the reign of Akbar, his court chronicle Abul Fazl states regarding the *sarkar* of Chambal: 'There is a game in plenty and the rhinoceros is found. It is an animal like a small elephant without a trunk and having a horn on its snout, with which it attacks animals. From its skin, shields are made and from its horn finger-guards for bowstrings, strings and the like.' Further, Abul Fazl includes this beast in his fauna of Hindustan, where it is described; 'The rhinoceros is a spectacular creature; he is twice the size of a buffalo, and much resembles a horse in amour.[48]

The Emperor Jahangir mentions that he was hunting the rhinoceros from an elephant in the Kul Nuh Ban (forest) in the neighbourhood of Aligarh. He says, 'A rhinoceros appeared, and I struck it with a bullet on the face near the lobe of the ear. The bullet penetrated for about a span. From the bullet, it fell and gave up its life. In my presence, it had often happened that powerful men with good shots with the bow have shot 20 or 30 arrows at them and not killed.' This took place about the year AD 1622. It has been stated that this animal was a wolf, but this is incorrect. In Persian, *gurg* is a wolf and *kurg* is a rhinoceros. A wolf certainly would not require 20 or 30 arrows to kill it.

The Zebra

In 1621, a delegation came to the court of Jahangir and presented the emperor with rare and exotic birds and animals. One was an African zebra, an animal peculiar to Jahangir as Jahangir had never seen a zebra before, it seemed like a horse painted with stripes. He wrote, 'One might say the painter of fate, with a strange brush, had left it on the page of the world'. He intended it to be sent to 'Shah Abbas of Iran, with whom he regularly exchanged valuable or rare presents, but there are no mentions of the artist's name to whom he gave the order to record the zebra's appearance. However, on the right of the painting, the emperor himself had written in his distinctive spidery hand, see Fig. 3.6, which was the work of one of his two leading artists, Mansur and includes details of how and when the zebra came to court.

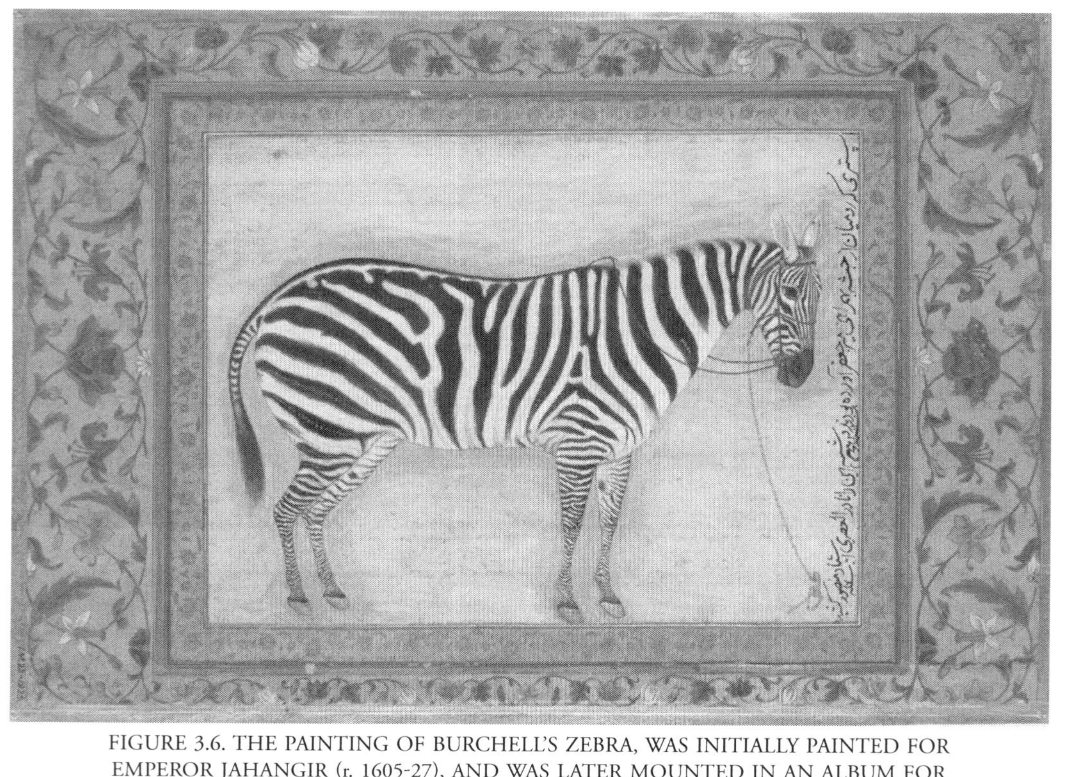

FIGURE 3.6. THE PAINTING OF BURCHELL'S ZEBRA, WAS INITIALLY PAINTED FOR EMPEROR JAHANGIR (r. 1605-27), AND WAS LATER MOUNTED IN AN ALBUM FOR HIS SON AND SUCCESSOR, SHAH JAHAN (*COURTESY:* VICTORIA AND ALBERT MUSEUM [IM. 23-1925], LONDON).

FAUNA IN MUGHAL ART

Other essential sources for studying fauna are Mughal miniature paintings. Mughal artists paid close attention to nature, especially animal and bird habitats and gave them an aesthetic context. Paintings of animals and individual studies were not famous before the Mughal Empire. During the sixteenth century, it became feasible to see nature through the eyes of an artist. Indeed, from the start of Mughal rule in the early sixteenth century, there was a strong interest in the flora and fauna of India. Babur, Humayun, and Akbar enjoyed nature's variety and their court artists drew inspiration from it. This art flourished during Jahangir and Shah Jahan's reigns. Later Mughal emperors followed this trend. Still, towards the end of Aurangzeb's rule in the latter part of the eighteenth century, a qualitative degradation was apparent, probably due to the decline of royal patronage.

Babur's description of Hindustan gives detailed information about varied species of birds, animals, trees, plants and flowers of the country. Babur carefully notices the habitat, characteristic physical features and anatomy of both plants and animals and variations in the parts of male and female species. For example, while writing about the bull, Babur says:

> It may stand as high as a horse but is somewhat lighter in build. Because the male is bluish-grey, people refer to him as *nil-gau.* It has two rather small horns. A nine-inch long tuft of hair on its throat resembles yak hair. Its hoof is cleft like the hoof of cattle. The doe is of the colour of the *bughumaral;* she, for her part, has no horns and is plumper than the male.[49]

Contrary to Babur, Jahangir, too, took much interest in wildlife. He writes in his memoirs: 'I had never seen anything like this before, and until now, no one had been able to figure out what they were called. Although King Babur mentioned the looks and forms of various creatures in his chronicles, he never ordered the artists to paint them. As these animals looked to me to be somewhat unusual, I both described them and ordered that artists depict them in the *Jahangirnama* so that the amazement that arose from hearing of them might be increased'.[50]

The Mughals were fascinated by the elephant. Migrating from the remote central Asian state of Farghana, they did not have much familiarity with this vast, strange-looking animal. The Emperor Babur was impressed with its sharp intelligence, precise nature and indispensability on the battlefield.[51] Abul Fazl deals with elephants in his seven-section long text in *Ain-i-Akbari*. Every detail about them, their classification, upkeep, food, and how Akbar handled them is described.[52] Akbar's sprawling *taswirkhana* (atelier) painters showed many of these elephants in illustrations of biographical works like the *Akbarnama* or individual studies of favourite animals for mounting in an album.

Though Jahangir's interest in elephants was not as all-pervading as Akbar's, it was more than usual. He maintained a large *filkhana* containing many prize animals and presented particular elephants to leading nobles. Among the portraits of prized elephants identified by Jahangir, three stand out for special mention: Alam Guman, Gaj Ratan and Pawan Gaj. When Jahangir travelled through the elephant forest near Dohad, he wanted to participate in elephant trapping with Gajpat Khan, the *filkhana* and Baluch Khan, chief huntsman. The pick of the catch of 185 male and female elephants was Pawan. On order from Emperor Jahangir, it was kept near the *jharokha* on the riverside when brought to the court.[53] Recently, an excellent shaded drawing of this elephant has been found (Fig. 3.4).

Besides, Jahangir's descriptions are conspicuous for their precision and brevity. He wastes no words, nor does he dilate upon the object of his admiration; instead, he takes note of the essential features to distinguish between species. He speaks of the animals' scheme of colouration, shape, physical features, anatomical peculiarities, habitats, climatic conditions, food habits and behaviours—all the features of external morphology, even getting them measured and weighed. The text also includes local names, wherever available. The animal is commonly known by people; Thus, he describes a Malaysian monkey (*Macacus cynomolgus*) in the following terms:

its hand, feet, ears, and head are like those of a monkey and its face like that of a hawk's size larger (Fig. 3.7). It measures an ordinary cubit from its head to the end of its tail. It is shorter than a monkey but stands higher than a fox. Its hairs are like a sheep's wool, and the colour is ashy. From the lobes

FIGURE 3.7. MALAYSIAN MONKEY (*MACACUS CYNOMOLGUS*), DRAWING BY ISHAQ MUHAMMAD, 1977 (*COURTESY:* MRS NASREEN HUSSAIN, CENTRE OF WILDLIFE AND ORNITHOLOGY, AMU, ALIGARH).

of its ear to the chin, it is red like wine. The tail is two or three fingers larger than half a cubit. Quite different from other monkeys, the tail of this animal hangs down like the tail of a cat. Sometimes, it utters a sound like a young antelope. In short, it is an extraordinary animal.[54]

The Slender Loris (*Loris tardigrades*) is unknown in northern India (Fig. 3.8). It is a native of Sri Lanka and is rarely found in peninsular India, where different names know it: *even* in Tamil, *devanga* in Telegu, chin-kul in a Corgi. In Sinhalese, it is called *unahappolava*. Jahangir calls it *devnak*. It is nocturnal in its habits. A Sri Lanka hermit presented it the emperor who had its likeness hermit presented it to the emperor, who had its likeness painted and described it in his memoirs:

Its face was exactly like a large bat and the whole shape like a monkey. But it had no tail. Its movements were like those of a black tailless monkey, which they call *ban-manush* in Hindi. Its body was of the size of a young monkey, two or three months old. It had been with the dervish (*hermit*) for five years. It appeared that the animal would not grow longer. Its food is milk, and it eats plantains also.[55]

HUNTING-AGRICULTURAL LAND AND FOREST NEXUS

Some argue that the Mughals viewed the hunting ground as a transitional zone between the cultivated land and uncultivated forest, as it established continuity between hunting practices and agriculture. Hunting usually took place in gardens, such as Darhra Bagh in Agra. Imperial hunters also incorporated many garden components into the hunting ground, significantly altering its natural character. Moreover, the natural environment of the forest cover areas was also appropriated and transformed through deforestation and the addition of features such as irrigation to enhance agricultural production and, as a result, to form a conducive environment for hunting.

Irrigation work is primarily meant to enhance cultivation in those lands where monsoon rain is a deficit, particularly in the arid zone, often deforested land. The creation of lakes and dams, technological upgrades to existing traditional water systems and the construction of canals not only enhance cultivation but also attracted abundant

FIGURE 3.8. SLENDER LORIS (*LORIS TARDIGRADUS*). ARTIST'S NAME IS NOT KNOWN (*COURTESY:* MRS NASREEN HUSSAIN, CENTRE OF WILDLIFE AND ORNITHOLOGY, AMU, ALIGARH)

wildlife from the wastelands in the vicinity, thereby creating thriving hunting grounds. *Arthashastra* by Kautilya also suggests that the nexus between agricultural land, hunting ground and forest cover—the king's hunting park, which is a dry but irrigated agricultural space filled with the game with claws and teeth removed, which should ideally border an immense animal preserve and timber forests; elephant forests along riverbeds or marshy tracts on the borders.[56] Delhi Doab exemplified the forest between the Sutlej and Yamuna rivers, bordered by the Siwalik Mountains. Their modified forests were fertile hunting grounds for the Mughals. *Anupa,* or marshy, mountainous, forested land, receives less rainfall than the *jungle* and is not ideal.[57] Forests protected agricultural villages at their boundary. Hence, the town or countryside was both 'inside' the jungle and 'different' from it: spatially included but ecologically separate, since both regions were interconnected.[58]

The great famine of 1630-2 was the worst ever famine in the history of Mughal Era, and it was compounded by pestilence; over three million people lost their lives in Gujarat and the Dakhin.[59] Grain brought over from Malwa was sold at high prices, resulting in huge gains for the imperial treasury. Peter Mundy, a British traveller stationed in India from 1628 to 1634, adds that the supply was also disrupted to feed Shah Jahan's army, encamped in Burhanpur near the worst-affected areas.[60] Although Shah Jahan's historian Lahori[61] and 'Inayat Khan[62] offer some details regarding the calamity and imperial remedies. Lahori[63] is more effusive in highlighting the emperor's lion in Burhanpur *Bagh-i-Zaynabad Shikargah* (Fig. 3.9) in the novel use of a net during the height of the famine in 1630. Shah Jahan's actions seem to have been motivated by the symbolic notion of the two interdependent spaces: agricultural lands and hunting grounds. The emperor was expected to be a champion of both activities to fulfil his kingly duties in their entirety.

The Lakhi jungle in the Panjab is another example of cultivation made possible by canal irrigation at the expense of forests, thus resulting in the creation of several imperial hunting grounds. As Sujan Rai Bhandari, a court historian of the Mughal, writing in 1695-6, explains, periodic flooding of the river Beas and Sutlej created a

FIGURE 3.9. SHAH JAHAN WAS HUNTING LIONS BAGH-I-ZAYANABAD SHIKARGAH USING THE NET, BURHANPUR, 1630. PAINTING RELATED TO DAULAT, *c.* 1635, THE WINDSOR PADSHANAMA, F. 220B, RCIN 1005025. AU. (*COURTESY:* ROYAL COLLECTION TRUST /© HM QUEEN ELIZABETH LONDON).

wasteland called the Lakhi Jungle. It is also acknowledged by Irfan Habib.[64] Since the tributaries of the Indus flowed in deep channels lower than the ground surface, two distinct blocks of cultivation developed in Punjab: one above the 200 metres mark; the other is the Son River channels created the south-easterly came together and contained cities such as Pakpattan.[65] The two areas were connected at several places along the riverbed; elsewhere, they were separated by the Sindsagar Doab (between the Chenab and Ravi rivers) and the Lakhi Jungle,[66] the natural habit for *cheetahs* and grazing grounds for the wild horses and onagers (Asiatic wild ass). The construction of irrigation canals eliminated the Lakhi wastelands and substantially increased the acreage of cultivated lands; it also created the favoured *shikars* of Pakpattan and Bathinda.

An extraordinary feature of the Indian subcontinent is the proximity of forested areas and wild animals at the edge of cultivated land and urban contexts, favouring *shikargah-i-mugarrars.* Court paintings frequently explore the hunting ground-agricultural lands narrative. In the Bodleian, *c.* 1660, an image depicts a Mughal prince pursuing blackbucks in a chariot near an irrigation tank. In the geographical zone of the Panjab, the province of Lahore is watered by the five tributaries of the Indus, whose 'agricultural fertility is rarely equalled'.[67] Its main *shikargah-i-muqarrars* include Hassan Abdal, Rohtas, Girjhak, Bhera, Jahangirabad, Kahnuwahan and Bhimbar were all situated in well-cultivated areas and many in proximity to urban centres. The area around Rajaur was famous for its high-quality rice and worthy of a mention by Jahangir. In this region, three *qamargha* hunts were organized for him in Bhimbar, Girjhak and Makhila in quick succession in 1620.[68]

James Forsyth, an English traveller who visited India in 1850, mentioned the proximity of wildlife and agricultural belts.[69] He also notes that antelopes were found in considerable herds in central India's corn districts, the most cultivated areas. Further, Forsyth also states that nilgai was often seen on 'the old sites of deserted villages and cultivation, unfortunately so common', adding that nilgai is 'never found very far from cultivation area.[70] Irfan Habib cites a section of the *Muntakhab-ul-Lubab* written by Khafi Khan in 1720 that many districts in the Mughal Empire that used to yield total revenue were rendered ruined and devastated because of the oppression of authorities and had become forests infested by wild animals such as lions and tigers. Therefore, cultivated lands reappropriated by woods and wildlife seem common place.[71] The relationship between agricultural land and forested areas was not simply one of outright confrontation, adding that 'the two were simultaneously engaged in a silent and fluctuating struggle of encroachment upon and retreat from each other's living space'.[72]

As a fact, dense forest cover seems to have been an object of a hindrance to hunting. While stating about the area between Pattan and Baroda in Gujarat, Abul Fazl notes a fertile belt of high-quality fruit orchards such as mango, musk-melon, fig and other fruits and flowers. He also adds that *cheetahs* are found in significant quantities in the nearby forests and that 'form the thick growth of forest sport is not satisfactory.[73] This suggests that woodcutters cleared either the forest before the hunt could occur or drum beaters had to drive the animals from the forests into a designated hunting ground. Jahangir's elephant trapping incident in the hilly, marshy, thick jungles of Gujarat and Malwa in 1618 also shows how the hunt failed due to the the terrain. An advance party of foot soldiers and horsemen had surrounded a large herd of elephants 'as in a *qamargha*' (battune ring hunt), which were then driven by specialist elephants-drivers from the Jarga tribe from the jungle towards Jahangir's presence, indicative of the fact that the hunt did not take place in the dense forest but an altered environment. Jahangir notes that the *qamargha* chain was broken due to the hilly terrain and thick growth of vegetation.[74] The imperial newsletters (*Akhbarats*) written during Aurangzeb's reign, such as the *Akhbarat-Darbar-i Mu'alla, Akhbarat-i Shahzada Muhammad Azam* and *Akhbarat-i Bahadur Shah,* also contain several reports of jungle clearance to facilitate the hunts of Princes Azam and Bahadur. These included laying paths, clearing the forested land for decoy hunts and driving animals towards the cleared land.

In the Mughal Empire, dense forests in hilly terrain with a large fresh water stream and scrub forest cover were the two types of forest cover found. These forest surfaces were interspersed with cultivation or lay on the periphery of cultivation zones and wastelands. Hunting grounds were found in both forests, whose natural landscape was extensively altered for imperial use. Abul Fazl spoke about many elephants being found in the *suba* of Agra, parts of Berar, Allahabad, Bihar, Bengal and Orissa.[75] Based on information collected from *Ain* and other Mughal literary sources, following the Mughal emperor's elephant trapping movements across the Mughal Empire, the description of forests about the hunt, and the understanding that elephants need dense stretches of tree forests and freshwater streams. Irfan Habib has mapped a broad belt of forest stretching from Gujarat in the west, covering Malwa, across the Upper and Middle Gangetic Basin to Bihar, Orissa and Bengal in the east; he calls this belt the 'Great Central Indian forest'.[76] After an extensive survey of the topography of Awadh *suba* in the 1830s, Butter pointed out that the dense forestation of the many higher-lying jungles is interspersed with cultivated land and that the forest was bordered by cultivation.[77]

Scrub forests were another type of forest cover prevalent in the Mughal Empire. These forests were typically semi-desert, with scrub jungles and grassland, occasional tree growth, rocky tracts and low rugged hills, often sharing a border with the wastelands of cultivated zones. The essential characteristic of these forests is seen as the natural habitat of *cheetahs*, antelope, chinkara (Indian gazelle) and blackbuck. The cheetah's swiftness means that its favoured habitat allowed it to sprint with minimum obstruction by features such as trees while it brought down its prey.[78] The semi-arid regions of western and central India were the most fertile cheetah-hunting regions. Pakpattan, Bathinda and Hissar Firuza are *shikargah-i-muqarrars,* where significant *cheetahs* being trapped.

MUGHAL AGRARIAN POLICY AND ITS IMPACT

The main objective of the Mughals was to extend and improve agriculture as it constituted the primary source of state income. In pursuit of this goal, the Mughals frequently changed and put into practice agricultural policies, with the main focus on bringing wasteland and forests under cultivation. Different categories (*polaj, chacha, parauti* and *banzar*) of the land area is based on production in *Ain-i-Akbari.*

The agricultural surplus produced appropriated from the peasantry was shared between the ruler and the landlord (*zamindar*). For the efficient administration and military contingent work, the sustained flow of land revenue was essential.[79] However, misuse, corruption, and peasants' exploitation by *zamindar* during the Mughal period were common phenomena and required constant scrutiny by authorities. The hunting expedition gave the emperor ample opportunity to redress the grievances of the peasantry. Regarding hunting, Abul Fazl justified hunting expeditions that Akbar always makes hunting because of increasing his field knowledge of his realm. Besides, he uses hunting parties as occasions to inquire, without having first given information about his coming, about the condition of the people and the army's action. Akbar travels in cognition and examines the matter related to taxation impact, *sayurghal* lands or state affairs connected with the household. On such account of this reason, His Majesty indulges in hunting expeditions.[80]

During Akbar's reign, some hunting practices were detrimental to the development of agriculture because of the two famous hunting practices and severely tested the emperor's role as a guarantor of prosperity and fertility. Both *qamargha* and decoy-drive hunts required large swathes of land to be cordoned off for several days and involved animals being driven in from substantial distances over cultivated lands into the arena (see Fig. 3.10, Akbar participates in *qamargha* hunt in Palam, Delhi, 1568). A monumental *qamargha* organized for Akbar in Lahore in 1567 entailed over 15,000 animals driven in from neighbouring hills for a month by 50,000 beaters into a 16 km circumference circle created especially for hunting. *Amirs* from the vicinity of 160 km in every direction were mobilized to oversee the closure of several provinces.[81] Animals driven in from great distances, especially on paths called *nihilam,*[82] would have invariably cut through cultivated lands and extended the spaces of the immediate hunting arena. Many workers employed in hunt-related jobs, such as beaters, would have been drawn from the agricultural sector. The closure of about 80,000 sq. km of agricultural land for over a month to accommodate the 1,567 *qamargha* meant not only disruptions to cultivation: it seems fair to presume that large quantities of agricultural lands and crops would have been destroyed due to the trampling of personnel and animals.

FIGURE 3.10. EMPEROR AKBAR PARTICIPATED IN A *QAMARGHA* HUNT IN PALAM, DELHI, IN 1568. (*COURTESY:* VICTORIA AND ALBERT MUSEUM, LONDON, V & A IS.2:70-1896).

The rulers were also well aware that there was polarity in the relationship of their hunting culture with agriculturalists. By their submission, emperors relate to the inevitability of crops and land being damaged or destroyed as a result of the movement of troops during hunting expeditions. Jahangir mentions hunting in the Agra vicinity at one of his favoured hunting places (*shikargahs*) in early 1610; since it was the session of crop planting, he assigned a sergeant and troops of soldiers to protect crops grown by peasants from damage by the passage of a royal army. However, aware of the futility of even such precautionary measures, he ordered several officers to inspect the trampling 'stage by stage' and award the peasants cash compensation.[83] Inayat Khan mentioned that 'despite every vigilance and precaution', his troops had destroyed standing crops on both banks of the Yamuna to Mukhlispur in 1627 and accordingly bestowed Rs. 30,000 from the royal treasury to the peasants as compensation for crops ruined.[84]

IRRIGATION AND ANIMAL HUNT

The construction of canals, dams, large tanks, and stepwells (*baoli*) near lakes and river bodies were always a fascinating place to attract abundant wildlife from the scrubs nearby. Irrigation-induced imperial hunting was not an early colonial phenomenon. However, ancient text, for instance, Kautilya's *Arthashastra,* notes that the ideal place for hunting should be by a lake, which promoted agriculture extensively.[85] Writing in the early fourteenth century, Farishta argued that the growth of agriculture was one of the principal objectives of Sultan Firuz Shah; as a result, he built fifty dams, thirty reservoirs, ten public wells and several aqueducts and channels. Several hunting grounds and hunting places were built around these water bodies.[86] Anthony Welch[87] notes that in Mahipalpur, south of Delhi, a *bund* and sluice gate created a natural hunting environment for Sultan Firuz. The latter was as fascinated by hunting as he was by hydraulic water engineering.

The Mughals inherited an extensive network of wells, dams, artificial lakes and tanks from the Delhi Sultanate and several hunting palaces. During Jahangir's reign, Ranthambhore in Ajmer *suba* was a favoured *shikargah* placed around a lake that supported sorghum and legume cultivation.[88] When Jahangir marched from Ajmer to Malwa in 1616-17, he encamped and hunted at several irrigation tanks on the route. The *Tuzuk* provides detailed information on the crops, fruits and vegetables for the market grown in the region.[89] The forests surrounding water bodies in Hissar had a favoured *shikargah* of Mughal Emperor Shah Jahan for hunting antelopes and nilgais.[90]

Indeed, the court historian of Shah Jahan, Abdul Hamid Lahori, notes in *Padshahnama* that, in 1638, Emperor Shah Jahan shotted a record fifty-two blackbuck and deer near the bank of the *bund* on Karnal stream at the Paḷam area (Fig. 3.11).[91] This shows the location of Palam *shikargah-i-mirror*. The painting Shah Jahan hunting in the Windsor *Padshahnama* was initially inserted to illustrate an earlier 1635 hunt in Palam (Fig. 3.12).

Rivulets, streams and irrigated canals were blocked for the imperial family to facilitate an imperial hunt. In *Nigarnama-i-Munshi,* cited by Irfan Habib, mentions a royal *farman* issued to the districts' officials concerned to block all smaller rivers from Delhi to Khizrabad to prepare for royalties family member's hunting expedition and local officials were asked to provide labour for hunt.[92]

GARDEN-BASED HUNTING GROUND OR *SHIKARGAH*

The Mughal hunting ground or *shikargah* is always proximate to the concept of the 'garden'. Traditional scholarship has considerably focused on the spatial and symbolic aspects of the so-called Mughal *char bagh* garden, broadly perceived as a protected, paradise space featuring a cross-axial layout and water channels and its use in funerary, pleasure and retreat contexts. However, the fact is that the Mughal Garden involved modifications to the environment and interactions with the extensive landscape and surroundings, which likely included sites where hunting took place.[93] For instance, the palace of Lal Mahal in Bari was one of the better-preserved hunting palaces near Dholapur in Rajasthan, which Shah Jahan developed in 1624-36. This hunting palace was famous for the lion hunt earlier. It had also been used as a *shikargah* by Babur, Akbar and Jahangir.[94] The Bari *Shikargah* was

FIGURE 3.11. 'SHAH JAHAN HUNTING ANTELOPE', UNKNOWN ARTISTS, INDIA, MUGHAL, THE 1640S, FROM THE *PADSHAHNAMA*, FO. 165R (*COURTESY:* ROYAL COLLECTION TRUST/© HM QUEEN ELIZABETH, LONDON).

FIGURE 3.12. THE PAINTING IS ONE FROM THE PAIR OF LACQUERED ALBUM COVER OF MUGHAL ALBUM BINDINGS c. 1740. IT PORTRAYS CHAND BIBI, THE WARRIOR QUEEN WEARING A PLUMED TURBAN SHOOTING BLACKBUCK WITH A MATCHLOCK. THE BARREL OF HER MATCHLOCK RESTS IN THE FORK OF A SMALL TREE AND HER COMPANION RESTS ANOTHER MATCHLOCK ON HER KNEE WHILE HOLDING A FLAMING WICK. (*COURTESY:* ROYAL COLLECTION TRUST, CAT. NO. 37)

the scene of a dramatic encounter when the young Shah Jahan rescued the Hindu courtier Anup Rai from the clutches of a lion in daring personal combat while hunting with his father Jahangir in 1610.[95]

Dahra Bagh, later renamed Nur Manzil Bagh in Agra, was another fascinating hunting garden and favoured halting palace. Jahangir and Shah Jahan encamped and hunted here frequently.[96] Jahangir mentioned that in 1619, Dahra had an area of 330 *jaribs* in *gaz-i-ilahi* (about 198 acres) and that the garden had magnificent buildings, pavilions, terraces and pools fed by an irrigation canal which brought in water from twelve large wells, whose water was drawn continuously by thirty-two pairs of oxen. Other than Dahra Bagh, Ana Sagar, Pushkar and Nalchha were many *bunds* around which cultivation and architectural infrastructures developed and were fertile hunting grounds.[97]

LEGITIMIZING HUNTING

The real purpose of hunting wild animals seems to have been to consolidate their authority over vast stretches of territories or intimidate restive provinces, lead military campaigns, inspect agricultural lands and assess the conditions of their subjects without intermediaries.[98] Abul Fazl claimed the hunt was a means of gathering intelligence about the state of the realm.[99] Furthermore, emulating their Timurid ancestors, the emperors led nomadic lifestyles as they travelled between the capital cities of Agra, Delhi and Lahore, the Kashmir valley in the summer months and beyond to distant provinces, encamping in gardens and *shikargahs* while hunting en route. Abul Fazl describes they appealed to Akbar for justice, advice and enlightenment:

> But when His Majesty leaves Court, to settle the affairs of a province, to conquer a kingdom, or to enjoy the pleasures of the chase, there is not a hamlet, a town or a city that does not send forth crowds of men and women with vow offerings in their hand, and prayers on their lips, touching the ground with their foreheads, praising the efficacy of their vows, or proclaiming the accounts of the spiritual assistance received.[100]

Jahangir encamped in the neighbourhood of Ajmer that there was a man-eating tiger about who had already accounted for several lives of humans. The prince, Shah Jahan, was detailed to 'save the people from its wickedness' and before nightfall, that tiger was shot down and brought to the emperor.

Sir Thomas Roe, who visited Jahangir's court as ambassador from James I of England, mentions how a lion and a wolf broke into his quarters one night while encamped at Mandu and fell upon some sheep in the courtyard. He says, 'exclusivity of hunting lions as he had to get permission from Jahangir in 1617 before he could kill'.[101]

Like his father, Jahangir also kept a record of his animal hunts. The registers showed that from the twelfth year (1580) of his age to his fiftieth lunar or forty-eight solar years, 28,532 animals had been taken in his presence, including 17,167, which the emperor himself had killed. These are tabulated thus:

Tigers (and lions)	86
Bears, leopards, foxes, otters (ubdilao) and hyaenas	9
Blue bulls	889
Blackbuck, chinkara, cheetah, mountain goats, etc.	1,670
Rams (quj) and red deer	215
Wild buffaloes	69
Wild Pigs	90
Mountain sheep	22
Wild asses	6
Total	3,073[103]

Of the 13,954 birds that constituted the whole bag during the period:

Pigeons	10,348
Lagar-jhagar (a species of hawk)	3
Eagles	2
Qaliwaj (kites)	23
Owls (chugd)	29
Qautan (goldfinch)	12
Sparrows	41
Doves	41

Ducks, geese, cranes and wildfowl	150
Crows	3,276
Total	13,935[102]

Besides, Jahangir was exceedingly fond of good hunting dogs and collected them from distant parts. Sir Thomas Roe records that once the emperor mentioned to him, 'I only desire you to help me to a horse of the greatest size, and a male and female of mastiffs and the tall Irish greyhounds and such other dogges as hunt in your lands.'

HUMAN-ANIMAL CONFLICTS DURING COLONIAL PERIOD

Various factors caused human-animal conflicts as agricultural land increased at the cost of forest land under the British administration. Consequently, wild animal species' habitats became more constrained and human confrontation became unavoidable; this might be one explanation. Another cause this rift could be an attack on cattle and people. Fields needed to be protected from predatory herbivores, and when they were killed, their meat could supplement the human diet. Larger carnivores were also hunted and killed because they attacked cattle and at times, people. For years, rural populations on the edges of forests have hunted animals with spears, bows and arrows. They possessed muskets, at least from the seventeenth century.[103] However, the absolute onslaught and the final extermination of our wildlife began only with introducing modern firm arms by the British. The British soldiers, planters and administration wiped out the royal game of the Indian lion over northern India during the second half of the nineteenth century. The Nawab of Junagarh had to pretend that there were only a few lions left in his Gir forest to protect them from every Governor, Viceroy and General who wanted his share of the booty.[104] The advent of the jeep during the Second World War threw open the remote corner of the forest to even the laziest hunter, and the last thirty years have witnessed the final plunge of our wildlife towards ultimate extinction.[105] In the 1860s, a British planter is claimed to have killed around 400 elephants in the Nilgiris. Wild asses—who had been chased and were numerous and quick-footed enough to

EXPLAINER

The complexities of introducing African cheetahs to India

Why are environmentalists upset with the plan to bring vulnerable big cats from the African savanna to Kuno national park

THE GIST

■ Historically, Asiatic cheetahs had a very wide distribution in India. There are authentic reports of their occurrence from as far north as Punjab to the Tirunelveli district in Tamil Nadu. The cheetah's habitat was also diverse, favouring the more open habitats: scrub forests, dry grasslands, savannas and other arid and semi-arid open habitats.

■ The consistent and widespread capture of cheetahs from the wild over centuries, its reduced levels of genetic heterogeneity due to a historical genetic bottleneck resulting in reduced fecundity and high infant mortality in the wild, its inability to breed in captivity, 'sport' hunting and bounty killings are the major reasons for the extinction of the Asiatic cheetah in India.

■ The main goals of the cheetah Action plan is to make cheetahs perform its functional role as a top predator and to use the cheetah to restore open forest and savanna systems. Both of which are already being done by extant species like the Asiatic lion and the leopard.

RAVI CHELLAM

The story so far: The cheetah, which became extinct in India after independence, is all set to return with the Union Government launching an action plan. According to the plan, about 50 of these big cats will be introduced in the next five years, from the Africa savannas, home to cheetahs, an endangered species.

What was the distribution of cheetahs in India? What were the habitats?
Historically, Asiatic cheetahs had a very wide distribution in India. There are authentic reports of their occurrence from as far north as Punjab to Tirunelveli district in southern Tamil Nadu, from Gujarat and Rajasthan in the west to Bengal in the east. Most of the records are from a belt extending from Gujarat passing through Maharashtra, Madhya Pradesh, Uttar Pradesh, Chhattisgarh, Jharkhand and Odisha. There is also a cluster of reports from southern Maharashtra extending to parts of Karnataka, Telangana, Kerala and Tamil Nadu. The distribution range of the cheetah was wide and spread all over the subcontinent. They occurred in substantial numbers.

The cheetah's habitat was also diverse, favouring the more open habitats: scrub forests, dry grasslands, savannas and other arid and semi-arid open habitats. Some of the last reports of cheetahs in India prior to their local extinction are from edge habitats of sal forests in east-central India, not necessarily their preferred habitat.

In Iran, the last surviving population of wild Asiatic cheetahs are found in hilly terrain, foothills and rocky valleys within a desert ecosystem, spread across seven provinces of Yazd, Semnan, Esfahan, North Khorasan, South Khorasan, Khorasan Razavi and Kerman. The current estimate of the population of wild Asiatic cheetahs is about 40 with 12 identified adult animals. They occur in very low density spread over vast areas extending to thousands of square kilometres.

What caused the extinction of cheetahs in India? When did they disappear?
The cheetah in India has been recorded in history from before the Common Era. It was taken from the wild for coursing blackbuck for centuries, which is a major contributor to the depletion of its numbers through the ages. Records of cheetahs being captured go back to 1550s. From the 16th century onwards, detailed accounts of its interaction with human beings are available as it was recorded by the Mughals and other kingdoms in the Deccan. However, the final phase of its extinction coincided with British colonial rule. The British added to the woes of the species by declaring a bounty for killing it in 1871.

The consistent and widespread capture of cheetahs from the wild (both male and female) over centuries, its reduced levels of genetic heterogeneity due to a historical genetic bottleneck resulting in reduced fecundity and high infant mortality in the wild, its inability to breed in captivity, 'sport' hunting and finally the bounty killings are the major reasons for the extinction of the Asiatic cheetah in India.

Range of the Asiatic cheetah during the British period and after in the Indian subcontinent

Pakistan

India

1954

1940

1932

1967

1919

1912

1994

1967

Historical range of the cheetah

The decision to introduce African cheetahs sidelines conservation priorities, an order of the Supreme Court, socio-economic constraints and academic rigour

It is reported that the Mughal Emperor Akbar had kept 1,000 cheetahs in his menagerie and collected as many as 9,000 cats during his half century reign from 1556 to 1605. As late as 1799, Tipu Sultan of Mysore is reported to have had 16 cheetahs as part of his menagerie.

The cheetah numbers were fast depleting by the end of the 18th century even though their prey base and habitat survived till much later. It is recorded that the last cheetahs were shot in India in 1947, but there are credible reports of sightings of the cat till about 1967.

What are the conservation objectives of introducing African cheetahs in India? Is it a priority for India? Is it cost effective?
Based on the available evidence it is difficult to conclude that the decision to introduce the African cheetah in India is based on science. Science is being used as a legitimising tool for what seems to be a politically influenced conservation goal. This also in turn sidelines conservation priorities, an order of the Supreme Court, socio-economic constraints and academic rigour. The issue calls for an open and informed debate.

Eminent biologist and administrator T.N. Khoshoo, first secretary of the Department of Environment, spoke out strongly against the cheetah project in 1995. "The reintroduction project was discussed threadbare during Indira Gandhi's tenure and found to be an exercise in futility," he said, pointing out that it was more important to conserve species that were still extant such as the lion and tiger, rather than trying to re-establish an extinct species that had little chance of surviving in a greatly transformed country.

Mr. Khoshoo's views are in sync with the 2013 order of the Supreme Court which quashed plans to introduce African cheetahs in India and more specifically at Kuno national park in Madhya Pradesh.

The officially stated goal is: Establish viable cheetah metapopulation in India that allows the cheetah to perform its functional role as a top predator and to provide space for the expansion of the cheetah within its historical range thereby contributing to its global conservation efforts.

African cheetahs are not required to perform the role of the top predator in these habitats when the site (Kuno) that they have identified already has a resident population of leopards, transient tigers and is also the site for the translocation of Asiatic lions as ordered by the Supreme Court of India in 2013. In other open dry habitats in India there are species performing this role, e.g., wolf and caracal, both of which are highly endangered and need urgent conservation attention. Even the Government's official estimate is expecting, at best only a few dozen cheetahs at a couple of sites (that too only after 15 years) which will require continuous and intensive management. Such a small number of cats at very few sites cannot meet the stated goal of performing its ecological function at any significant scale to have real on ground impact. Clearly, there are far more cost-effective, efficient, speedier and more inclusive ways to conserve grasslands and other open ecosystems of India.

Apart from establishing a cheetah population in India, the stated objectives include: To use the cheetah as a charismatic flagship and umbrella species to garner resources for restoring open forest and savanna systems that will benefit biodiversity and ecosystem services from these ecosystems.

Asiatic lions and a variety of species already found in these ecosystems can very well perform this role and more. If the government is serious about restoration and protection of these habitats, it first needs to remove grasslands from the category of wastelands and prevent further degradation, fragmentation and destruction of these habitats. Investing directly in science-based restoration and inclusive protection of these ecosystems will yield results much more quickly and sustainably than the introduction of African cheetahs.

Another goal is to enhance India's capacity to sequester carbon through ecosystem restoration activities in cheetah conservation areas and thereby contribute towards the global climate change mitigation goals. Experts contend that this objective does not require the introduction of African cheetahs, at a cost of ₹40 crore, with the attendant risks of diseases which haven't really been dealt with.

What is the current status of this project? What are the chances of it succeeding?
According to the Government, Kuno is ready to receive the cheetahs. About a month ago a team of government officials visited Namibia to inspect the cheetahs that would be sent to India, review the arrangements and to reach an agreement for the transfer of the cats. It is being reported that Namibia wants India's support for lifting the CITES ban on commercial trade of wildlife products, including ivory. The draft memorandum of understanding shared by Namibia reportedly contains a condition requiring India to support Namibia for "sustainable utilisation of wildlife". Negotiations are currently underway to finalise the MoU and it is expected to be signed by the end of March.

The cheetahs are to be provided by the Cheetah Conservation Fund, an NGO, and not the Namibian government. Three to five cheetahs are expected to be part of the first group of cats and these are expected to arrive as early as May 2022 and released in the wild by August 15.

Given all the challenges, especially the lack of extensive areas extending in hundreds if not thousands of square kilometres with sufficient density of suitable prey, it is very unlikely that African cheetahs would ever establish themselves in India as truly wild and self-perpetuating populations. A likely unfortunate consequence of this initiative will be the diversion of scarce conservation resources, distraction from the real conservation priorities and a further delay in the translocation of lions to Kuno.

Ravi Chellam is CEO, Metastring Foundation, and member, Biodiversity Collaborative

FIGURE 3.13. RANGE OF THE ASIATIC *CHEETAH* DURING THE BRITISH PERIOD AND AFTER IN THE INDIAN SUBCONTINENT (*COURTESY: THE HINDU,* MONDAY, MARCH 21, 2022, DELHI EDITION).

withstand the old methods—stood little chance against the new weaponry. Around 1900, seventy to eighty wild asses were machine-gunned at Bahawalpur to provide meat for the local army.[106] In 1933-40, the king of Nepal and his guests killed approximately 53 rhinoceros and 433 tigers. This may be considered a small haul over seven years compared to others. In Nepal, in 1911-12, his Britannic Majesty George V (assisted by his entourages) shot and killed 39 tigers in eleven days.[107]

Indeed, the story of the tigers illustrated best what wildlife was now faced with. A serious chargesheet undoubtedly is framed against the beast for being a danger to human life, even if only a small proportion of tigers and tigresses turned into 'man-eaters'. In 1877, out of 3,400 persons reportedly killed by wild animals in British India, 819 were killed by tigers. In 1903, the latter toll was put at 866. But in 1922, out of 3,263 deaths from wild beasts, 1,603 were from attacks by tigers; in 1927, the respective figures were 2,285 and 1,033. Presumably, the statistics from the 1920s cover the whole of India, hence the increase over earlier figures for tigers' human victims. The numbers of cattle killed all over the country by tigers are not recorded, but they must have been many times more, and this was why anyone who killed tigers was popular with villagers. As strychnine became available, the villagers used it to kill tigers. Until the 1930s, within the government-controlled forests and duly under license, hundreds of tigers were killed annually (1,074 tigers were so killed in Uttar Pradesh alone, in 1929-39); the numbers of those killed illegally in these controlled areas or killed outside of them, are not known; nor the number of those tigers which, wounded, died untraced by hunters. Individual well-placed hunters, white and brown, kept proud records of tigers shot, supported by the animals' skin for proof, sometimes running into hundreds. By an estimate accepted by Salim Ali, the probable number of tigers in India declined from 40,000 to 4,000 over the fifty years 1900-50. In the Indus basin, where the tigers appeared on the Indus seals over four thousand years ago, the last known member of the species was shot in 1886.

The tiger population was, by 1947, confirmed to be scattered in small, forested territories.[108] But the lion, already small in numbers since it preferred drier areas with fewer game and more exposure to hunter's guns, became extinct over the region where it used to be hunted as late as the nineteenth century: the Punjab, Haryana, Rajasthan and part of central India. By 1880, the lion's only surviving habitat was the small Gir forest in Saurashtra (Gujarat), where their number in 1930 was stated to be about 200. (A community of lions still survives rather perilously in that sanctuary.)[109] Another big-cat family, the leopard, also suffered significant diminution, but the cheetah (hunting leopard) became extinct; the last three animals of the species in the wild were reportedly shot in 1948.[110]

As for other animals, the one-horned rhinoceros, which was still in the nineteenth century, survived in sub-Himalayan forests of the Gangetic basin, was practically eliminated there and stayed only in Nepal and north-east India. The wild asses were killed off in most of their habitats in the dry zone of north-western India and survived with declining numbers in the inhospitable saline waste of the Rann of Kutch and Baluchistan.

The wild ruminant mammals, notably the deer, undoubtedly suffered from the hunter's assault, made mainly for their meat and because stags with horns were especially prized.[111] If they remained widely distributed over the country, this was because of their ability to live off the cultivated crops and the protection the agricultural zone offered to their herds from major wild predators. This is especially marked also with the nilgai. But no protection was gained from the hunter's gun, and the large deer herds still seen in the late nineteenth century in the Punjab and the Upper Gangetic Plains were either seen no more, or only in much-dwindled herds, by 1947.[112]

The elephant[113] stands in a class apart because it is both a wild and domesticated animal. The tusker became a particular target of the ivory-seeking poacher's gun by continuing to retreat from the forest itself. One effect of the destruction of tuskers was that the male-female ratio was affected, probably contributing to a decline in reproduction.[114] By 1947, the captive population of elephants did not likely exceed wild stock since elephants do not breed well in captivity. Therefore, elephant domestication has not been of much help in balancing elephant's depopulation in the wild.[115]

HABITAT DESTRUCTION

The most severe impact of man on wild animals arises from his destruction of the habitat—this must have begun ever since man took to cultivation some ten thousand years ago. The river valleys were the first to be put plough. The episode of the burning of the Khandava forest by Arjun in *Mahabharat* times describes forest clearing in the Gangetic plain for cultivation.[116] Man's demand for land then spread to drier and more undulating tracts until he finally reached the most challenging terrain for constructing reservoirs and mining.

ORNITHOLOGY THROUGH MUGHAL ART AND LITERATURE

India comes in the top ten of the world's biodiversity-rich nations. Its immense biological diversity represents about 7 per cent of the world's flora and 6.5 per cent of its fauna. There are over 600 species of amphibians and reptiles, nearly 1,300 species of birds and 350 species of mammals in India.[117]

Among all the groups of animals globally, birds are most enjoyed owing to their rich colouration, song, easy recognition and liveliness. Birds are represented everywhere from forests, grasslands and wetlands to crop fields and urban gardens. Fortunately, India is very rich in bird life. Of nearly 10,000 different birds in the world, 1,300 species, or about 13 per cent of the world's birds, are found on the Indian subcontinent.[118]

Depicting a bird's life in legends, myths and folklore must often have been based on real-life observation and experiences. Birds' observation was given a significant boost in the period between the thirteenth to seventeenth centuries, many of whose emperors were keen naturalists. They often recorded their experiences and observations in minute detail, with ornithological gems embedded in works such as the *Baburnama*, the *Ain-i-Akbari* of Abul Fazl and the *Tuzuk-i-Jahangiri* or *Memoirs of Jahangir*. Emperor Babur was known to closely observe animals even while at war. Babur recognized that four or five quail species were new.[119] Jahangir, who ruled from 1605 to 1627, had unique wildlife added by Mansur. Mansur painted a Siberian crane, *Grus leucogeranus,* about one hundred and sixty years before it was described for Western Science by the Russian zoologist Pallas![120] In a series of paintings known as the Company School, these realistic portrayals were carried on after the Mughal Empire by the British and Indians working under the colonial rulers.

The Mughal emperors' observations of birds' ecology and biodiversity are too many to deal with comprehensively here, but some examples are illustrative. Jahangir, in his memoirs, says of the Pied crested cuckoo *Clamator jacobinus:*

> In Hindustan, there is a bird called Papiha of a sweet voice, which in the rainy season utters soul-piercing lament. As the Koyel lays its eggs in the nest of a crow and the latter brings up its young, so I have seen in Kashmir that the Papiha lays its eggs in the nest of the Ghaughai and the Ghaughai brings up its young.[121]

Main Habitats

The bird habitats of northern India can be roughly divided into forest, scrubs, wetlands, grassland, desert and agricultural land. Some habitats overlap, for example, mangrove forests can also be considered wetlands, as can seasonally flood grasslands. Many bird species require mixed habitat types.

Forests

There is a great variety of forest types in the region. Tropical forests range from coastal mangroves to wet, dense, evergreen, dry deciduous and open desert thorn forests. Temperate forests in the Himalayas include mixed broadleaves, moist oak and rhododendron and dry coniferous forests of pines and firs. Higher up are subalpine forests of birch, rhododendron and jumper.[122]

The region's forests are vitally important for many birds, including globally threatened and restricted-range species. The tropical deciduous forest once covered much of the plains and lower hills of the sub-continent, including moist and dry *sal* and teak forests and riverine and dry thorn forests. Several widespread species endemic to the subcontinent are chiefly confined to these forests, including the Palm-headed Parakeet, which prefers moist deciduous forests and the White-bellied Drongo, which favours open dry deciduous forests.

Scrub

Scrubs have developed where trees cannot grow in the region because soils are poor, thin, or too wet, such as at the edges of wetlands or in seasonally inundated floodplains. Scrubs also grow naturally in extreme climate conditions, such as in semi-desert or at high altitudes in the Himalayas.[123] In addition, there are now large areas of scrubland in the region where forests have been over-exploited for fodder and fuel collection or grazing.

Wetlands

Wetlands in the region are abundant and support a rich array of waterfowl. As well as providing habitats for breeding resident species, the subcontinent's wetlands include primary staging and wintering grounds for waterfowl breeding in central and northern Asia. The region possesses a wide range of wetlands, including mountain glacial lakes, freshwater and brackish marshes, large water storage reservoirs, village tanks, saline flats, coastal mangroves and mudflats.[124] The vast saline flats of the Rann of Kutch in north-west India are essential for migratory waterfowl and support breeding colonies of the Lesser Flamingo, herons and egrets. Other wetlands in the region valuable for birds include the marshes, *jheels* and *terai* swamps of the Gangetic plain. Small water-storage reservoirs or tanks are a distinctive feature in India. These tanks' aggregation provides important feeding and nesting areas for a wide range of waterbirds in some places.[125]

Grasslands

The most critical grasslands for birds in the subcontinent include the seasonally-flooded grasslands along the Himalayan foothills and in the floodplains of the Ganges River, the arid grasslands of the Thar desert, and grassland managed for animal fodder in Gujarat and

Rajasthan.[126] These lowland grasslands support distinctive bird communities with several specialist endemic species.

Desert

The Thar desert is the largest in Asia, covering an area of 2,00,000 km^2 in northwest India and Pakistan. Nearly 80 per cent of the Thar lies in Rajasthan, and it also extends into parts of Panjab, Haryana and Gujarat.[127] The far northern mountain regions, which the monsoon winds do not penetrate, experience a cold desert climate.[128] Hot deserts in the region are extensions of the Saharan and Arabian deserts and are also connected with semi-arid parts of peninsular India.

Agricultural Habitats

The region is remarkable for the abundance of birds in agricultural habitats in many areas because of non-intensive agricultural systems and low levels of hunting and persecution, which can appear abundant on road and rail journeys.[129] However, this changes as farming becomes more intensive and higher levels of pesticides are applied.[130]

Carrier Pigeons

Much has been heard of the Baghdad pigeons that were called Carrie during the Abbasid caliphs.[131] Carrier pigeons are a third larger than wild pigeons. Jahangir says: 'I ordered the pigeon raisers to teach them and they trained several pairs so that when we let them fly from Mandu at the beginning of the day if there was a lot of rain, they reached Burhanpur in a maximum of two and a half watches, or most arrived in a look and others came in four Charis's'.[132]

Starlings

It was solid black, and its body was larger and round than a lark.[133] Another kind of starling was more slender and had red around its eyes.[134]

The Grey Til (*Porus major Linnaeus*)

It is found throughout the Indian Empire, in the plains and hills of about 6,000 feet. However, the grey til avoids heavy evergreen forests.[135]

Bustards

'There were thought to be two kinds of bustard, one black and spotted and the other dum-coloured. Recently, it was learned that they are not two types: the spotted black one is male and found in the spotted eggs in the dun-coloured one.'[136] The experiment was done repeatedly by Jahangir.

Partridge

The partridge is not peculiar to Hindustan but is found in warm climates. However, certain kinds are not found anywhere except in Hindustan.[137] The black partridge's body was the size of a snow cock. The male's back was the colour of a female pheasant. Its throat and breast were black, and it had bright white sport. Red lines come down either side of its eyes. Another kind of partridge was the gray partridge, which had a body the size of a black partridge, but its sound was much shriller. The male and female had only a slight difference in colouration.[138]

Water Fowl

Hunting down water fowl is indeed a lot of fun. The following is a relatively unusual method of capturing them. They create a fake duck with wings, a beak and a tail made of waterfowl skin. Two holes are drilled into the skin for viewing. The body has a hollow interior. The hunter dipped his head into it and stood up to his neck in the water. He cautiously approaches the birds and pulls them one by one into the water. However, they may be clever and fly away at any moment. The birds will hold a duck down and perch on it while swimming and returning to the hunter's or hawk's boat.[139]

Another method was to let buffaloes into the water while the hunter hid between them and thus caught the birds.[140]

Falcon

Jahangir was fascinated by the Falcon, and he was indeed familiar with different kinds of hawks and falcons, as seen from the accurate observations in his memoirs. Among the most used falcons in falconry was the shaheen (Falco Peregrinus peregrinator), 'king among raptors', a resident bird in India, followed by *Bahari* (Falcon peregrinus calidus), a winter visitor.[141]

Siberian Crane

Crane, *Kulang* or *Sarus* could not be hunted by ordinary people. Somewhat, their hunt was exclusively reserved for the emperor. Mannuci notes, 'This animal, like the cat, approached near the *palk* of the *Kulangs*, and finding itself within the straightforward approach of the prey, sprang at it. When others flew, the hunters thought their prey was safe.[142] Hawks or Molchis also caught them.[143] While Emperor Jahangir was praising the falcon's heart and courage, he noted Crane could seize such strong-bodied animals, and with the strength of kits, talons would subdue them.[144]

Besides, their numbers are steadily declining because of the increasing degradation of forest cover and woodlands, especially in the Himalayas and other hilly areas. Unfortunately, habitat destruction, illegal shooting, and trapping put many of our birds at risk of extinction. Pink-headed Ducks and Himalayan Quail are probably already extinct. Some magnificent birds are heading that way, such as the Indian Bustard, White-bellied Heron, White-winged Duck, Siberian Crane, Bengal Florican and Lesser Florican.

NOTES

1. Zahiruddin Muhammad Babur, *Baburnama,* tr. Annette Susannah Beveridge, 1921, rpt., New Delhi: Orient Books Reprint Corporation, 1970. See also the Turkish transcription, Persian ed. and trans. Wheeler M. Thackston Jr. published in three parts by the Department of Near Eastern Languages and

Civilization, Harvard: Harvard University, 1993: and the *Baburnama: Memoirs of Babur, Prince and Emperor,* trans. and ed. Wheeler M. Thackston Jr. (New York and Oxford University Press in association with the Freer Gallery of Arts and Arthur M. Sackler Gallery, Smithsonian Institution, 1996).

2. 'Although Emperor Babur has described in his memoirs the appearance and shapes of several animals, he had never ordered the painters to make pictures of them. As these animals (a turkey and monkey brought by Muqarrab Khan from Goa in 1612) appeared to me to be very strange, I have described them both and ordered that painters should draw them in the *Jahangirnama*', Jahangir, trans. 1: 215. For a discussion of the naturalistic interests of the Mughals, see also Ebba Koch, *Shah Jahan and Orpheus: The Pieter Dure Decoration and the Programme of the Throne in the Hall of the Public Audiences at the Red Fort of Delhi* (Graz: Akademische Druck-u. Verlaganstalt, 1988), esp. pp. 8-9, 22, with further literature.
3. Toby Falk and Mildred Archer, *Indian Miniatures in the India Office Library,* London: Oxford University Press, 1981, cat. no. 68, pp. 72-81.
4. William Dalrymple, *The Last Mughal: The Fall of a Dynasty, Delhi, 1857,* New Delhi: Penguin, 2006, p. 14.
5. Mahesh Rangarajan and K. Sivaramakrishnan, *Shifting Grounds: People, Animal, and Mobility in India's Environmental History,* New Delhi: Oxford University Press, 2014, p. 89.
6. Sumit Guha, *Health and Population in South Asia: From the Earliest Times to the Present,* New Delhi: Permanent Black, 2001, p. 34: also see Mahesh Rangarajan, *India's Wildlife History: An Introduction,* New Delhi: Permanent Black, 2001, p. 16.
7. Ibid., p. 60.
8. K.K. Trivedi, 'Estimating Forests, Wastes and Fields, *c.* 1600', in *Studies in History,* no. 14, New Delhi: Sage, 1998, pp. 301-11: Shireen Moosvi, in her paper 'Man and Nature in Mughal Era' Symposium Paper 5, *Indian History Congress,* 1993, gives somewhat different picture of agriculture in and around Agra, lands between Yamuna and Ganga and Gujarat. However, Bernier's description of the path of the Mughal cavalcade to which we shall come presently is relevant for our purpose. Trivedi in *Estimating Forests...* and Guha in *Health and Population in South Asia,* give us a later analysis of the landscape than the period covered by Moosvi's paper. She has, however, developed the argument on lines her 1993 paper, in a later work: *People Taxation and Trade in the Mughal India,* New Delhi: Oxford University Press, 2008. Rangarajan, *India's Wildlife History,* p. 16.
9. François Bernier, *Travels in the Mughal Empire by Francois Bernier 1656-1668 A.D.,* trans. Archibald Constable, 2nd edn., revised by Vincent A. Smith, New Delhi: Oriental Reprint, 1983/1934, p. 374.

10. Sir William Foster, *The Embassy of Sir Thomas Roe to India, 1615-1619 as Narrated in His Journals and Correspondence,* New Delhi: Munshiram Manoharlal, 1990, p. 297.
11. Jahangir, *Tuzuk-i-Jahangir or The Memoires of the Jahangir,* tr. Alexander Rogers, ed. Henry Beveridge, New Delhi: Munshiram Manoharlal, 1980, p. 233.
12. *Imperial Gazetteer of Indian:* Provincial Series; *Punjab*, vol. II, *The Lahore, Rawalpindi and Multan Divisions; and Native States,* Calcutta: Superintendent of Government Printing, 1908, p. 2.
13. Ibid., p. 3.
14. Ibid., p. 3.
15. M. Gadgil and Ramchandra Guha, *The Fissured Land: An Ecological History of India,* New Delhi: Oxford University Press, 1999, p. 116.
16. W.W. Hunter. *A Statistical Account of Assam,* vol. I, London: Trübner & Co., 1879, p. 108.
17. *100 Years of Indian Forestry 1861-1961*, vol. I, issued on the Celebration of the Indian Forest Century, Forest Research Institute, 18 November 1961.
18. B. Ribbentrop, *Forestry in British India,* Calcutta: Office of the Superintendent of Government Printing, 1900, p. 78.
19. For more detail see Thomas Rosin's 'The Tradition of Ground Irrigation in Northwestern India', he argued that the central Aravalli Hills of Rajasthan, is important for several reasons: the practice of groundwater irrigation which was once pervasive and dominant across a vast stretch of India.
20. E.P. Gee. *The Wild Life of India,* London: Collins, 1964, p. 82.
21. Madhav Gadgil. 'Wildlife Resources of India', *National Academic of Science, India*, 1980, pp. 2-10.
22. History of Asiatic lion—Flipbook by | FlipHTML5. https://fliphtml5.com/acng/ccph.
23. Abul Fazl, *Ain-i-Akbari,* vol. III, tr. H.S. Jarrett, Calcutta: Royal Asiatic Society, 1978, p. 143.
24. Foster, op. cit., p. 365.
25. François Bernier, *Travels in the Mughal Empire,* op. cit., Westminster: A. Constable, 1842. p. 374.
26. Wheeler M. Thackston, *The Jahangirnama, Memoirs of Jahangir, Emperor of India,* Freer Gallery of Arts/Arthur M. Sackler Gallery, New York/Washington: Oxford University Press, 1999, p. 216.
27. A double page painting titled 'Akbar slays a tigress which attacked royal cavalcade from the *Akbarnama,* preserved at the Victoria and Albert Museum, London; see Geeti Sen, *Paintings from the Akbarnama: A Visual Chronicle of Mughal India,* Varanasi: Lustre Press and New Delhi: Rupa & Co, 1984, pp. 48-49, 163.

28. Rai Krisnadasa, *Anwar-i-Suhaili: Iyar-i-Danish,* Varanasi: Bharat Kala Bhavan, Banaras Hindu University, Pl. B, C, E; Pl. III, Fig. 10; A.K. Das, *Paintings of the Razmnama: The Book of War,* Ahmedabad: Mapin Publishing, 2005, pp. 59, 69, 81, 115.
29. Jahangir. *Tuzuk-i-Jahangir* or *Memoirs of Jahangir,* by Alexander Rogers, ed. Henry Beveridge, vol, I, New Delhi: Munshiram Manoharlal, 1978, p. 157.
30. Abul Fazl. *Akbarnama,* tr. H. Beveriadge, Calcutta: P.L. Printers, 1912; rpt., Delhi, 2003, pp. 186-7, 508-9.
31. R. Skelton. *Pers.comm,* Windsor Castle manuscript, 1993, f. 165 v.
32. Irfan Habib, *An Atlas of the Mughal Empire,* New Delhi: Oxford University Press, 1982, Sheet No. 4B, 6B, 7B, 8B.
33. Bilal Habib, 'Ecology of Leopard: In Relation to Prey Abundance and Land Use Pattern in Kashmir Valley', *Wildlife Institute of India,* 2014, p. 8.
34. Abul Fazl, *Ain-i-Akbari,* vol. II, H.S. Jaretta, ed. J.N. Sarkar, Calcutta, 1949, p. 351.
35. Valmik Thapar, *Wild Fire: The Splendours of India's Animal Kingdom,* New Delhi: Aleph Book Company, 2014, p. 93.
36. Ibid., p. 93.
37. This information has been cited from the Chester Beatty Library, Dublin.
38. Simon Digby, 'War Horse and the Elephant in the Delhi Sultanate: A Study of Military Supplies', *Journal of Royal Asiatic Society,* Cambridge: Cambridge University Press, 1973, pp. 178-9.
39. A town of great historic interest on the right bank of the Jumna in the Jalaun district, UP.
40. A town on the left bank of the Jumna in Allahabad District.
41. A town in Partabgarh district, Delhi.
42. Abul Fazl. *Ain-i-Akbari,* tr. Blochman & Co. H.S. Jaretta, vol. I, New Delhi: Orient Book Reprint Corporation, 1992-4, pp. 123-40.
43. Ashok Kumar Das, 'The Elephant in Mughal Painting', in *Flora and Fauna in Mughal Art,* ed. Some Prakash Verma, Mumbai: Marg Publications, 1999, pp. 36-54.
44. R. Sukumar, *Elephant Days and Nights: Ten Years with the Indian Elephant,* New Delhi: Oxford University Press, 1994, p. 153; G.P. Sanderson, *Thirteen Years among the Wild Beasts of India,* London: W.H. Allen & Co., 1896
45. See, R. Sukumar, *Living Elephants,* Cambridge: Harvard University Press, 2006, p. 403.
46. Irfan Habib, *An Atlas of Mughal Empire,* New Delhi: Oxford University Press, 1982, Sheet 13 B, p. 52.
47. Zahiruddin Muhammad Babur. *Baburnama* or *Memoires of Babur,* tr. Beveridge, New Delhi: Publications Division, Government of India, 1979, p. 210.

48. Abul Fazl. *Ain-i-Akbari*, tr. S.H. Jarrett, ed. J.N. Sarkar, vol. III, Calcutta: Asiatic Society, 1940, p. 344.
49. *Baburnama,* op. cit., pp. 490-1.
50. *Tuzuk-i-Jahangiri*, op. cit., p. 215.
51. *Baburnama*, vol. II, op. cit., pp. 488-9.
52. *Ain-i-Akbari*, vol. I, op. cit., pp. 123-9.
53. *Tuzuk-i-Jahangiri*, op. cit., p. 216.
54. Ibid., Preface, p. V.
55. Ibid., p. 143.
56. Kautilya. *The Kautilya Arthashastra* II, trans. R.P. Kangle, pt. III, 1969, rpt. New Delhi: Motilal Banarsidass, 2014, pp. 59-60.
57. Francis Zimmermann, *The Jungle and the Aroma of Meats: An Ecological Theme in Hindu Medicine,* rpt. 2011, New Delhi: Oxford University Press, 1999, pp. 47-9.
58. Ibid., p. 51.
59. William Foster, *The English Factories in India, 1630-1633,* vol. XIII, Oxford: Clarendon Press, p. XXI.
60. Peter Mundy. *The Travels of Peter Mundy in Europe and Asia 1608-1677,* vol. II, *Travels in Asia 1628-1634,* London: Hakluyt Society, 2014, p. 56.
61. Abdul Hamid Lahori. *Lahori's Padshahnamah 1592-1638,* trans. & ed. H.A. Siddiqi, vol. II, New Delhi: S. Chand & Company, 2010, pp. 106-7.
62. Inayat Khan. *The Shahjahannama of Inayat Khan,* trans. & ed. A.R. Fuller, W.E. Begley and Z.A. Desai, New Delhi: Oxford University Press, 1990, p. 42.
63. *Padshahnama*, op. cit., pp. 80-1.
64. Irfan Habib, *The Agrarian System of Mughal India,* New Delhi: Oxford University Press, 2014, p. 16.
65. Andre Wink, *Al-Hind: The Making of the Indo-Islamic World,* vol. II, Brill Leiden, New York, Kolu, 1997, pp. 240-1.
66. Ibid., pp. 240-1.
67. *Ain-i-Akbari*, vol. II, op. cit., p. 316.
68. *Tuzuk*, op. cit., p. 350.
69. James Forsyth, 'Game Animals and Birds of the Plains', *The Oxford Anthology of Indian Wildlife,* vol. I, ed. Mahesh Rangarajan, New Delhi: Oxford University Press, pp. 36-53.
70. Ibid., pp. 36-53.
71. *The Agrarian System of Mughal India*, op. cit., p. 373.
72. Chentan Singh. 'Forests, Pastoralists and Agrarian Society in Mughal India', in *Nature, Culture, Imperialism: Essays on the Environmental History of South Asia,* ed. David Arnold and Ramchandra Guha, New Delhi: Macmillan, 1995, p. 21.

73. *Ain-i-Akbar* II, op. cit., p. 246.
74. *Jahangirnama*, op. cit., , pp. 258-9.
75. *Ain-i-Akbari*, vol. I, op. cit., p. 658.
76. *An Atlas of Mughal Empire*, op. cit., Map 9 B.
77. Donald Butter, *Outlines of the Topography and Statistics of the Southern District of Oudh and of the Cantonment of Sultanpur-Oudh*, ed. G.H. Huttmana, Calcutta: Bengal Mily, Orphan Press, 1839, p. 4-7.
78. Divyabhanusinh, *The End of a Trail: The Cheetah in India*, New Delhi: Oxford University Press, 1995, p. 2.
79. Syed Inayat Ali Zaidi, 'Akbar and the Rajput Principalities: Integration into Empire', in *Akbar and His India*, ed. Irfan Habib, rpt. 2011, New Delhi: Oxford University Press, 1997, pp. 15-24.
80. *Ain-i-Akbari*, vol. II, op. cit., pp. 292-3.
81. Khwaja Nizamuddin Ahmad, *The Tabaqat-i-Akbari*, vol. III, trans. Brajendranath De, rpt. 1996, Calcutta: Asiatic Society, 1936, pp. 328-9; Abul Fazl, *Akbarnama*, II, pp. 416-17.
82. H. Beveridge, 'Meaning of the word *nihilism*', *Journal of the Royal Asiatic Society of Great Britain & Ireland*. 1900, pp. 137-8.
83. *Jahangirnama*, op. cit., pp. 105-6.
84. Inayat Khan, *The Shahjahannama*, trans. & ed. A.R. Fuller, W.E. Begley and Z.A. Desai, New Delhi: Oxford University Press, 1990, p. 537.
85. Kautilya, op. cit., p. 64.
86. Muhammad Qasim Firishra, *Tarikh-i-Firishta, History of the Rise of Mahamedan Power in India*, trans. J. Briggs, vol. IV, rpt. 1881, New Delhi, 1829, p. 269.
87. Anthony Welch. 'Gardens that Babur did not like landscape, water, and architecture for the Sultans of Delhi', in *Mughal Gardens: Sources, Places, Representations and Prospects*, ed. J.L. Wescoat & J. Wolschke-Bulman, Dumbarton Oaks Res Library & Coll, Washington DC, 1996, p. 74.
88. *Ain-i-Akbari*, vol. II, op. cit., p. 273.
89. *Tuzuk-i-Jahangiri*, op. cit., pp. 341-62.
90. *Shahjahannama*, op. cit., pp. 407, 412.
91. *Padashanama*, vol. II, op. cit., p. 36.
92. Irfan Habib's *Agrarian System*, op. cit., pp. 289-90.
93. John Dixon Hunt, *Greater Perfection: The Practice of Garden Theory*, London: Thames & Hudson, 2000, p. 29.
94. *Baburnama*, op. cit., p. 585; *Ain-i-Akbari*, vol. I, op. cit., p. 270.
95. For more details see Abdul Hamid Lahorei. *Padshahnamah I*, pp. 158-9; *Tuzuk-i-Jahangir I* or *Memoirs of Jahangir*, trans. Rogers, ed. Henry Beveriadge, p. 165.

96. *Tuzuk-i-Jahangiri I*, op. cit., pp. 182, 232, 234; *Tuzuk* II, pp. 75-6.
97. Jahangir hunted eleven times near Pushkar tank during his stay in Ajmer, 1613-16; *Jahangirnama*, p. 202.
98. *Agrarian System of Mughal India*, op. cit., p. 45.
99. Mahesh Rangarajan, *Indian's Wildlife History: An Introduction*, New Delhi: Permanent Black, 2001, p, 13.
100. *Ain-i-Akbari I*, op. cit., p. 173.
101. Sir Thomas Roe's 'Voyage to India', *Pinkerton's Voyages*, vol. VIII, p. 14.
103. Ibid., p. 2-10.
104. Ibid., p. 82
105. A.M. Smith, *Sports and Adventure in the Indian Jungle*, London: Hurst and Blackett, 1904, p. 103.
106. Irfan Habib, *Man and Environment: The Ecological History of India*, A People's History of India, New Delhi: Tulika Books, 2010, p. 130.
107. Ibid., p. 131.
108. Inderjit Badhwar, 'The Tiger Widows', *India Today*, 29 February 1988.
109. E.P. Gee. *A Glossary of Nature Conservation and Wildlife Management Terminology for Use in India*, New Delhi: IBWL, 1961, p. 45.
110. J.R. Ellerman, *The Fauna of India*, Mammalia, vol. III, Rodentia (pt. II), New Delhi: Manohar, 1961, p. 145.
111. R.C. Wroughton, 'Bombay Natural History Society's Mammal Survey of India', Report 1-45, *Journal of Bombay Natural History Society*, vol. 21, no. 2 to vol. 33, no. 3; 1912-29.
112. Lee Merriam Talbot, 'A Look at Threatened Species', *Oryx*, vol. 5, nos. 4 & 5, London: Fauna Preservation Society, 1960, p. 23.
113. For more detail see S.H. Prater's *The Book Indian Animals*, Bombay Natural History Society, 1965, p. 222.
114. Ibid., p. 229.
115. Gee, op. cit., p. 67.
116. Gadgil, Centre for Theoretical Studies, Indian Institute of Science, Bangalore, National Academy of Science, India, Golden Jubilee Commemoration Volume, 1980, op. cit., p. 14.
117. M.Z. Islam and A.R. Rahmani, 'Threatened Birds of India', *Buceros 7* (1 & 2). Compiled from *Threatened Birds of Asia*, Birds Life International, Red Data Book, 2001, p. 25.
118. *The Red Dada Book on Indian Animals: Vertebrate*, pt. 1, Calcutta: Zoological Survey of India, Government of India, 1993, p. 25.
119. *Baburnama*, op. cit., p. 343
120. Ashish Kothari. *Birds in Our Lives*, Hyderabad: Universities Press, 2007, p. 65.
121. *Tuzuk-i-Jahangiri*, op. cit., p. 245.
122. Indian State of Forest Report 2019: Forest Survey of India, *Ministry of*

Environment, Forest and Climate Change, Government of India, vol. I, Dehradun, 2019, p. 1.

123. Mayank Kumar. *Monsoon Ecologies: Irrigation, Agricultural and Settlement Patterns in Rajasthan during the Pre-Colonial Period,* New Delhi: Manohar, 2013, pp 15-40.
124. Ramsar Sites of India-Factsheet, Wetlands Division, *Ministry of Environment, Forest and Climate Change*, Government of India, 2019.
125. Richard Grimmett, *Birds of Northern India,* New Delhi: Oxford University Press, 2003, p. 6.
126. Monsoon Ecology, op. cit., p. 145.
127. Tanuja Kothiyal, *Nomadic Narratives: A History of Mobility and Identity in the Great Indian Desert,* New Delhi: Cambridge University Press, 2016, pp. 1-5.
128. Salim Ali, *The Book of Indian Birds,* Bombay: The Bombay Natural History Society, 1941, p. XII.
129. Abdul Jamil Urfi, ed., *Birds of India: A Literary Anthology,* New Delhi: Oxford University Press, 2008, pp. XVI-XXVII.
130. *Birds of India*, op. cit., p. 14.
131. The Abbasid caliphs ruled, mostly from Baghdad, from AD 749 until the house was extinguished by the Mughals in 1258.
132. *Jahangirnama*, op. cit., p. 343
133. The Indian grackle, or hill myna (*Eulabes intermedia*).
134. Wheeler M. Thackston, *The Baburnama: Memoirs of Babur,* trans. Paperback edition, New York: Modern Library, 2002, p. 532.
135. *The Book of Indian Birds*, op. cit., p. 12.
136. Wheeler M. Thackston, *The Jahangirnama: Memoirs of Jahangir,* New York: Oxford University Press, 1999, p. 34.
137. Salim Ali, *Book of Indian Birds*, op. cit., p. 45.
138. *Baburnama*, op. cit., p. 455.
139. *Ain-i-Akbari,* vol. I, op. cit., p. 307.
140. Ibid., p. 307.
141. *Tuzuk-i-Jahangiri*, op. cit., p. 107.
142. Nicola Manucci. *Storia do Mogor 1656-72,* tr. William Irvin, vol. III, London, 1907-8, pp. 89, 90.
143. About this animal, Abul Fazl says that 'it is an animal more like a sparrow, of yellow plumage like the Shaheen.
144. *Tuzuk-i-Jahangiri,* vol. I, op. cit., p. 53, vol. II, p. 60.

CHAPTER 4

Forest Ecology of Mughal North India in Awadh

HISTORICAL BACKGROUND

ABUL FAZL'S *Accounts of Twelve Provinces* lists the region of Awadh as one of the Mughal *subas*.[1] The length of the *suba* Abul Fazl describes in *Ain*; 'is 135 *kos* from Gorakhpur *sarkar* to Kanauj. It stretches for 115 *kos* from the northern mountains to Sidhpur, on the outskirts of Allahabad *suba*. Bihar lies to the east, the hills are to the north, Manikpur is to the south, and Kanauj is to the west. Its main streams are the river *Saru* (Sarju), the *Ghaghar* (Gogra), the *Sai* and the *Godi* (Gumti).'[2]

Awadh, under the nawab rule, asserted its origins in Persia. The founder of the Awadh kingdom, Saadat Khan Burhan al-Mulk (1680-1739), belonged to an elite Saiyid family of Nishanpur, a place well known for its cultural and intellectual life in the Islamic world since the time of the Samanids (874-999) and Seljuqs (1037-1157).[3] Immigrants from Nishapur had enjoyed high esteem at the Mughal court. The family, well-trained in the imperial traditions of Safavid Iran, had migrated to India during the early years of the eighteenth century. Additionally, they benefited from the rich traditions of the Mughals, who were deeply knowledgeable about Persian culture.

S.Z. Jafri has argued that Awadh, during the eighteenth century, saw a transformation in its position for two different reasons. First, as the Mughal emperors more or less confined their courts to Delhi from the time of Farrukh Siyar (*c.* 1713) onwards, holding possession of adjacent provinces became very important for exerting influence at the Court.[4] Thus, the three successive governors of Awadh, Sa'adat Khan (1722-39), Safdarjung 1739-54), and Shuja-ud-Daula (1754-75), sought to use their control over Awadh and its resources as the springboard for pursuing their ambitions at Delhi. Second, as the Mughal Empire contracted, Awadh became subject to threats from the Afghans, Marathas, and the English. For both these reasons, Awadh re-entered and remained in the realm of political annals with a new prominence.[5]

After the battle of Buxar, Shuja-ud-Daula finally settled down in Awadh, after which the Awadh court asserted its distinct cultural and political identity. Intensive building activity was started in Faizabad. A contemporary historian remarked that 'Shuja-al-Daula was very keen to advance the prosperity and enhance the beauty of his capital. Had he lived for a few more years, there would have grown another Shahjahanabad (here).'[6] The nawab engaged the service of Antoine Louis Polier, the Company's chief engineer at Fort William, Calcutta, to look after some civil works and significantly improve the city's defense.

The style and culture of the court were redefined by the rule Asaf-al-Daula (1775-97). According to the contemporary traveller Thomas Twinning, the Awadh court was at its most magnificent under Asaf-al-Daula.[7] The centre of art and culture now shifted from Faizabad to Lucknow. Ghazi-al-Din Haider, who ruled from 1814 to 1827, declared Awadh an independent state on 9 October 1819. He broke away from Mughal court cultural tradition, and he was the first Indian ruler to adopt the European symbols of kingship. His crown coat of arms and coronation robes had a clear European origin.

The East India Company annexed Awadh to their possessions in less than thirty years. During Nasir-al-Din Haidar's region (1827-37), 'Awadh shrank from a major component in the political world of north India to an isolated subordinate within the Company's influence'.[8] The government exercised 'pure despotism' only in name; it was 'restrained' by 'the fear of offending the British government'.[9] It was now the Governor-General who claimed the responsibility of protecting the people of Awadh from the 'tyranny and oppression' of their rulers. After Nasir al-Din Haidar's death, Awadh was ruled by three rulers: Muhammad Ali Shah (1837-42), Amjad Ali Shah (1842-47) and Wajid Ali Shah (1847-56). Their power, authority, and resources dwindled until the last ruler was dethroned for incompetence. A British brigade marched to Awadh, encountered no armed resistance, and the king was exiled to Calcutta. The British annexed the state's territories to their possessions in India on 13 February, 1856, thus ending an era of great creativity.[10]

Besides the political turmoil in Awadh, the region possessed a rich natural geography, characterized by rivers, tributaries, varied soil types, and large forest belts at the edges of farmland. With ample natural resources at the disposal of the Mughal Empire.[11] Mughal rulers never seemed to have enacted any regular forest policy. The expansion of the cultivation remained an index of achievement for them. Despite the unchecked exploitation of forests, especially for timber cutting and cattle grazing, the extent of forests remained quite impressive in Mughal Awadh. In contrast, agriculture was predominantly the backbone of the Mughal economy.

With the growing intervention of the English East India Company in the regional politics of Awadh, the agro-forest balance or relationship suffered a significant change. Before 1857, since there was nawab rule in Awadh, the British openly criticized the state of agriculture, especially the revenue administration and depletion of old forest cover in the region. They considered these factors as affecting the natural landscape of Awadh.

THE GEOGRAPHY SETTING OF AWADH

Awadh was recognized as one of the twelve Mughal *subas* in 1580. It extended over the territory comprising of alluvial plains, lying between 79.6^0 and 84^0 longitude E. and 26^0 and 28.4^0 latitudes N.[12] The limits of the *suba* are described by Abul Fazl in his *Ain*. The provinces of Bihar bound it on the east and to the north lay the northern mountains; *sarkar* Manikpur of *suba* Allahabad was situated on the south of the area, while on the western side was *sarkar* of Kannauj of *suba* Agra. The distance from the limits of *sarkar* Gorakhpur to Kannauj was calculated to be 135 *kos*, while they said that the northern mountains and the southern boundary of the *suba* were only 115 *kos* apart. In the Mughal period, the geographical extent of Awadh remained more or less intact, but it was subjected to changes after the growth of nawabs'[13] rule in the region. The landmark changes in the geographical position of Awadh came in 1775, 1801 and 1857.[14]

NATURAL DIVISION

We have divided Awadh, which encompasses the central part of north India, into three separate natural divisions, each possessing its own distinct physical characteristics, which we will briefly describe below:

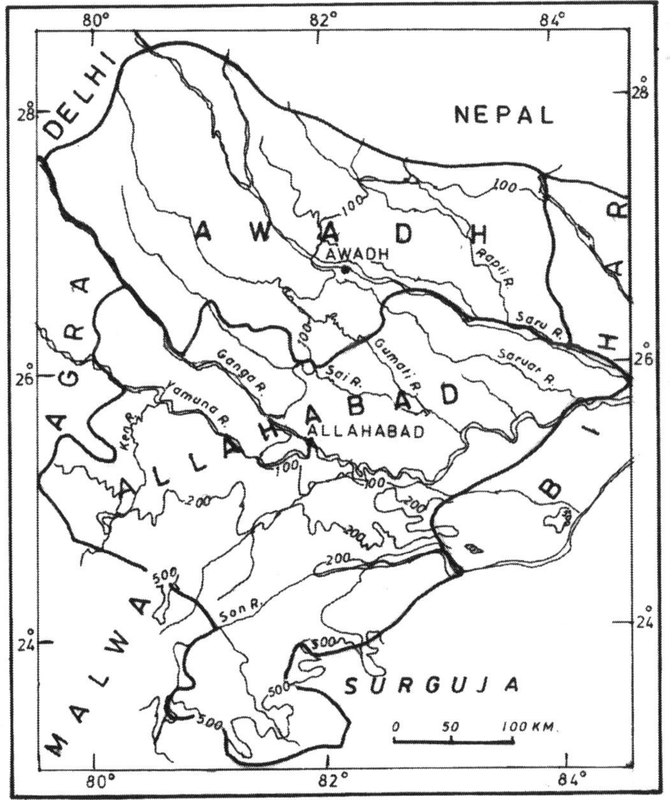

MAP 4.1: BOUNDARIES OF AWADH *SUBA* DURING THE MUGHAL PERIOD. *COURTESY*: IRFAN HABIB'S *AN ATLAS OF THE MUGHAL EMPIRE*, NEW DELHI: OXFORD UNIVERSITY PRESS, 1982, SHEET NO. 8B

(I) Three ranges, intersect the Himalayan Tract whose snow-capped summits supply the Jumna, Ganges, Ramganga, and Sarda rivers. In Nepal, the Rapti and Gandak rivers rise. The topmost elevations of the Himalayas are best characterized as snow deserts, since they are entirely devoid of vegetation. They sustain nothing other than arctic vegetation further down. From a height of 12,000 feet lower, tree growth starts, with the most valuable forest of oaks and conifers restricted to altitudes below 10,000 feet.[15] The best forest of *sal* (*Shorea robusta*) and other vital species may be found in the foothills, particularly the sub-montane tract. The *bhabar*, a waterless track that runs alongside the Gangetic alluvium, comprises debris deposits at the foot of the hills. Hill streams that vanish into the massive, porous mass of residues known as the *bhabar* resurface in the *terai*, making it wet and malarious.[16] Both *bhabar* and *terai* were home to essential forests and abundant wildlife. The climate in the Himalayan zone ranges from freezing temperatures to shifting damp heat in the *terai*. Rainfall is abundant.[17]

(II) The Gangetic Basin lies like a trough between the Himalayas in the north and the central India Plateau in the south. The sub-recent alluvium estimated at 6,000 to 15,000 feet deep gives this track its characteristic flat appearance, fertility, and maximum population density. The older *doab* lands between the Jumna and the Ganges, which endured early Aryan colonization, have been impoverished continuously under the plough and, are less productive than soils of more recent origin in the east of the Ramganaga.[18] In its lower latitudes, the western region is geologically older, has less rainfall, and is drier than the eastern districts. Studded with many historical cities along the bank of navigable rivers, the Gangetic Basin is the melting pot of many a civilization, the nodality of which gives this region the importance it enjoys. The climate is characterized by well-defined seasons—winter, summer and rainy season, with continental temperature extremes. The bulk of the rainfall is confined to the rainy season, which lasts from the 15th of June to 15th of October.[19]

(III) The Central India Plateau covers a rough, broken and picturesque countryside to the south of the Jumna. The rugged spurs of the

Vindhyas and Kaimurs terrace down from an elevation of about 3,000 feet in awkward steps to about 100 feet. The region is traversed by numerous streams, the chief among which from west to east are the Betwa, the Dhasan, the Ken, the Tons and the Son.[20] Except for rich alluvium deposits in the valleys, the soil derived from the hard, infertile rocks of Archean and Vindhyan origin is generally poor. The climate resembles that of the Gagentic Basin with the modification that the summer is more extended and hotter and the rain more pleasant.[21]

Rivers

Many rivers and their tributaries flowed through the province of Awadh. Abul Fazl lists four significant rivers across the province's plains. Sarju, Ghaghar, Sai and Godi (Gumti) were among them.[22] This list is short. According to Butter, the Ganges, Deoha (Ghaghar), Gomti, Sai, Tons and Lon rivers are significant waterways in Awadh's southern regions. He does a great job of describing the distinct characteristics of each of these rivers.[23] The Ganges and Deoha had a low bed with an average width of 4 miles, and the channels changed almost every year. Within four or five years, the rivers' courses had significantly changed. Compared to these, the smaller rivers had essentially set narrow channels and minimal variation in their courses. A few rivers had sufficient depth to prevent flooding during the wet season. The banks of these rivers were made up of high *kankar* ridges, making them navigable. However, they discovered that the summer shrinkage of the *kankar* ridges severely reduced the depth of the rivers. Butter believed it was the responsibility of the nawab-wazir administration to remove the debris from such collapsed cliffs to maintain the stream's accessibility.

The river Gomti, notwithstanding its small size, was the third most important river in India, after the Ganges and the Deoha. Its right bank comprised solid *kankar*, giving it the appearance of a mountain range, while the left bank was low and sandy, stretching for 3 miles and serving as an arid waste. The land was very fertile outside this zone. The yellowish mud in the water made it unfit for drinking. Fish were plentiful at all times of the year. The Sai could handle boats up to 300 maunds in certain areas during the wet season, but navigators avoided it because of its zigzag route, preferring the Ganges and Gomti instead.[24] Ravines broke the surface of the region. Near the rivers were found sandy dunes almost wholly devoid of irrigation and fit for nothing but the cultivation of poor crops of *bajra* and *moth* or merely thatching grass. Elsewhere lie vast stretches of barren *usar*, which sometimes extend for miles and present no sign of vegetable growth. These *usar* plains were found in the west and south of the region, and their influence often affects the cultivated fields in the neighbourhood.[25]

Soils

Another ecological factor that deserves to be mentioned is the soil. Soil relates human relationships to the environment. The Awadh province's soil was made up of different varieties. Occasionally, it contained siliceous and calcareous earth, as the form of *kankar,* which occurred in the limited horizontal layers at 6 to 8 feet. The *kankar* ridges were generally found along the right banks of rivers. In many places, *kankar* constituted the surface of the soil as well. The sites of the 'primaeval forests of Oudh' and the regions between the Ganges and Deoha had rich and dark soil. In the southern districts of Awadh, the soil of *pargana* Salon, Jayis, Rampur and Manikpur were judged as the best and very productive for different varieties of the grain.[26]

The soil of the Awadh region resembles that of the rest of Oudh, being a light alluvia loam. There are, as usual, many local variations in the soil, ranging from pure sand to heavy clay.[27] The best soil was a mixture of these two. It is known as loam or *dumat,* as used by the cultivators; it was most comprehensive, including soil that appears to be almost all sand, on which meagre crops can only be raised by a liberal application of manure and water and the fertility is evident in the excellence of the produce which it bears. As a whole, the district is not remarkable for its natural productiveness. Round the city and the smaller towns where the population was thickest and the supply of manure most abundant, it has been brought to high fertility, but there are large areas of inferior and precarious land in the neighbourhood of the rivers; in the south-western *parganas,* there was much heavy clay which was only suitable for rice. These clay tracts were ordinarily the accompaniment of defective drainage; they were studded with tanks and usually contained large areas of *usar* land, a sure sign of saturation.[28]

Classification of Soil

Two soil classification systems are employed in different parts of the *suba*. In *pargana* Lucknow, the conventional system is adopted, the soils being demarcated as *goind*, *manjhar* and *palo*.[29] The first is the richly manured land immediately adjoining the homestead; *manjhar*, or the middle land, was the ordinary well-cultivated land of the village that received a small amount of manure and was responsible for the bulk of the staple crops. *Palo* was the outlying land that was imperfectly cultivated and never manured from its position. In the rest of the district, the old distinction into natural soils was followed, with the addition of *goind* as a separate class. They were known as *dormant* or loam, *matiar* or heavy clay and *bhur* or sand. The proportion of the expected from the proximity of the city. Here it amounted to 20.78 per cent, while in the rest of the district, it was 16-51 per cent, giving an average of 17.26 per cent; for the entire area. Of the rest, in *pargana* Lucknow, 28.52 per cent was classed as *manjhar*, 37.85 per cent, as *palo* and 12.85 per cent, as *tarai*, the latter being the low-lying alluvial soil on the banks of the Gomti. In the other six *parganas*, 54.9 per cent was demarcated as loam, 19.98 per cent as clay, 8.29 per cent as sandy *bhur* and the small remaining proportion of .32 per cent consisted of *tarai* land along the Gomti and Sai rivers.[30]

FOREST COVER

The forest history of the subcontinent varies enormously from region to region. It is essential to highlight this deviation and recognize the regional and local variations. This chapter has sought to comprehend the people's experiences of ecological pressure and their responses to the changes over time. Indeed, the forest was utilized as a basis for social, economic and political initiatives. They had also served a commercial and strategic purpose from Mughal times to the colonial period.

The forest resources in Awadh were not only exploited for their flora and fauna, but it was used as a political domain by the *zamindars* or *taluqdars*[31] of the region. As reported from the Mughal accounts up to the British records of the nineteenth century, forests were used as a natural defense by this landowning class to resist central authorities, either mainly for tax evasion or to throw off their allegiance to their rulers. Before Manucci's seventeenth-century accounts of *zamindars* living in forests, we have a reference from Bayazid Biyat's *Tarikh-i-Humayun,* who in 1566, mentions that 'after the imperial force took over Gorakhpur, Raja Sansar Chand who was injured fled to his "own" forest (*Jangal-i khud*)'.[32] Manucci, in the Mughal period, observed about the forested dominions of *zamindar* that 'The roads are not direct, owing to the forest and mountains and interposition of territories belonging to the different rajas and *zamindars*, who allow no travellers to pass through, out of the fear they have of the Mughals.'[33] In this way, forests served as a political asylum for refractory *zamindars*.

In the eighteenth century, when the *raja* of Banaras, Balwant Singh, to strengthen his position in the region, adopted a policy of rooting out the power of local chieftains, he faced resistance frequently but only the resistance from the Sengar Rajputs of *pargana* Lakhnesar in Ballia was successful owing to the presence of forest for their defense as forest made their region most inaccessible.[34] Thus, Balwant Singh had to enter a compromise, the Sengars being left in possession of their estates at a low revenue.[35] In his settlement report of Banaras in 1795, Jonathan Duncan reported the *zamindars* of *pargana* Khareed in Ballia deliberately kept the jungle as a place of asylum where they differed from the *amil* of Khareed; they found a place of retreat.[36] Due to the effects of this problem, Duncan ordered to grant *patta* to the *ryats*, who could root up all the jungle and cultivate the land in three years.[37]

In the first half of the nineteenth century, Donald Butter and W.H. Sleeman give a more detailed account of *zamindars* and their forested abodes in Awadh. Donald Butter (1836) observed that the so-called primaeval forest of Awadh went carefully preserved from the axe by the neighbouring *zamindars*, to whom they have long afforded a secure asylum from the tyranny and greed of the *chakledars*.[38] He also gives details of particular *zamindars* who used to hide in the neighbouring jungles with their families and immediate dependence to evade taxes or challenge nawab's authority. The most detailed account has been given about the Tiloin *rajas* of Nain in Salon.[39]

Sleeman (1849) writes that Awadh (excluding the *terai* region) was geographically a level plain. Still, there were deep ravines at places where river Gomti cut the soil to 50 feet. The landholders along the border overcome these natural difficulties by planting and preserving trees to hide themselves and their followers when they rebelled against their government.[40] Landholders in the open plains and on the banks of rivers with no ravines also made artificial jungles for the same purpose.

In these jungles, the landholders found shooting, fishing, and security for themselves and their families, grazing ground for their horses and cattle, and fuel and grass for their followers.[41]

TYPE OF FOREST COVER

An essential feature of the natural geography of Awadh in the sixteenth to eighteenth centuries was a large forest belt. It is possible to map the main forest tracts by drawing upon diverse sources.[42] We find the terai forest spread between the city of Gorakhpur and the Himalayan range, as depicted in James Rennell's *Bengal Atlas* (1780). In his memoir of the Gorakhpur district (1810), Ghulam Hazrat tells us that forests surrounded the city of Gorakhpur. He says that the *tappa* of *parganas* Anola, Bansi, Silhat, Basti, Maghar and Gorakhpur were desolate owing to the scarcity of peasants and the denseness of jungles and the inroads of the wild elephants. Owing to the depredations of these elephants, the peasants abstained from the cultivation of sugar cane.[43] Francis Buchana, who surveyed the district in 1807, estimated that out of the total area of 7,438 sq. miles, about 1,450 sq. miles were covered with forest.[44] Besides these forests, several patches studded with long grass were found here and there.[45]

Another category of the forests consisted of the jungle situated either on the low land (*kachar*) or the higher grounds. These were carefully preserved from clearing by the *zamindars* of the area. These offered them a safe place of 'asylum from tyranny and the capacity of the *calendar*.[46] The face of the county was a level plain, but river

Gomti had cut the soil at some places creating ravines to the depth of 50 ft. The *zamindars* used these ravines, planted trees to create jungles and made hideouts for themselves. Amid these forests, every land-holder of consequence used to build mud-forts (*garhis*) 'surrounded by a ditch and dense fence of living bamboos, through which cannon shot cannot penetrate'.[47] The *chakledars* were always helpless against such fortifications of the *zamindars*, as the jungles were too green to be set fire to and 'being within the range of matchlocks from the parapet, the besieging force cannot cut them down.[48] Sleeman laments that such defence could easily be broken down, but 'Oudh force seldom had the means or the skill for such purpose'.[49] Sleeman has listed twenty-four belts of forests in the kingdom of Oudh (1850), which were being used by the *zamindars* to challenge the authority of the government officials. They were spread over all parts of the kingdom, and it was computed that such forests covered about 886½ sq. miles of area.[50] Sleeman offers us the figures for the estimated area under forest in the districts of the Awadh kingdom in square miles.[51]

TABLE 4.1: ESTIMATED FOREST AREA IN THE DISTRICT OF THE AWADH

S.No.	*Chakla (Dist.)*	*Forested area (in sq. miles)*
1.	Sultanpur	279 sq. miles
2.	Uldemau	102 sq. miles
3.	Daruabad	76 sq. miles
4.	Dewa-Jahangirabad	64 sq. miles
5.	Bangar	72 sq. miles
6.	Salon	72 sq. miles
7.	Bainsware	30 sq. miles
8.	Hydergarh	7½ sq. miles
9.	Khyrabad Muchreyte	30 sq. miles
	Total	888½ sq. miles[52]

The government encouraged clearing the forest for cultivation to increase revenue and perhaps remove the *zamindars*' hide-out. Several incentives were given to the peasants to carry out the reclamation work. Forest land was lightly assessed by the revenue officials of the nawab-wazirs 'free for the first year of occupancy, charged at only two *annas* per *bigha*, the second year, 4 *annas*, the third year, 6 *annas*; fourth and fifth year, 10 *annas*; beyond which, as an encouragement to the settlers, the abundantly as the water-table was found just at a depth of 10 feet, and wells and tanks could be dug quite easily.[53] Until the year 1833, Butter describes the destruction of a *chiul* jungle which was 20 miles and 8 miles broad, between Niwurdipur and Manikpur. 'The soil, which is covered, has been found of good quality, and there is little difficulty in cutting down *chiul* jungle, which is free from thorns. Nearly the whole of it has been destroyed since that period, and the remainder is rapidly disappearing.[54]

COLONIAL FOREST POLICY LED TO DEFORESTATION

The British inherited the pre-colonial attitude towards the forest and began experiments within it. Notwithstanding the inherited wisdom and tradition, the Company, influenced by the philosophy of the agricultural revolution and its rapid success in England, showed a unique vision of forests. The Company's aims were clear: adequate and profitable supply of timber, tree-feeling and expansion of cultivation. The latter was achieved with marked rapidity until the 1850s, when the apprehensions of deforested Gorakhpur overcame the Company. The Company made rigid plans to conserve forests to save and preserve timber and create a balanced ecosystem.[55]

However, the histories of Indian forestry written by British officials, E.P. Stebbing and B. Ribbentrop have argued strongly in favour of the benefits of scientific forestry and scientific supervision and management of forests.[56] Conversely, scholars like Vandana Shiva, Ramchandra Guha and Madhav Gadgil have argued that the colonial forest policy had a reason for deforestation. They argued that these forest use and management systems led to ecological decline and agrarian protest.[57] Emphasis on the conflict between state forestry and peasantry, these scholars have suggested that the colonial forest policy had led to deforestation and that the colonial law had alienated the communities living in the forest areas by depriving them of the right to manage the forests.

The dominant burden of agricultural policy was to extend cultivation, and 'the watchword of the time was to destroy the forest with this end in view'. When the East India Company annexed the ceded and conquered provinces at the beginning of the nineteenth century, it gained one of India's most fertile agricultural regions. Under the Mughal rule, this area had been amongst the most exhaustively worked land in northern India, and the rate of revenue demand was high.[58] However, the *doab*'s most crucial natural landscape was under its dense forest cover. The centuries-old farming and irrigation projects under the Mughals had already adversely reduced the areas in the upper *doab*. Still, the central and lower *doab* from Bulandshahr to beyond Kanpur, interfluvial lowlands, was under thick forest cover until the nineteenth century. However, British rule led to the adverse impact on this natural landscape due to the extraction of forest resources.

Awadh, under the nawab's government, remained conscious of the fiscal value of the forest and asserted their claim as the state's share of revenue to be paid by the *zamindars*. To extend cultivation and enhance revenue, the nawabs ordered the clearing and settling of lands under forests. To ensure speedy reclamation, like the Mughal emperors, they served as an incentive to clear and cultivate the land; and gave the *zamindars* the privilege to keep the revenue after paying the regulated *jama* to the government.[59] Enhancing revenue was one objective; expanding the government's political power and control over the forests was equally significant. The nawabs asserted the states' rights over all such wastelands and jungle areas, which had no claimant of established proprietors. They used these lands to confer *madad-i ma'ash* and *ma'afi* grants. The nawabs also maintained the forests as hunting reserves and organized hunting parties.[60]

By 1840, with over half of the district cultivated, expansion could not be predictable. The rest of the *dhak* forest vanished in the second half of the nineteenth century. By 1880, there were hardly any trees left outside the properties of *taluqdars*.[61] According to contemporary observers, the forest belt up to 3 miles wide vanished in the ten years following the British arrival there. Around 1850, there was no remaining forest in the area beyond a small patch of Bharatpur.[62]

The consolidation of British power and the country's opening up in the first half of the nineteenth century synchronized with an unprecedented assault on the forest, which came to be destroyed as never in the Awadh region. The government granted large tracts of forest to enterprising speculators for a small fee, allowing them to clear the land for farming. In Basti, Gorakhpur and other eastern districts where the population density was high, cultivation in areas once under a forest of Gorakhpur was known as the '*zabti* jungle' (resumed-confiscated-forest) because it represents not the area reserved as such. In Bundelkhand, only inaccessible forests and rugged terrain unfit for cultivation were declared 'reserved' or 'protected'. At the same time, those on the level ground were handed over to landlords to bring them under cultivation.

The destruction of forests became more acute in the early nineteenth century when timber was required for railway sleepers. Forests were farmed out to European merchants at a fixed sum annually. The privilege of extracting dammer from the *sal* trees by inciting a few feet above the root was also farmed out to European merchants. Even though the growth in timber value was rapid, the Company felt no compulsion to assume the royalty of forests. The reasons were obvious. The advantages poured in smoothy and steadily by a levy of 2.5 per cent on the value of timber when exported.[63] Thus, to facilitate timber supply to the British, Dr. Brandis was appointed as the first Inspector-General of forests in India in 1864. Shortly afterwards, a forest department was made in these provinces under his guidance. Valuable timber-bearing regions were progressively declared as 'reserved' or 'protected' under the Forest Act VII of 1878 (now Act XVI of 1927).[64]

However, because of the ongoing destruction of the forests, adverse effects were produced on the general climate. Donald Butter argued that the annual average rainfall declined, and the water table went down, thus creating difficulties for irrigation. A systematic artificial planting could have certainly controlled this situation to counteract the parching effects produced by removing these natural protectors of the soil. But the reclamation continued unabated. The agricultural statistics of 1885-6 show no forest area in that district, where Sleeman estimates forest area as 882½ sq. miles. It may be assumed that by 1885-6, such extensive tracts of forest comprising about half a million acres had come under cultivation.[65]

BRITISH MILITARY OPERATION AND DEFORESTATION

Weekly narratives of British military operations in the districts during the revolt of 1857 quite often reported a hindrance in their movement, and that was forests, 'Until the fugitive rebels from Baiswara have been entirely driven out or reduced to submission, the country around Jagadishpur will be more or less disturbed as the extent of the jungle gives shelter to marauders.'[66]

Few rebels 'for some weeks past infested the jungles of the Gondah district bordering on Gorakhpur, where it is difficult to come up with them.'[67]

However, the military campaign against rebel forces exposed the actual strength of the forest in Awadh. It aroused such fear in the minds of the British that they adopted a comprehensive policy of its destruction.

We find, parallel to the combining operations, British authorities again started re-structuring their forest policy in Awadh. A report dated 26 November 1858 declares that 'to those who had cleared land within the forests, the Governor-General in Council directed a proprietary right should be given and a fair proportion of wasteland also be added'.[68] Further Revised Rules for the guidance of the Superintendent of Forests in Awadh, 1858, declared that 'such tracts of forests as contained timber, not worth preserving and are not required for the formation of the plantation will be assigned in clearing leases by the district officers, and the Superintendent should early define and separate such tracts'.[69]

However, in 1859, fresh leases were granted to *taluqdars* for bringing jungle and wasteland under cultivation. According to the Secretary to the Chief Commissioner Awadh's report to the Secretary to the Government of India, 1859. However, the *taluqdars* had already been made to clear a specific space around their forts; the jungles were far more extensive, and it was an hard task to have them removed speedily.[70] Also, the Chief Commissioner of Awadh thought it was no use cutting down the jungle faster than the land could be cultivated.[71] They worried that 'the plough must keep space with an axe, or an impenetrable brushwood spring up in place of the tall trees, which is infinitely more difficult to remove'.[72]

Thus, it is inaccurate to characterize colonial periods uniformly as the most dramatic phases of ecological devastation for the countries concerned. The first official measures for protecting nature, whatever their motives and effectiveness, arose in these countries on the initiative of colonial governments. In Awadh, the forest areas were declared as state forests and came under the Conservator of Forest in 1861. In 1563, Brandis toured Awadh forest, and in 1879, the ravines in Etawa districts, because of which afforestation in United Provinces began.[73] Several measures had been taken on the recommendation of Brandis for the preservation of timber and its regular supply.

Demarcation, which is one of the important technologies of scientific forestry, denoted for foresters the division of a forest into reserved and protected forests. The survey and the maps made were central to the project of controlling the boundary envisaged.[74]

The next step was the 'simple form of working plan' in forest conservancy. A simple form of the working plan means the idea of fixing and forecasting the annual yield based on some form of computation of the contents of the forests combined with the rate of growth of trees. Stabbing assumed that 'the credit of having been the first to introduce a simple form of forest working plan in India must go to Mr Munro'.[75]

FAUNA

Wild animals found their way into these deep and long stretches of green belts. The *terai* forest of *sarkar* Gorakhpur was famous for containing many elephants, a menace to cultivation.[76] Tigers, too, were found in significant numbers between Gorakhpur and the mountains. Before the cession of this territory to the English, their number was still more critical. After 1801, because of forest clearing operations, many were hunted down by English civilians and military officers. These animals lived primarily on cattle that in 1769, the year of great famines, most of the 'herbivorous animals' perished so that the tigers were famished. The tigers in a large hoard fell upon the town of Bhewapor and, within no time, killed about 400 of its inhabitants. The city remained deserted for an extended period.

Wolves and jackals were widespread in these forests, posing a constant threat to the peasants and domestic animals.[77] The wolf was quite a menace in the southern districts of Awadh when Butter compiled his survey. He says that they carried away several children from the small bar attached to the Cantonment of Sultanpur. Superstition among the 'native population' prevailed that they were being killed, and their dens were observable along the sides of the 'ravines' throughout the country.[78]

The wild animals of the district were conspicuous by their absence. As usual, the commonest were gig, but even these are scarce. Jackals, of course, abound, but these, except a few blackbuck, who have as yet escaped extermination and a nilgai or two in the Mohanlalganj *pargana*, practically exhaust the list. The large *jhils* usually contain a fair number of wildfowl in the cold weather, and snipes, too, were found in places but they were usually much harried owing to the number of sportspersons in Lucknow and the cantonments. See Appendix IV on page 217 for the list of fauna found in Awadh.

AGRICULTURE AND CLIMATE

In essentials, the agricultural practices of the Indian peasants seemed similar to those pursued by their counterparts in Europe, given the difference in crops and climate.[79] Another feature of Indian agriculture was artificial irrigation to supplement rain and flood. Wells and tanks were the primary sources of such irrigation. In regional distribution, the food grains and cash crops show quite different tendencies when we compare the conditions of the seventeenth century with those of the late nineteenth. The regional distribution of the food crops seems hardly to have altered: climate and the volume of seasonal floods set the limits, as they do now, to the rice and wheat zone.[80]

Suppose the absolute size of the agricultural products, or even the per capita product, in Mughal India was impressive, still it does not follow that agricultural production was carried on at a smooth or even pace. Two natural and other human factors created serious interruptions or violent setbacks for agricultural life. The first factor was climatic, essentially, the untimeliness and scarcity of overabundance of rain. The dependence of Indian agriculture on the monsoons is proverbial.

Explicitly the fact that Donald Butter, in the first quarter of the nineteenth century, in his topographical and statistical survey of the southern district of Awadh, stated that 'in the ill-contrived and worst administered revenue system of Oudh, and the prevailing insecurity of life and property, may be found the abundant reasons for the present miserably depressed state of the agriculture of this kingdom'.[81] Butter noticed the decreased trends in the *rabi* and *kharif* crops, which attributed to a significant change in the climate owing to a declining trend in the region's rainfall.[82] Butter thought that the annual average rain had gradually declined, and the water- table went down, creating difficulties for irrigation. He attributed such a change to the destruction of the old forest in the region by peasants to bring more land under cultivation.[83]

Donald Butter has appended tables showing the diminishing pattern of the *rabi* and the *kharif* crops. At the time of his report writing (AD 1836), even the 'produce in a good year' was much less than what it was 'before the significant change in the climate. The ecological concern of Donald Butter in the first half of the nineteenth century makes it possible to compare how in the second half of the nineteenth century, i.e. after the revolt of 1857, the British responded to these issues when they worked over the charge of Awadh administration responded to these issues.[84]

TABLE 4.2: *KHARIF* CROPS, SOWN IN THE RAINY SEASON[85]

S.No.	*Name of the crop*	*Sers of the seeds per bigha*	*Mans of the produce in a good year*	*Mans of the produce in a bad year*	*Former produce in man*
1	Kodo	4	10 to 12	4 or 5	15 or 16
2	Makra	4	8 to 9	2 or 3	10 or 11
3	Sanwa	3	8	2 or 3	10 or 12
4	Asahan *kharif*	30	15	8 or 9	20

Source: Mufti Ghulam Hazrat, *Kwaif-i-Zila-i Gorakhpur (1810 AD)*, MS Aligarh, Subhan Ullah Collection, pp. 57-8.

TABLE 4.3: *RABI* CROPS SOWN IN THE WINTER SEASON

S.No.	*Name of the crop*	*Sers of the seeds per bigha*	*Mans of the produce in a good year*	*Mans of the produce in a bad year*	*Former produce in man*
1	Kodo	30	14 or 15	5 or 8	18
2	Makra	50	14 or 15	7 or 8	18
3	Sanwa	40	20 to 22	10 or 13	20

Source: Mufti Ghulam Hazrat, *Kwaif-i-Zila-i Gorakhpur (1810 AD)*, MS Aligarh, Subhan Ullah Collection, pp. 57-8.

The average annual rainfall in Awadh, according to Donald Butter, followed a very irregular pattern. It was 'steadily decreasing on an average of 5 or 6 inches every year.[86] Butter attributed such a change to the 'Dylan vesture' destruction by the peasants to bring more land under cultivation. Experts predicted that the country would slowly but surely become 'barren ravines' because the lack of forest left it vulnerable to the sun's intense rays and prevented due deposition, which in turn prevented the formation of springs. The green belts of the region had detained water in meshes, but such land was now 'ploughed into barren ravines'. As a result, the province lost 'its springs and parental streamlets'. Its springs and parental streamlets, the distance of water from the earth increased and its rainfalls and the volume of its rivers diminished.[87]

The accompanying map is drawn to show the Isohyets projects, that the annual average rainfall of the province ranges from 54.7 inches.[88] It is heavier as we move towards the north-west and lighter as we go westward. Butter in 1836 estimated the average annual rainfall in southern Awadh at between '70 to 30 inches within four months but is steadily decreasing on average of five or six years'.[89]

The statistical account of the Mughal Empire contains valuable information about the total *arazi* and the *jama* of each *sarkar*. An

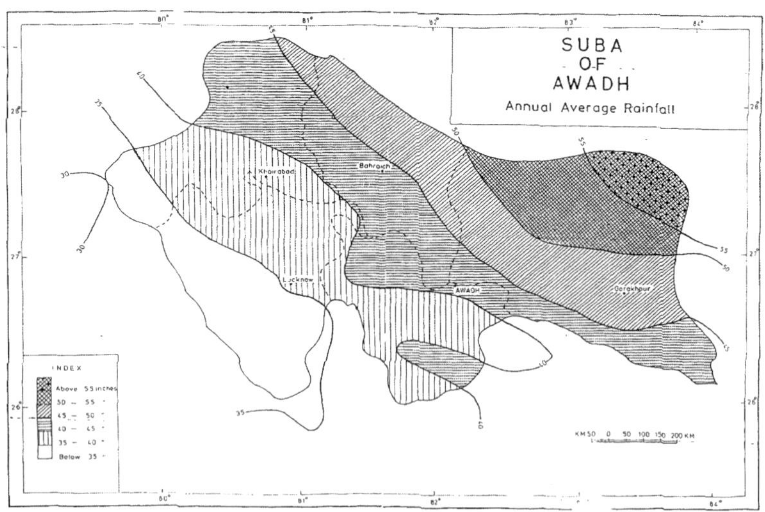

MAP 4.2 MAP SHOWS ANNUAL AVERAGE RAINFALL IN THE *SUBA* OF AWADH *c.* 1860. (*COURTESY*: S.Z.H. JAFARI, *AGRARIAN CONDITION OF AWADH UNDER THE MUGHAL AND NAWAB*), GYAN PUBLISHING HOUSE, NEW DELHI.

analysis and comparison of these statistics with data from British-period agricultural statistics may lead to some provisional conclusions.

The *sarkar* boundaries and the *pargana* headquarters of the province of Awadh were by Irfan Habib in *An Atlas of the Mughal Empire.* As measured by his maps and figures converted into *bigha-i-Ilahi*, the total area of each *sarkar* may be compared with the *arazi* of the respective *sarkars* in the *Ain.*

TABLE 4.4: MEASURED AREA CONVERTED INTO *BIGHA-I-ILAHI* [90]

S.No.	*Sarkar*	*Measured Area in bigha-i-Ilahi (A)*	*Map Area in bigha-i-Ilahi (B)*	*As % of (B)*
1.	Awadh	27,95,946	32,38,466	86. 33 %
2.	Lucknow	33,04,905	61,01,955	
3.	Khairabad	19,80,714	52,98,558	
4.	Bahraich	18, 23, 435	44,49,800	40.97 %
5.	Gorakhpur	2,44,681	90,97370	20.68 %
	Total	1,01,49,681	2,81,86,198	36.00 %

The exceptionally low *arazi* figure for *sarkar* Gorakhpur was mainly because of it bordering on the Himalayas. The large tracts of *terai* forests and other forest belts spread all over *sarkar*. Even during the early years of the nineteenth century. Francis Buchanan informs us that an area of 1,450 sq. miles out of 7,483 sq. miles, or 19.36 per cent of the whole, was covered with dense forests.[91] Similarly, Ghulam Hazrat pointed out *c.* 1810 that the city of Gorakhpur itself was surrounded by 'forest on two sides and rivers on two sides.[92] If we exclude the map area and *arazi* figures of *sarkar* Gorakhpur, the *arazi* of the rest of the *suba* of Awadh will rise to as high as 51.88 per cent of the map area.

TABLE 4.5: RISE OF AGRICULTURE LAND IN AWADH[93]

S. No.	Suba/Sarkar	Jama *in the 43 c. 1656*	Jama *in Add. 6586, c. 1707*	Jama *in Chahar Gulshan*	Arazi *in Chahar Gulshan*	Arazi *as a percentage of Map area in Chahar Gulshan*
1	Suba Awadh	180,72	197.89	161.21	124.80	66. 45 %
2	Sarkar Bahraich	127.20	161.60	104. 45	100. 48	41.22 %

3	Sarkar Gorakhpur	361.25	368.25	467.03	-	-
4	Sarkar Lucknow	167.47	19.08	136.59	109.65	59.44 %
5	Sarkar Khairabad	204.01	224.90	187.34	219.52	82.36 %

The agricultural statistics of British India, which was issued in 1885-5, offer us valuable data for comparing the extent of cultivation during the nineteenth century with that of Akbar's time. For our purposes, the figures for 1885-6 are more appropriate as in the statistics the current follows are separately given and not included in cultivable waste as in the 1884-5 figures. *Sarkar*-wise comparison is, of course, not possible, as the modern figures are for British districts. For this reason, the statistical returns of all those districts within the limit of the Mughal *suba* of Awadh, either wholly or partly, have been pooled together. The modern returns' area units (areas) have been converted into *bigha-i-Illahi*.

The fact that the measured area increased substantially during the seventeenth century is confirmed because the total number of the villages recorded in oriental manuscripts M.S. Fraser 86 housed in the Bodleian library at Oxford University, *Dastur al-amal* provides the numbers for the *suba* Awadh is 52,691 while 33,842 towns or 64.22 per cent of the total number of villages were said to have fully measured.

TABLE 4.6: MAP OF CULTIVATED AREA IN 1885-6[94]

S.No.	*District*	*Map-area in* bigha-i-Ilahi	*Cultivated area in* bigha-i-Ilahi	*Cultivated as % of Map area*
1.	Lucknow	10,42,133	6,09135	58.45
2.	Unnao	18,57,733	10,88,318	8.77
3.	Barabanki	18,43,200	12.41,416	67.35
4.	Sitapur	23,53,066	16,66,668	70.82
5.	Hardoi	24,38,400	16,35,153	67.70
6.	Kheri	31,49,386	15,17,840	48.14
7.	Faizabad	17,58,933	11,46,583	65.18
8.	Gonda	28,21,333	15,92,455	56.44
9.	Bahraich	30,12,266	20,40,091	67.72

10.	Rae-Bareli	16,68,800	10,13,588	54.32
11.	Sultanpur	18,14,400	10,26,456	56.57
12.	Partapgarh	15,55,200	8,43,536	54.23
13.	Gorakhpur	49,04,640	32,74,066	66.75
14.	Basti	29,36,320	19,84,300	67.57
15.	Ballia	12,11,733	5,08,178	41.93
16.	Pilibhit	14,64,533	7,63,848	52.15
17.	Farrukhabad	18,33,600	11,67,668	63.68
	Total	3,81,86,189	1,01,63,360	61.04

Note:	*Compare:*			
	Ain	2,81,86,189	1,01,63,360	36.00
	Chahar Gulshan		1,26,84,872	66.45

The table shows that cultivation had dramatically increased in areas of the old *sarkar* of Gorakhpur (district Gorakhpur, Gonda and Basti). There was a notable extension in cultivation in the district of Mughal *sarkar* Khairabad (notably the district of Sitapur and Hardoi), though Kheri remained backwards in cultivation.

It appears safe to assume that the total span of the area under cultivation during the sixteenth century was appreciably high. It ought to have been about 50 per cent of what it was during the nineteenth century.

The extent of cultivation should probably have been over 10 per cent less in 1856, the year of annexation, than in 1885-6. Part of this must have been under the forest. The presence of forest alongside rivers, deep ravines, and open plains of south Awadh are described by Butter in 1836 and by Sleeman in 1849-50. Since the agricutural statistics of 1885-6 do not show any area under forests in these districts, it may be assumed that these were cleared in the thirty or thirty-five years after 1850, and we may then safely allow a margin of 10 per cent growth in cultivation during this period.

Agricultural Production

Several bowls of cereal and cash crops were raised in the provinces of Awadh.[95] Some new crops were introduced during the fifteenth century, compared with the traditional crops of Awadh; these were only grown over a small area by the end of the nineteenth century.[96]

The *dastur* rates given in *Ain-i-Akbari* show that twenty-one *rabi* crops are listed for the six revenue circles of *sarkars* Awadh and Bahraich. In contrast, the crops on which *dastur* are recorded under *sarkars* Khairabad, Lucknow and Gorakhpur are fewer.[97] Even crops such as wheat, barley and mustard seeds, grown in the localities during the nineteenth century, have been omitted from the *dastur* list.[98] Among the twenty-nine *kharif* crops, fourteen have been mentioned in all the twelve *dasturs*. In comparison, eleven minor crops are listed in only six *dasturs* of the *sarkars* Awadh and Bahraich, Kharonsa, Khairabad, and Pali; for the other two, lobiya and carrots, the rates are provided only for one circle (i.e. Ibrahimabad). Kur (a wild grain) found its mention in Ibrahimadad and Bahraich circles.[99]

The cereal crops cultivated in Awadh can be broadly divided into rice, wheat and millet. Many pulses were also grown in the *rabi* and *kharif* harvest.

Rice constituted the chief cereal crop of the region since its cultivation suited the low-lying area subject to inundations. It was cultivated throughout the *terai* region and alongside the courses of major rivers traversing Awadh.[100]

During the eighteenth century, *sarkar* Gorakhpur, especially *pargana* Hansi, became quite famous for the high-grade varieties of rice raised there. These were called *bhairani, shamira, rajhans* and *ratkwal*. In the markets of Faizabad and Lucknow, these varieties were sold under the name of *pargana* Hansi.[101] The area under rice cultivation seems to have been much more significant than under wheat. The agricultural statistics of 1885-5 disclose a size of 21,59,424 acres (about 20.56 per cent of the total area) under rice, while under wheat, this came to 15,56,198 acres (about 16.56 per cent of the total).[102]

Another major crop of the province was wheat. Its cultivation suited only the higher grounds and drier areas. The high lands between the rivers were particularly well-suited for growing wheat. Significantly, Abul Fazl has not recorded the revenue rates for wheat in some higher regions, such as *sarkar* Khairabad and Lucknow. However, during the nineteenth century, these regions raised substantial wheat crops.[103]

Abul Fazl furnishes us with *dastur* rates for the coarse grain and most pulses in various revenue circles. But a comparison of the crop pattern during the sixteenth century with that of the nineteenth century is impossible, as these cereals have been put under a column headed by 'other food crops' in the agricultural statistics. But these made up the bulk of agricultural production during the nineteenth century, as the 'other food crops' are sown over an area (in Oudh, including *sarkar* Gorakhpur, of 76,27,739 acres as compared with 53,20,822 acres under rice and wheat.[104] Crops like *jowar*, *ahara* (bajara), and chana could be raised only on higher grounds, and the cultivation of those crops closely coincided with wheat. In this category, a new crop, maize, was introduced by the end of the fifteenth century, but as Butter had not noticed its cultivation in southern Oudh, it was still sparsely cultivated by 1838.

The chief crops raised in the province were oilseed, sugar cane, cotton, indigo and tobacco. The cultivation of the vegetables for the market and domestic use was also undertaken. The peasants belonging to some particular castes carried on it.[105]

Abul Fazl has provided the revenue rates for mustard seed only in six *dastur* circles. Although oil has been a part of the diet of every Indian, it was not considered to be an important crop of Awadh in the Mughal period. The agricultural statistics of 1885-6 show an area of 4,98,879 acres under oilseeds.[106] Possibly, the cultivation of oilseeds as a cash crop expanded after the annexation owing to European demand promoted by the construction of railways.[107]

Sugar cane was perhaps the most critical cash crop. *Ain* provides the revenue rates for high-quality and common sugar cane for all the *dastur* circles of Awadh. Mufti Ghulam Hazrat mentions extensive cultivation of these crops in *sarkar* of Gorakhpur; it was the best kind compared to the other places for 'its sweetness and delicacy'. In some *parganas* of *sarkar* Gorakhpur, however, its cultivation had to be abandoned because of the menace of the wild elephants.[108]

During the fifteenth century, Butter noticed the crop was raised in 'small patches here and there, particularly between the river Sai and Ganges and sugar was made in small quantities in the south-west part of Oudh.[109] Thornton described its cultivation as 'very circumscribed'.[110] However, while passing through the district of Sultanpur, six kinds of sugar cane were noticed by Sleeman, and he found its cultivation to be quite extensive there.[111] The agricultural statistics show as many as 2,40,975 acres under sugar cane.[112] This large acreage may be because of the subsequent extension in sugar cane cultivation after annexation.

The cultivation of potatoes does not seem to have made much progress in Awadh; a few Kunjras and Kachis planted it near Kanpur, Lucknow and Faizabad. People mainly exported the potato produce to the nearest British Cantonments. In the interior, the extension of this crop was checked by the prejudice felt by the people, predominantly the Brahman and Bachgoti Rajputs, against eating a new vegetable, especially a root. It also does not seem to have become a part of the town man's diet in Awadh.[113]

Poppy cultivation was noticed by Butter along the bank of river Gomati by some particular castes, particularly the Kachis. People, particularly the Kachis, exported poppy primarily to the nearby British districts.[114]

The situation changed as the population increased and cultivation expanded. The peasants in Awadh depended on it, and cultivation expanded. The peasants in Awadh turned on the *siul dhak* and other jungles to support their animals. During the eighteenth and nineteenth centuries, people reclaimed forests on a large scale to expand the area under cultivation and to get firewood. The scarcity of the 'grazing ground' led ultimately to the fall in the number of animals in the total human population. This deterioration in the southern districts was so acute that 'people who would formerly have possessed 100 oxen and 50 buffaloes have now only four or five of them.[115] The animals left with peasants were in no good condition because, 'exception along with the Sai and near Faizabad, where there is still a good supply of water and fodder, the oxen are most miserable animals of the kind- lean stunted and frequently diseased'.[116]

The scarcity of cattle had also become acute because of the 'universal practice of revenue collectors seizing and carrying them away when their owner fell into arrears'. The problem had assumed a dimension that when the fields had to be wanted, it was quite common to see 'all family members, male and female, working instead of cattle at the good rope'.[117] The fall in the number of livestock per capita ultimately raised the price of opec. It was, 'formerly sole at 20 *sers* the rupee, is now sold at a *sers* and half.'[118]

Manuring was done with the dung of cattle and horses. This was supposed to raise the fertility of the land and the productivity of the crop in 'triple measure'. But one would think that since there was some scarcity of cattle and reduced grazing grounds during the nineteenth century, the dung manure would also have become relatively less plentiful. Butter criticized the local peasants for not manuring scientifically, believing they had much to learn.[119]

Rains and Irrigation

The rivers flowing through the province and the rainfall were the primary sources of irrigation. The rivers Sarju, Ghaghar, Sai and Gumti, according to Abul Fazl, are the major streams that run through the province. Many water-lifting devices are strewn up these rivers, but there is no information. Floods were critical to rice farming. 'With the start of the dry season, it's wonderful how the floods from the Sarju and Ghaghar begin: they flood the area before the monsoon arrives,' Abul Fazl explains. 'Rice stalks grow and lengthen when the water level rises. Rice crops are only ruined if floods occur before ears have developed'.[120] Similarly, on small areas of cultivated land, artificial irrigation systems were also used, albeit in crude forms. According to Bhandari, 'Cultivation is supported in certain places by wells. However, the bulk of the land depends still on rainfall.' Earlier, the abundance of rainfall in the province was practised as it resulted 'in an extension of the cultivation, augmentation of crop-yields, the cheapness of the grains, and the large settlements in *parganas*'.[121]

But, with the extension of the cultivation through a continuous process of the reclamation of virgin land, the need for more artificial irrigation was felt. During the nineteenth century, irrigation was practised throughout the kingdom of Awadh to supplement the monsoon. The principal sources of artificial irrigation were wells, tanks and lakes. Butter thought that the need for artificial irrigation had been growing in Awadh and became a diminution of rainfall due to forest clearance. The rapid clearing of forests in the north-western parts of the kingdom had occurred. It was not accompanied by any artificial planting system that might counter-act 'the parching effects' produced by removing the great forest.[122]

Methods of Irrigation

The rainfall and the rivers flowing through the province were the primary sources of irrigation. Abul Fazl mentions the rivers, Sarju, Ghaghar, Sai and Gumti as the principal streams. There is no information about any water-lifting devices set up in these rivers. However, the floods were significant for rice cultivation. Abul Fazal says, 'With the dry season's beginning, it is wonderful how the floods begin from the Sarju and Ghaghar: they flood the land before the monsoon's onset. As the water rises, the rice stalks also grow and lengthen. Only if the floods take place before the ears grow is rice crop destroyed.'[123] Similarly, over a small area of cultivated land, artificial methods of irrigation were also applied, but in crude forms. Bhandari tells us that 'although at some places cultivation is supported by the wells; most of the land still depended on rainfall'. Earlier, the abundance of rainfall in the province has been practised as it resulted 'in an extension of the cultivation, augmentation of crop yields, the cheapness of the grains, and the large settlement in *parganas*.[124]

But, with the extension of the cultivation through a continuous process of the reclamation of virgin land, the need for more artificial irrigation was practised throughout the kingdom of Awadh to supplement the monsoon. The principal sources of artificial irrigation were wells, tanks and lakes. Butter thought that the need for artificial irrigation had been growing in Awadh and became a diminution of rainfall because of forest clearance. The forest clearing had been carried out rapidly in north-western parts of the kingdom. It was not accompanied by any artificial system of planting that might counteract 'the parching effects' produced by the removal of the forests.[125]

While going through the literary sources, some argue that Awadh was endowed with the richness of natural sources: rivers, tributaries, varied soil types and large forest belts at the fringes of agricultural fields. However, by that time, its forest resources were exploited for its flora and fauna, but it was used as a political asylum by the *zamindars*.

At the same time, the fact is that the creation of ravines to a depth of 50 feet due to soil cut by the river Gomti. The *zamindars* used these ravines and planted trees to create jungles for hiding themselves. Subsequently, forests spread throughout the kingdom and calculations showed they covered approximately 886½ sq. miles.

However, the government cleared the forest cover to root out hideous *zamindars*. The government offered several incentives to the peasants to reclaim the land. Besides this, the land revenue policy of the Mughals and British was another reason for deforestation.

Donald Butter describes the direct consequences of clearing forest cover in Awadh. The annual average rainfall declined, and the water table level went down, thus creating difficulties for irrigation. However, it may be assumed that by 1885-6, such extensive tracts of forest comprising about half a million acres of land had come under cultivation.

Although colonial forest policy handled deforestation in Awadh, it is inaccurate to portray colonial periods as the most dramatic phases of ecological devastation for the countries concerned. The first official measures for protecting nature arose from the colonial government's efforts.

NOTES

1. Abul Fazl, *Ain-i-Akbari,* vol. II, tr. H.S. Jarret, Delhi, 1978, p. 184.
2. Ibid., p. 181.
3. J.A. Boyle, ed., *The Cambridge History of Iran,* vol. 5, *The Seljuq and Mongol Period,* Cambridge: Cambridge University Press, 1968, pp. 9, 43, 56, 150.
4. Saiyid Zaheer Husain Jafri, *Awadh from Mughal to Colonial Rule: Studies in the Anatomy of a Transformation,* New Delhi: Gayan Publishing House, 2016, p. 26.
5. Ibid., p. 26.
6. Madhu Trivedi, *The Making of the Awadh Culture,* New Delhi: Primus Book, 2010, p. 2.
7. Thomas Twining, *Travels in India a Hundred Years Ago; With a Visit to the*

United States (1792), ed. W.H.G. Twining and James R. Osgood, London, 1893, p. 168.

8. Michael H. Fisher, *A Clash of Culture: Awadh, the British and the Mughals,* New Delhi: Manohar, 1987, p. 165.
9. Edward Thornton, *A Gazetteer of the Territories under the Government of the East India Company and of the Native States on the Continental India,* London: W.H. Allen & Co., 1854, Vol. IV, p. 36.
10. Sabina Kazmi, 'Colonial Intervention in Awadh: Indigenous Political Structures and Indirect Rule in Eighteenth Century', *Proceeding of the Indian History Congress (PIHC),* 74th Session, Cuttack, 2013, pp. 450-1.
11. Francis Buchanan, District Reports (1807-11), edited and abridged by Montgomery Martin, *The History, Antiquities, Topography and Statistics of Eastern India,* vol. III, London, 1838.
12. Jafri, op. cit., p. 33.
13. The term 'nawab' means a deputy of the Mughal Emperor and was only bestowed on his close nobles.
14. Nalini Singh, 'Forest, Fort and Arms: Resistance to Colonial Authority in Awadh during 1857-59', *PIHC,* 67th Session, Calicut, 2007, p. 610.
15. M.D. Chaturvedi, *Land Management in the United Province,* Allahabad: Government Press, 1938, pp. 61.
16. Ibid., p. 61.
17. Ibid., p. 62.
18. M.D. Chaturvedi, 'Roadside Avenue and Compounds', Bulletin No. 12, United Provinces, Forest Department, Allahabad: Government Press, 1938, p. 67.
19. Land Management, op. cit., p. 65.
20. M.P. Bhola and S. Hussain, 'Taungyas in the Gorakhpur Forest Division', Bulletin No. 4, United Provinces, Indian Forestry, July 1940, p. 78.
21. S.S. Negi, *Forest Development in the United Provinces,* Indian Forestry, July 1940, p. 88.
22. Abul Fazl, *Ain-i-Akbari,* vol. II, ed. Blochmann, Calcutta: Bibliotheca India, 1867-77, p. 78.
23. Donald Butter, *Topography and Statistics of the Southern Districts of Awadh,* ed. Safi Ahmad, Idarah-i Adabiyat-i Delhi, 2009, pp. 10-14.
24. Jafri, op. cit., p. 34.
25. *Lucknow Gazetteer: District Gazetteers of the United Provinces of Agra and Oudh,* vol. XXXVII, complied and ed. by H. R. Nevill, Allahabad, 1904, p. 1.
26. Ibid., p. 6.
27. Ibid., p. 6.
28. Ibid., p. 6.

29. Ibid., p. 7.
30. Ibid., p. 7.
31. *Zamindar* was a category of hereditary chief whose *pargana*-wise *zamindari* possession was recorded by Abul Fazl in *Ain-i-Akbari* whereas *taluqdars* could be divided into two categories. The first who belonged to the hereditary chief who had been in the possession of their estates since long and took advantages of their prime position to enlarge their landed possession in the form of *taluqa* tenures by the use forces, fraud and violence. The second consisted of those belonging to the bankers and traders possessing large capitals who came to enjoy a significant position in the official establishment of the revenue department. For further details see S.Z.H. Jafri, 'Land Control in Awadh: A Study of the *Taluqdari* Tenures up to *c.* 1850', in *UP Historical Review*, New Series, vol, I, April 2004, pp. 80-93.
32. Shireen Moosvi, 'Man and Nature in Mughal Era', Symposia Papers: 5, *Indian History Congress,* 1993, p. 13.
33. Niccolao Manucci, *Storia Do Mogor or Mogul India 1653-1708,* vol. II, tr. William Irvine, Calcutta, 1967, p. 414; Manucci uses the word *zamindar* in its usual sense of a petty, semi-independent chief. The great Rajahs even were called *zamindars* by the Mogul officials.
34. Wilton Oldham, *Historical and Statistical Memoir of the Ghazipur District,* vol. I, Allahabad, 1870, p. 103.
35. Ibid., p. 103.
36. A. Shakespeare, *Selection from the Duncan Records,* vol. I, Benares, 1873, p. 56
37. Ibid., p. 57.
38. Butter, op. cit., p. 5.
39. Ibid., pp. 109-10; Butter's account of Tiloin rajas of Nain (Salon) goes like 'About the year 1760, the son and successor of Balbhadar Shah (Tiloin raja) threw off his allegiance to the nawab who solicited the aid of the British government. Despite getting assistance from Britisher he was defeated and slain. His son and serving followers betook themselves to the jungles where they subsisted on the tribute levied from four or five villages. Such was the power of jungles when whole difficulties, the fugitive raja was invited to Lucknow and was invested with the government of the estates.'
40. W.H. Sleeman, *Sleeman in Oudh: An Abridgement of W.H. Sleeman's A Journey through the Kingdom of Oude in 1849-50,* ed. P.D. Reeves, Cambridge University Press, 1971, pp. 4-5.
41. Ibid., pp. 286-7.
42. Among the Indian works, only Haft Iqlim seems to refer to forest in Awadh; Irfan Habib, *An Atlas of the Mughal Empire*, New Delhi: Oxford University Press, 1982, Sheet No. 8A.

43. Mufti Ghulam Hazrat, *Kwaif-i-Zila-i Gorakhpur (1810 AD)*, MS, Aligarh Subhan Ullah Collection 954/12.
44. Francis Buchana, *District Reports (1807-11)* edited and abridged by Mantgomery Martin, *The History, Antiquities, Topography, and Statistics of Eastern India,* vol. 3, London: 1838: Indian reprint, 1976, vol. 5. The Survey of Gorakhpur is in Martins Abridgement, vol. II, p. 512.
45. Ibid., p. 513
46. Butter, op. cit., p. 5.
47. W.H. Sleeman, *A Journey through the Kingdom of Oudh during 1849-50,* vol. 2, London, 1858, pp. 279-87
48. Ibid., p. 289.
49. Ibid., p. 290.
50. Ibid., p. 293.
51. Ibid., p. 296.
52. Foreign Consultation, no. 136/52, dated 31 August 1865, New Delhi: National Archives of India, cf. A.A. Azmi, 'Position of Taluqdars in Oudh, 1814-1856', paper presented at the session of Indian History Congress, Allahabad Session, 1965. Only summery of paper was published in the proceeding, p. 323. For details, see the cyclostyled paper, p. 16.
53. Butter, op. cit., pp. 7-8.
54. Ibid., p. 7.
55. Meena Bhargava, *State, Society and Ecology: Gorakhpur in Transition, 1750-1830,* New Delhi: Manohar, 1999, pp. 54-9.
56. E.P. Stebbing, *The Forests of India,* vol. I, London, 1921, p. 532; also see B. Ribbentrop. *Forestry in British India,* Calcutta, 1900, p. 126.
57. Ramchandra Guha and Madhav Gadgil, *The Unquiet Woods: Ecological Change and Peasant Resistance in the Western Himalaya,* New Delhi: Oxford University Press, 1989, p. 8.
58. G. Ch. Divedi, *The Jats,* Bangalore, 1989, pp. 224-6.
59. Extract of a letter from Secretary to Government to the Court of Directors, 4 October 1815, Pre-Mutiny: Revenue Correspondence, Letters received from Government by the Board of Revenue, vol. I, 1810-16, Lucknow: Uttar Pradesh State Archives.
60. Irfan Habib, *Agrarian System of the Mughal Empire,* New Delhi: Oxford University Press, p. 248; he argues that for the sake of the hunting expeditions of the Mughal emperors and the royal princes, jungles were cut and paths cleared.
61. *Final Report on the Revision of Settlement in the District of Aligarh,* Allahabad, 1882, para. 10.
62. *Report on the Settlement of Mainpuri District,* Allahabad, 1875, para 10.
63. Bhargava, op. cit., p. 45.

64. For more detail see article of Nalini Singh, 'Forest, Forts and Arms', published in Proceeding of Indian History Congress, 2007, p. 623.
65. Agricultural Statistics of British India, 1885-6, Calcutta.
66. Foreign Department, Political Branch 'C' consultation, 17 December 1858, F. No. 247, 249, New Delhi: National Archives of India (NA).
67. Foreign Department, Political Proceeding, 30 December 1859 F. No. 498, NAI.
68. Foreign Department, Political Proceeding, 21-26 January 1859, F. No. 104, NAI.
69. Ibid., F. No. 105.
70. Foreign Department, Political Proceedings, 10 June 1859, F. No. 252.
71. Ibid., F. No. 252.
72. Ibid., F. No. 252.
73. *Oudh Forest Report for 1861-1862,* Public Work Department, Revenue and Forest Branch, National Archives of India, April, 1865, F. No. 83.
74. Ajay Skaria, 'Timber Conservation, Desiccationism and Scientific Forestry: the Dangs 18405-19205', in Sangwan Damodran and Richard Grove, eds., *Nature and Orient: The Environmental History of South East Asia,* Delhi, 1998, p. 608.
75. In 1837 Munro, superintendent of forest in Travancore, estimated that in season about 1,00,000 trees of teak were fit to be felled in the forests. It is true he based his figure on his 'personal observation and experience of nearly twenty years in the woods; *100 Years of India Forestry 1861-1961,* vol. II, Issued on the Occasion of the Celebration of Indian Forest century, 18th Nov. 1861, FRI, Dehradun, pp. 91-2.
76. Hazrat, op. cit., f. 9a.
77. Ibid., p. 52.
78. Ibid., p. 56.
79. Tapan Raychaudhari and Irfan Habib, eds., *The Cambridge Economic History of India,* vol. I: *c.* 1200-*c.* 1750, Cambridge: Cambridge University Press, 1982, p. 214.
80. Ibid., p. 223.
81. Butter, op. cit., p. 58.
82. Ibid., p. 57-8.
83. Ibid., p. 9.
84. Ibid., p. 18.
85. Hazrat, op. cit., pp. 57-8. The tables contain information about several other crops, but entries are provided against the last column only for the crops listed in our table.
86. Butter, op. cit., p. 16.
87. Ibid., p. 9

88. Albert T. Walker, *Memoirs of the Indian Metrological Department (from Records up to 1920)*, vol. XXIII, pt. VII, Calcutta, 1924.
89. Butter, op. cit., p. 16.
90. S.Z.H. Jafri, 'Agrarian Condition of Awadh under the Mughal and Nawab Wazir' (unpublished doctoral thesis), Aligarh Muslim University, Aligarh, 1985, p. 10.
91. Montgomery Martin, vol. II, p. 66.
92. Hazrat, op. cit., f. Aa. b
93. Jafri, *Agrarian Condition of Awadh*, op. cit., p. 13.
94. Ibid., p. 15.
95. W.H. Laurance, The Kingdom of Oude', *Calcutta Review*, pt. III, 1845, p. 382.
96. Agricultural Statistics of British India, 1885-6.
97. *Abul Fazl, Ain-i-Akbari*, vol. I, ed. Blochmann, Calcutta, 1877, pp. 354-6.
98. Agricultural Statistics op. cit.
99. *Ain-i-Akbari*, vol. I, op. cit., p. 433.
100. Ibid., p. 433.
101. Hazrat, op. cit., f. 126.
102. Agricultural Statistics, op. cit., p. 26.
103. Ibid., p. 26.
104. Agricultural Statistics, op. cit.
105. The peasants who carried on garden cultivation were mostly Kachis, Morais, Kunjra and Luniya or Muniya. They raised almost every vegetable on the, richest soil immediately around the village, in enclosed and reserved fields: Gardens cultivation needed much manuring, the land around the village, was very fertile in having 'natural waste. See Butter, p. 69; Sleeman I, pp. 125-6.
106. Agricultural Statistics, op. cit.
107. Irfan Habib, 'Colonization of Indian Economy', *Social Scientist*, no. 22, 1992.
108. Khaif-i-Gorakhpur, op. cit., f. 12 a.
109. Butter, op. cit., p. 61.
110. Thornton, op. cit., pp. 28-9.
111. Sleeman, I, op. cit., pp. 162-3.
112. Agricultural Statistics, op. cit.
113. Butter, op. cit., p. 76.
114. Ibid., p. 77.
115. Butter, op. cit., p. 65.
116. Ibid., p. 64.
117. Ibid., p. 65-6.
118. Ibid., p. 64.

119. Ibid., p. 63.
120. *Ain-i-Akbari* I, op. cit., p. 433; Sujan Rai Khattri, *Khulastut Tawarikh*, tr. Sir J.N. Sarkar in *India of Aurangzeb*, Calcutta, 1901, p. 45.
121. *Khulastut Tawarikh*, op. cit., sp. 10.
122. Butter, op. cit., p. 48.
123. *Ain-i-Akbari*, vol. I, op. cit., p. 433; *Khulastut Tawarikh*, op. cit., p. 45.
124. Ibid., p. 10.
125. Butter, op. cit., p. 48.

CHAPTER 5

Ecological Change and the Calamitous Events of North India: A Historical Overview

INTRODUCTION

This chapter examines the ecological concerns in north India because of natural resource exploitation. To comprehend the environmental change that occurred between 1556 and 1860 it is essential to envisage a global climate anomaly in Europe in the seventeenth century. Besides, this chapter will emphasize human ecology, which denotes the relationship between human groups and their physical environment. Various historical and scientific evidence clearly shows that climate played a role in seventeenth-century Europe. The hardcore historical and collaborative evidence showed that it went through an inactivity in the latter half of the seventeenth century. In contrast to the European situation, the Mughal state arguably thrived during the same period. The Mughal period reached its territorial expansion, and characterized as a tightly-knit and bureaucratically robust kind of state. So, it doesn't mean that India did not experience global climate change. The question is how Indian agriculture got affected over a period because of the global climate anomaly.

The seventeenth-century document suggested that the sun's energy has diminished and its energy is reduced, which led to the Little Ice

Age in European history. During the coldest phase of Ice Age, there are indications that the average winter temperature in Europe and North America was 6°C, lesser than the present temperature that we find in Europe. So, the entire northern hemisphere, especially Europe, had experienced the severity of winter. As a result, summers were cooler, winters lasted longer, and the summer months were shorter. There are records that suggest that the summers were often very cool, and it was not only cool but also wet. When this phenomenon took many years it led to the shortening of agricultural months in Europe, which led to the seventeenth-century crisis.

LITTLE ICE AGE: A DEBATE BETWEEN GEOFFREY PARKER AND DAGOMAR DEGROOT

We know many historians talked about the seventeenth-century crisis climate, as it was an essential factor that historians have thoroughly researched and proposed to be one of the key factors in the seventeenth-century turmoil that we have read about. One historian named Geoffrey Parker looked at this 'maunder minimum'[1] phenomenon, the global cooling phenomena, from a global perspective. In his book *Global Crisis: War, Climate Change and Catastrophe in the Seventeenth Century,* he blames seventeenth-century cooling as the cause of catastrophes worldwide. When he mentions all this, he also mentions the Indian subcontinent. He says that the seventeenth-century period was a crisis worldwide because of the seventeenth-century climate changes. His central argument in his book is that the cooler conditions led to different crop failures all around the globe, and he also says that there was the failure of the States because of this lesser revenue coming to the State. He also points out that wars became more frequent during that period. The seventeenth century was when other parts of the globe experienced wars worldwide.[2] In India, a drought followed by floods killed over a million people in Gujarat between 1627 and 1630. A vicious war in the Mughal Empire intensified the impact of another drought between 1658 and 1662.[3]

Parker appropriates the term to refer to climate conditions between the 1610s and the great winter of 1708-9. In this period, he argues, three natural forces combined to generate cooler temperatures and more significant climatic variability, reduced solar energy reaching the earth (the result of an interruption in the ordinary course of sunspot cycles), increased volcanic activity, which periodically intensified this cooling process, and greater frequency of the El-Nino-Southern Oscillation, which disrupted Asian monsoon and North American rainfall and, perhaps, intensified volcanic activity. As a result, almost every decade experienced a 'blocked climate' of two or more years of frigid winters and excessive rain or severe drought. These climatic insults generated the episodes of distress that stand at the heart of Geoffrey Parker's work.

Recently, another environmental historian, Dagomar Degroot has emerged. He has written a fascinating book, *Frigid Golden Age,* Degroot although is very against such kind of sweeping generalization that, this man Geoffery Parker has done and he says that this kind of generalizations cannot be done for the entire globe and Degroot is quite right, in fact he thinks that the economic implications of the Ice Age were very complex.[4] Now, his work is particularly useful, although it mainly focuses on the Dutch Republic and does not discuss other regions in detail. However, he does highlight some interesting points on why the Dutch Republic prospered. In contrast, the other European countries were not growing; they faced a crisis. So, he said that there cannot be climate change and cannot be the reason for the problem worldwide. So, different parts of the world would have other implications. The Little Ice Age also coincides with the maritime expansion of Europe in the Indian Ocean and the creation of the Colonial Empire. So, we find that other different colonial empires also prospered. There was some conflict between these colonial empires for the dominance of the Indian Ocean.

EVIDENCE OF CLIMATIC AND ENVIRONMENTAL CHANGE IN INDIA

As part of historical research, it is exciting to investigate this kind of climate anomaly that could impact India. So, the question that comes before us is, did it have a similar impact on the tropical region like India or any other South Asian region? We have ocean currents and oceanic condensations; there are changes in the monsoon patterns the Indian Ocean. It leads to the succession of different climate events. Today, we read about the El Nino phenomena and the La Lina. All these oceanic activities are there. Research has shown that these oceanic phenomena have affected the Indian monsoon, which the Mughals considered the backbone of Indian agriculture. Agriculture was one of the primary sources of state revenue and the oceanic phenomena that had significant implications on the Indian monsoon. Many scientists have proven the effect of the El Nino phenomena, and El Nino has been a detrimental factor to Indian agriculture because it disturbs the Indian monsoon.

In the seventeenth century, many El Nino episodes occurred, and different scientists confirmed this through different ways of interpreting those periods. So, they have used various logbooks of the descriptions given by the moving ships in the oceans, and they say that there were twice as many El Nino episodes in the seventeenth century. Usually, warm ocean conditions arise along the tropical west coast of South America. Because the entire ocean is connected, a phenomenon happening on the western coast of America can affect the Indian Ocean. So, it is a phenomenon of the rising surface temperature of the Pacific Ocean, which causes the flopping of the rainfall in India, and this has been proven in the logbooks of the British ships. Each of these ships was supposed to maintain the logbooks. If we examine all these, they would suggest that the monsoon was very irregular between the period 1550 to 1590, and the ratio of drought occurrences was much higher during these years. There is evidence suggesting that there was a possibility of one drop every three years. This gradually came down to one drop every six years in the second half of the seventeenth century, but in the second half of the seventeenth century, we observed that these drops were continuous for two years. So there is a drop taking place in one particular year, it continues in the second year, and this frequency of double drops is happening so much in the second half of the seventeenth century. This means that during this period of the second-half of the seventeenth century frequent El Nino phenomena, recorded during the second half of the seventeenth century, led to the decline of the Indian monsoon.

Based on the empirical data of this kind of frequency of drops or the rain failure in the second half of the seventeenth century, we can assume perhaps this might have affected the state in terms of revenue.

So, if we believe the Mughal documented accounts have given a different and contrary picture, for instance, if we read the Mughal Shah Jahan's account, who ruled from 1627 to 1658, it provides another view altogether. It says that the Mughal Empire was prospering during those days. It is also true because he could not have undertaken massive construction projects if he did not have such enormous revenue as the Taj Mahal, the Lal Qila that he constructed and Shahjahanabad.[5] So, this was not possible without massive revenue at his disposal. When he made Shahjahanabad the new capital city, Shahjahanabad was arguably the only capital city in the world in the mid-seventeenth century. Many of the accounts of that time mentioned that not only in the Mughal documents but even travellers who came during the reign of Shah Jahan also noted that the empire was a vast empire with a massive length in terms of territories.[6] When they talk about these immense territories, they say that it had given them a tremendous amount of income in terms of agricultural revenue.

One of the travellers of that time Withington, wrote in the mid-seventeenth century that the Mughals had ruled the area, which was almost half of the size of Europe. So, one of the added knowledge for the Mughals was that it had a vast area that they controlled and had an immense peasant population that lived in a vast fertile plain. The fertile land they possessed now had extended from the Indus to the Ganga basin down to Bengal. If we look at the Mughal accounts, they also glorify the vast extent of the Mughal Empire, but we have to take such descriptions with a pinch of salt.

Such documentary evidence has influenced many recent writings. One of the books which has become very popular in terms of global history is Victor Lieberman's *Strange Parallels*. He used two phrases in that book; he calls this a protected zone and the exposed zones. He kept the European countries in the category of the protected zone, whereas South Asia, India, he put in the category of the exposed zone. According to him, the exposed zone has been called the exposed zone because it was a vast stretch of Indo-Gangetic plain, easy to invade by the Mongols whose chief strength lay in the cavalry.[7] This kind of sweeping generalization for the entire Indo-genetic zone plane by Victor Lieberman is not correct. Still, looking at the geography of the stretch of land in the Indo-Gangetic area that the Mughals possessed, there were geographical abstractions and rivers. So, this did not allow the Mughal rulers to have firmer control over the region.

However, we must acknowledge that the most interesting aspect is that the three rulers of seventeenth century, Jahangir, Shah Jahan and Aurangzeb, ruled over a vast stretch of territories. The title of their name itself manifested the great conquerors of the world. These three Mughal emperors took was in the seventeenth century that all these Mughal rulers had to maintain a vast military to lionize their image as world conquerors. This was not possible without invading far-off territories.[8]

The shortening of the monsoon period benefited the Mughals, and all the three Mughal emperors went on campaigns every year; if we read the Mughal sources, it would be suggested that they would all proceed after the South-East monsoon had receded and they had returned to the capital ahead of the onset of the annual monsoon. Their travel radius was also very calculated because the Mughals travelled all the time with all their paraphernalia and with their entire courts. So, they could not move more than 4 or 5 miles a day. So, looking at the kind of movement that the Mughals had in the seventeenth century, we can see that it was essential for the Mughal rulers to travel to these far-off areas, control these territories, and bring revenue from those subjugated areas. We also need to look at the period of Shah Jahan and Aurangzeb from the point of view of frequent monsoon failures because of the El Nino phenomenon. During that period, many Mughals' accounts had suggested monsoon failures. So, there were failures of rainfall from 1630 to 1632, then similarly from 1658 to 1660, there were continuous failures for two years, and again it happened in 1685 and 1687. All these failures produced widespread famine. This has been well documented in the Mughal accounts. The most affected area by the monsoon failures was the western parts of India, particularly Gujarat and a considerable part of the Ganga Plain. Ganga Plain is the area from where a significant amount of revenue came for the Mughals.

One of the worst catastrophes in the 1630s continued even in 1631 and 1632. There was virtually no rain that had taken place. Logbooks show that these dry periods coincided with El Nino events in the Pacific Ocean. So, 1630 to 1632 was when the El

Nino effect took place. Mughal accounts and European travellers both noted that this period was marked by rain failures. Peter Mundy talked about the death of law's massive population wipeout because of the famines that had taken place.[9]

When Shah Jahan faced climate-induced challenges, he immediately responded to the disaster as a responsible ruler. He took a series of measures when famines took place; he established the soup kitchen and the arms house as recorded in the Mughal documents. Shah Jahan fully understood the possibility that these peasants who could not cultivate their land and the peasants were the backbones of the state's revenue when the good monsoon years would come. So, the question arises: how was it possible for Shah Jahan to spend a considerable amount of money on his glorification? When we say glorification, it means the amount of money spent on the Peacock Throne, the amount spent on the construction of the Taj Mahal, and the structure of the Shalimar Garden. All these vast expenses were not possible without the invasion of the new territories. Abdul Hamid Lahori has devoted well over half of his pages and images to the campaigns of Shah Jahan forces. Shah Jahan was able to seize Kandhar; he went to Afghanistan and crossed the Khyber Pass. There is evidence suggesting that he failed in the Bulk region of Afghanistan because of the severe winters in that part of Afghanistan. Massive snowfalls were happening in the 1640s, reducing his campaign season.[10]

When Aurangzeb became the Mughal ruler, there were other continuous famines from 1658 to 1660 and monsoon failures were cited as the reason. The prices of goods increased in Delhi and different other parts of India. Aurangzeb is also one ruler who is said to have abolished many of the taxes to give relief to the hardship faced by the people. Nevertheless, the fact remains that the State has been met by these challenges of climate and rainfall failures, so perhaps the treasury of the State would be affected; if we read the sources of that time, it would suggest that the revenue of Aurangzeb treasury fell almost by 20 per cent during these continuous famines from 1658 to 1660. It has been recognized that famines and natural calamities had a bothersome effect on the Mughal Indian economy[11] with the development of the market and the cash nexus and abundant harvest and the resulting fall in prices could equally appear as a 'calamity.[12]

However, Shireen Moosvi has argued that the 1658 to 1660 period crisis was a watershed for the Mughal expansion and decline in the eighteenth century.[13] When faced with these challenges, a ruler like Aurangzeb had to enhance his revenue to sustain his empire. So, to meet state expenditure, Aurangzeb followed a policy of expanding the Mughal territories as his predecessor did. He remained to campaign in the Marathwada region for many years.[14]

When the Mughals faced climate challenges, they took different other measures. Their vast army gave them the power to expand into new territories, which they were forced to replenish their treasury during financial crises. It could be possible that the Maunder minimum and the climate changes had not very similar impacts on India. In contrast to the European situation during the same century, the Mughal treasury increased during the same period. The Mughal Empire is considered the most prosperous. Shah Jahan and Aurangzeb periods are considered to be the magnificence of the Mughal Empire taking place.

POSSIBLE IMPACTS OF CLIMATE CHANGE IN INDIA

The period of the great Mughals was not immune from natural catastrophes such as famines, inundation, epidemics, earthquakes fires, etc., which had a baneful effect on the people and the society of that period. These natural calamities occurred because of various factors such as failure of monsoon, excessive rainfall, flood, fire, pestilence, earthquake and epidemics. They brought with them a series of miseries for millions of people, resulting in severe agricultural depletion and disruptions in trade and commerce, which led to a significant reduction in production.

Besides the effect of global climate anomaly, severe environmental damage and an increased malfunction of ecosystems sometimes appeared in the tracks of European expansion to Asia and America. In the 'New World', it has been argued that the Spanish and Portuguese arrival, followed by North Europeans, saw the almost total collapse of a hitherto broadly balanced ecological environment. New species of animals, plants, bacteria and viruses, which the Europeans both wittingly and unwittingly brought, caused a far-reaching ecological transformation. The death on a massive scale of plants, animals and people was an unavoidable consequence.[15]

Not only did the developing ecological consciousness of the 1970 expressed vehement and comprehensive criticism of the consequences of dependent commercial systems after his stay in South America (1795-9), Alexander von Humboldt drew attention to uncontrolled colonial commerce, which functioned at the expense of the climate, the water supply of entire regions, and ultimately the indigenous population. When Humboldt wanted to travel to India at the beginning of the nineteenth century, the EIC Court of Directors refused him entry, rightly fearing that he might come across the first signs of fundamental deterioration of the environment and eco-systems.[16]

Floods and famines were always counted as natural calamities. A brief study of their occurrences in North India:

Flood

In 1658, the first year of Aurangzeb's reign, the water in the Ganges and the Jamuna at Allahabad rose so high that it submerged nearly the entire town. The rising waters killed many people. By the end of October 1701, on account of the tidal effects, about fifteen villages on the coast of Masulipatam were destroyed. Niccolo Manucci, referring to this catastrophe, says, 'I have always noticed in this country that when such disasters occur, they are a prelude to war and coming misfortunes. Thus, after the inundation at the above town in 1680, we saw the destruction of the kingdom of Golconda and Bijapur, a calamity which put the people to extreme misery.'[17]

Allahabad suffered another severe flood in August 1671. Sir John Marshall, while describing it, writes, 'At Elllahabsse (Allahabad) which is from Bonorras (Benaras) towards Agra 3 days' journey, towards the latter end... In August 1671, there was a significant flood because the Ganges and Gemini (Jamuna) overflowed, which met there. They overflowed in the night so much and encompassed the town so that few could escape. Many went to the castle to preserve themselves.

Famines

There is no direct reference to famines in Mughal India during the reigns of Babur and Humayun. But during this period, famines occurred in Kashmir and Vijayanagara, which did not form part of the Mughal Empire. In 1534, during the reign of Muhammad Shah, king of Kashmir, there occurred an acute famine because of the failure of crops in the Kashmir valley. The foodstuffs became so scarce that a *khari* of paddy could not be procured even for 10,000 *dinars.*[18]

Akbar's accession to the throne in AD 1556 synchronized with the occurrence of a famine, which was exceptionally severe. Abul Fazl writes, 'The capital was devastated, and mortality was enormous.'[19] In 1556, the whole country presented a desolate look. Two years of continuous warfare after the death of Islam Shah, whose reign preceded that of Akbar, resulted in complete political and economic confusion. A terrible famine devastated many of its cities and towns, especially those of Delhi and Agra. The scarcity of food was so great that men took to eating even one another. Some would join together, carry off a solitary man, and make them their food.[20] Some other events, too, made the prevailing tension and confusion all the more severe. Abdul Qadir Badaoni, who was an eyewitness to the famine, says, 'Men ate their kind, and the appearance of the famished sufferers was so hideous that one could scarcely bear to look at them.... The country was desert, and no husbandmen remained to till the ground.' Badaoni's description seems to be highly exaggerated, the horrors of the famine the less terrible. Abul Fazl also describes the horrors of the famine, saying that in his family of seventy persons, only one *seer* of grain was supplied. His father boiled this grain in water and distributed a few grains with a cupful of boiled water, which was the only meal for the entire day and night.[21]

This famine occurred because of failure of the monsoon and the consequent destruction of crops. V.A. Smith says, 'The occurrence of famines resulting from the absolute non-existence of crops was inevitable in a country where the possibility of sowing and reaping of crops depended upon seasonal rains which often failed and where the masses of the population had been impoverished.'[22] The *suba* of Allahabad suffered severe famines from the years 1595-8. V. Smith says, 'At this time, the whole of Hindustan or Northern India suffered from a terrible famine, which lasted continuously for three or four years, beginning in 1595-96. A kind of plague also added to the horrors of this period.'[23]

In AD 1614-15, during the reign of Jahangir, a severe famine occurred in Punjab.[24] It ravaged Punjab as far as east of Delhi. But Moreland maintains that the drought was localized in Punjab.[25] The famine of 1618-19 spread in the Deccan and on the Coromandel Coast. During Shah Jahan's reign, a few famines occurred. In the early years of his reign, i.e. 1630-1, a severe famine occurred, affecting Golkunda, Ahmadnagar, Gujarat and some parts of Malwa. Referring to this famine, Abdul Hamid Lahori says, 'The regions above suffered terribly from this famine of AD 1630. For twenty years, they remained in deplorable conditions with a falling revenue demand, which was still far more than the collection.'[26]

TABLE 5.1: FAMINES DURING THE SEVENTEENTH CENTURY

Year	*Areas Affected*	*Cause*	*Mortality*	*Remarks*
1613-14 and 1614-15	Panjab, Sirhind, Delhi, Doab, Mewar.	Drought	Severe, mainly from the bubonic plague, which followed the scarcity	
1622	Vijayanagara Empire	Drought	Not stated	Parents sell children owing to starvation
1630-2	Gujarat, Sindh, Deccan and Coromandel	Drought in 1630, followed by unseasonal rains, 1631 and accentuated by attacks on crops by nice and locusts	Heavy toll and large-scale depopulation. There were 2 million deaths in Gujarat and 1 million in Ahmadanagar and 30,000 dead reported in Surat	Even cannibalism was reported
1634	Malabar	Drought and civil wars	Not stated	–
1636-7	Panjab	Drought	-do-	–

1640	Kashmir	Excessive rain and flood	-do-	–
1641-2	Kashmir	Excessive rain	-do-	Thirty thousand people migrate from Kashmir to Lahore
1642	Coromandel and Orissa	Drought	-do-	–
1644	Agra	Drought	-do-	–
1646	Punjab and vicinity of Agra	Drought	-do-	–
1646-7	Coromandel	–	Severe: 15,000 die in Punjab town, the same number in St. Thome and 4,000 in Madras	Parents sell children
1647	Marwar	Drought	Considerable depopulation	
1650	North India	Drought	Not stated	–
1651	Punjab (Lahore and Multan provinces) and Kashmir	Drought, followed by excessive rain	-do-	–
1655	Balaghat (Deccan)	Kharif crop damaged by late monsoon	-do-	–
1658-9	Sindh	Drought	Very severe	Accompanied by plague.
1659-61	Gujarat, Punjab, Agra, Malwa.	Drought and warfare Drought?	Extensive distress	–

(Contd.)

TABLE 5.1: (Contd.)

Year	*Areas Affected*	*Cause*	*Mortality*	*Remarks*
1662	Dhaka	Interference in transport	Not stated	
1663	Gujarat	Drought	90,720 reported dead in Patna alone	

Source: This table is based on Irfan Habib, *Agrarian System of Mughal India*, 2nd edn., pp. 112-22, supplemented by a new survey of the source material.

In 1647, the rains failed, causing a famine in some parts of Rajputana. On account of human mortality and the exodus of the people, those areas become wholly depopulated, deserted and impassable.[27] Referring to natural calamities in Rajputana, Col Tod spoke, 'There was no longer a distinction of caste, and the Shudra and the Brahmin were indistinguishable. To appease their hunger, people consumed fruits, flowers, vegetables and even stripped trees of their bark. Men ate men. Cities were left depopulated. Families died out, fish became extinct, and all hope extinguished.'[28]

Bihar witnessed a severe famine in 1670-1. This famine broke out in October 1670 and lasted until November 1671.[29] It covered a wide area. Patna and its suburbs were severely affected. The famine affected the areas extending beyond Banaras; to the east of Patna, and the tracts lying up to Rajmahal were in its grip.[30] This famine had occurred because of the failure of crops resulting from the drought of 1670.[31] That year, there was practically no rain in south Bihar. The famine brought untold miseries to the people.

Another effect of this devastating famine was the large-scale migration of people from Patna and its suburbs to other places. Most survivors left Patna and went to Deccan, in search of employment and food.[32]

Between 1765 and 1860, the country saw twelve famines and four severe scarcities over ninety years. From 1860 to 1906, scarcities were widespread in one part of the country or another, numbering twenty in all over forty-nine years.[33] According to many reports from the Famine Commission and the *United Provinces District Gazetteer*, famine increased under British rule, and several famines occurred in north India and Awadh. The country's first famine occurred in 1802-

4. The Bombay Presidency, Hyderabad and the North-Western Provinces were all severely hit. Awadh deteriorated severely due to exorbitantly high land tax demand and insufficient rainfall.[34] The drought returned in 1805-6 because there was no rain until the middle of August. The worst famine of the first half of the nineteenth century struck in 1837-8, affecting many of the doab area and upper India. It affected the entire country between Allahabad and Delhi and Rajasthan's neighbouring states as far west as Jaipur.[35] The famine affected an area of around 11,300 sq. miles, with 56,000 sq. miles falling within British control. According to Colonel Baird Smith's estimate, there were 2,86,00,000 people affected, with about 8,00,000 deaths due to starvation. Mr. Jhon Lawrence's statement might also evaluate it. 'I have never seen such destruction as that which is now spread across the *parganas* of Hodar & Palwal,' wrote the author. In several places, including Kanpur, Fatehpur, and Agra, dead bodies were lying on the roadside, not eaten by wild animals.[36] It was caused by the total failure of rains in 1837 after a series of bad seasons but was worsened by an excessive revenue demand. Baird Smith correctly observed that 'the native society had to face the 1873 famine debilitated by a fiscal system that was oppressive in its influence. The agrarian class was in a state of great unrest. The complete failure of rainfall in 1837, following a series of terrible seasons, was the reason, but an excessive revenue demand exacerbated it. 'The native society had to face the 1873 famine crippled by a fiscal system that was repressive and dismal in its influence,' Baird Smith correctly observed. As a result, the agrarian class became increasingly agitated.[37]

During the rainy season of 1838, the famine persisted. The government offered low-wage work as alleviation, but money was in short supply. As a result, the government halted work during the rainy season, leaving thousands without jobs.[38] A public charity was entrusted with providing gratuitous help. In February 1838, a relief association was established in Agra, and work on a brick-walled asylum was begun. Tickets were required for entry, and cooked food was distributed to the poor people.[39]

It can be clearly understood from the above table that the famines, from time to time, introduced into the stolid isolation of agricultural production a terrible element of fluidity and devastation. If there had been nothing else, this alone would have sufficed to explain the migratory characteristics of the peasantry, which were such a marked feature of the rural life of the time.

Earthquakes

Earthquakes have been documented throughout history, going back to the Harappan period. Even the Vedic people were aware of natural disasters such as earthquakes. The seismic cloud hypothesis and earthquake indicators are discussed in the 32nd chapter of the *Brihat Samhita*. The first recorded earthquake in the subcontinent occurred in the Delhi region in CE 893. Later, medieval chroniclers provided detailed accounts of the numerous earthquakes that struck Assam and Kashmir throughout the Sultanate and Mughal periods, making these events particularly well documented. Around 250 earthquakes were recorded in the region between CE 1800 and 2008.[40]

On 6 July 1505, the earthquake that struck Agra was so powerful that mountains shook, and tall buildings collapsed. Delhi, Agra, and villages across northern India felt tremors that day.[41] Another event occurred during King Shamsha Shah's reign (1537-9). Another historian, Suka, has also mentioned this event. J.C. Dutt (1887), a nineteenth-century historian, has also confirmed it. Another source, the *bakshi* of the kingdom, Nizamuddin Ahmad, has described it in *Tabaqat-i-Akbari*. This significant incident is also recorded in *Tabaqat-i-Akbari*, *Tarikh-i-Firishtah* by Ferishta. Muhammad Qasim Hindu Shah Astarabadi is another source. Haider Malik Chandma Raisul Malik further confirms it in *Tarikh-i-Kashmir*.[42]

Epidemics

Though the information regarding epidemics under the first two Mughal Emperors, Babur and Humayun, is insufficient, and no generalization can be made on its basis, it is certain that the country was not entirely immune to the occasional epidemics and pestilences. Babur writes, 'The year (1526) was scorching, violent and destructive; winds struck people down in heaps together, masses began to die off.'[43] While staying in Sambhal during Babur's reign, Humayun, his eldest son, fell ill. Babur brought him to Agra by boat so that the court physicians could attend to him, but the latter declared the case hopeless. Babur also had severe attacks of malaria. As his condition grew worse, Humayun's health improved.[43] In AD 1548, a severe plague struck Sindh, claiming the lives of many, including Sheikh Ali.

In AD 1556, during the reign of Akbar, most of the cities of northern India were affected by the plague, and many people died of it.[44] In the first quarter of AD 1616, the plague broke out in some places of northern India. Gradually, it became more violent in some *parganas* of Punjab and spread up to Lahore, as a result of which a large number of people gradually lost their lives. Then it proceeded towards Sirhind and through the Doab, reaching as far as Delhi and the surrounding areas. Most of the villages and *parganas* had become depopulated.[45]

During this period, the plague made its appearance here and there at the commencement of winter and disappeared in the hot season. Sometimes, indeed, as in 1617-18, its severity would decline for a time at the beginning of winter but reviewed again in the spring. In 1618-19 it devastated Agra and the neighbouring areas. It did not spread further than Ahmadabad. Curiously enough, Fatehpur Sikri, only about 25 miles ahead of Agra, remained entirely untouched. The complete desertion of the inhabitants' neighbouring areas probably saved India's old metropolis from its ravages.[46] In January AD 1617, Sir Thomas Roe noted that the number of plague victims in Agra had come down to one hundred per day.[47] The ravages of the epidemic in 1618-19 continued all through the spring of 1619.[48] In their reports to the emperor, the imperial officers in Agra estimated the daily mortality in the metropolis to average around one hundred, which can be considered accurate for that year.

In AD 1575, Abul Fazl recorded a devastating event. Malaria had turned into an epidemic, killing many people across the country. This disease spread rapidly, affecting most parts of the nation. He gave lists of officers who died of it at Gaur after their return from Orissa. The most important among them were Mirza Khan and Haji Khan Sistani.[49] In 1618, malaria swept through Ahmadabad during Jahangir's stay and visit to that city and caused heavy mortality among the Europeans and the Indians.[50] Anyway, the plague at Ahmedabad was mysterious. It was characterized by very high temperature and the appearance of large dark blisters on the victim's body. Death took place in a few hours, even the small English community lost seven. The emperors, Jahangir and Shah Jahan contacted the disease and could recover after a protracted recovery.[51]

During the reign of Shah Jahan, when a severe famine was ravaging the whole of the Deccan, the people's suffering was further aggravated by the outbreaks of plague, in the famine's wake. The epidemic practically depopulated the Deccan, and the inhabitants were compelled to take shelter in northern India.[52]

On the other hand, cholera caused significant mortality from Guptas through the Mughals; there were ample opportunities for infested wayfarers. It is a deadly water-borne disease, but apparently, it did not become uniformly endemic or frequently epidemic in Punjab and some other locales. Cholera proliferated there systematically only after the mid-nineteenth century. There was no lethal mutation of the microbe, no radical collapse of living standards and no dissemination of a dangerous vector paralleling the spread of *A. philipinnesis* and *A. maculates,* which propagated deadly *P. falciparum* epidemics of malaria. Instead, ecological disruption significantly continued.[53]

MEASURES ADOPTED TO FIGHT THE DEVASTATION CAUSED BY NATURAL CALAMITIES

It is beyond the power of man to have complete control over these natural calamities and save living beings from the irreparable devastations which come in their wake. However, the ruling monarch believed it was his sacred duty to do his best to save the people from the misery caused by such natural calamities.

The chief emergency relief measures adopted by Indian rulers for the benefit of the people included: free distribution of food grains, opening of free kitchens and grain godowns, remitting or reducing taxes, providing advances, constructing or repairing roads, creating irrigation facilities (such as digging and repairing of canals, ponds, wells, tanks, etc.) setting up embankments, annulling loans given by rich bankers to the poor during famines, making administrative changes, the introduction of new economic measures, bringing wasteland under cultivation, increasing the pay of the soldiers, plantation of the garden and planting trees on roadsides, creating jungle enclosures for providing firewood and arranging for the migration of people to areas comparatively richer in food and other necessaries of life.

Babur and Humayun, the first two emperors of the Mughal dynasty, were primarily focused on founding and consolidating their empires. A result, they could not fully address the internal problems of the state. Emperor Akbar was more solicitous of the welfare of the suffering masses than any other previous Mughal monarch. At times of drought and famine, he issued detailed instructions to his officers to grant remissions on lands newly brought under cultivation and send regular reports about the living conditions of the people, crops and local prices.[54] In 1583, Akbar opened three free kitchens outside the capital. One supplying food to the Hindus was called *Dharmapurna,* the second supplying food to the Muslims was known as *Khairpura,* and the third supplying food to the *jogis* was named *Jogipura.*[56] During this famine, additional kitchens were opened to feed the poor, the indigent, and the beggars and the rich were entrusted with their management.

The scarcity of rain caused a shortage of foodstuffs and a consequent rise in the prices, making life hard for the poor. Officers were appointed in every district to give relief to the poor. We learn from Abul Fazl that Akbar made the most commendable effort to relieve the people's distress during the Punjab famine of 1595-8, when Sheikh Farid Bukhari, a man of generally generous disposition, was put on special duty to superintend the relief measures. Shared kitchens were started. Experienced officers were dispatched in every direction to distribute food to the starving masses.[55]

The reign of Jahangir was also not immune from famines. In AD 1614-16, a famine occurred, considerably affecting Punjab, the areas adjoining Delhi and a portion of southern India.[56] In 1618-19, another famine devastated the Coromandel Coast. This famine, too, was very terrible, and the people suffered very great hardship.[57]

Jahangir did little to ease the suffering caused by the famines and other devastating havoc. He led an easy life and was not serious about helping the distressed people of his realm.

Shah Jahan also adopted various measures to fight the famines during his reign. In the nineteenth year of Shah Jahan's reign (AD 1646), Punjab was hit by a famine occurring because of scanty rainfall. The severity of the situation forced some impoverished individuals to sell their children to avoid starvation. The emperor ordered that the government treasury pay these people the value of their children, alleviating their suffering and preventing separation from their families. Following the emperor's orders, ten free kitchens were established in the province to distribute cooked food. Sayyid Jalal was commissioned to allocate a sum of Rs. 10,000 to the poor. In February 1647, Shah Jahan sanctioned relief work in Punjab.[58]

In Mughal India, the failure of rain was the most important cause of famine. So, the Mughals paid sufficient attention to irrigation works. They constructed wells, tanks, reservoirs and canals to irrigate agricultural land.[59] Babur has given a graphic description of irrigation in India from wells, which is true even today.[60] Humayun's concern for the farming problems is apparent because one important department of the state was exclusively devoted to land affairs.[61] Akbar constructed the lake at Fatehpur Sikri, which was 7 *kos* in circumference for irrigation purposes. Extending from Sikri to Bharatpur, the marks of its embankment can be seen even to this day.[62] In the twenty-second year of his reign, when Akbar returned from Ajmer, it was brought to his notice that the country was wasting because of the reservoirs' terrible condition. His Majesty himself visited the neighbourhood and had the reservoirs renovated immediately.[63]

Although, their magnificent building development marked the period of Shah Jahan's reign, that, they also paid great attention to the development of agriculture. A *pargana,* which yielded an only revenue of 3,00,000 dams in Akbar's time, began to yield 7,00,000 dams during his reign. This was due to improved irrigation, besides the enhanced rate of revenue and other *abawabs*. Aurangzeb's reign saw canals provide one-third of the country's irrigation. In one of his *farmans,* Aurangzeb instructed his *karoris* to get the old and disused wells renovated and sink new ones.[64]

POSSIBLE EFFECT OF CLIMATE CHANGE ON AGRICULTURE

The pre-colonial period was characterized by an agricultural society, with agriculture being the primary sector, heavily dependent on monsoon rains. Hence, the impact of climate change on agriculture is very crucial. Indeed, agriculture during medieval times was affected by natural evolution in climate rather than anthropogenic. However, the role of humans in inducing climate change has been visible since the late nineteenth century.

Almost every calamity ruins agriculture in one way or another. When drought occurs, the land becomes dry and barren, forests lose their cover, pools, tanks and lakes dry up. All these lead to a significant decrease in agricultural production. When men and animals die in large numbers, agriculture is severely adversely. During an earthquake, vast tracts of land become useless for agricultural purposes. In times of drought, rivers, ponds and streams dry up, leaving the earth arid and barren. As a result, crops are badly damaged and food becomes scarce.

In 1556, when there was a monsoon failure in northern India, the country felt its devastating effects. Describing its horrors, Abul Fazl narrates how, owing to the acute scarcity of foodstuffs, only one *seer* of grain could be given to a family of seventy persons.[65]

During the reign of Jahangir, the drought that occurred in Punjab in AD 1614-15 adversely affected agriculture, damaged the crops, and created a great scarcity of food, which resulted in a famine.[66] Again, in 1630-1, during the early years of the reign of Shah Jahan, when there was a complete failure of rains,[67] crops were destroyed and articles of daily need almost vanished from the market.

In 1650, India faced a significant drought due to minimal rainfall across most regions. This hurt agriculture and the result was an acute scarcity of food grains.[68] Again, in 1658, want of rains made grains very scarce and dear in northern and central India.

Excessive rains were equally responsible for bringing about the disruption of agriculture, destruction of crops and scarcity of food stuffs. When there was severe and continuous rainfall in 1630-1, most of the crops that had survived the attack of pests were submerged under the flood's waters and were utterly destroyed, making the scarcity of foodstuffs all the more acute.[69] Again, in 1641, heavy and continuous rainfall destroyed the *share* crops in Kashmir, and consequently, there was a great scarcity of food.[70]

Furthermore, the late eighteenth and early nineteenth century was not limited to legal and administrative reforms to restore local society's outer casing. A comprehensive solution to agriculture's fragile state—dependent on the unpredictable monsoon—was sought through large-scale development of agricultural resources and improvements in distribution of the augmented product using the latest canal, road, and railway-building techniques. Apart from that, this environment was characterized by a significant regional disparity—in climate and soil condition between Doab and Bundelkhand, Awadh and the eastern North-West Provinces. Centuries of rapid and extensive deforestation, most noticeable in the Doab from the beginning of the nineteenth century, bared vast tracts to the weeping monsoon rains and the months of scorching summer sun that preceded them; centuries of persistent agricultural settlement had left their mark on the land pattern formed by ages' geomorphic processes.[71]

To Western observers, the monsoon's power over the land's life and death combined with the peasantry's powerlessness to control its course exemplified India's benighted state. The erratic nature with which monsoon anomalies interrupted agriculture further added to this image. Colonel Richard Baird Smith was impressed by 'the desolate dreariness of its appearance' when riding through the tahsils (sub-divisions) of Khair, Chandaus and Tappal of Aligarh district during the drought of 1860-1. Usually, it is fertile land, but when I travelled through it in March 1861, only a few scattered plots of culture reflected the large fields one was used to riding across. Moreover, the country appeared to be devoid of inhabitants and widespread emigration.[72] Eight months later, the landscape transformed. Good and timely rainfall had replaced the bare patches and stunted crops with the rich vegetation of promising *rabi* crops.[73]

Another far-reaching ecological consequence in the Doab areas was the harmful agricultural practices by the British, which dramatically affected the soil, the water supply, plants, animals and people. As a result, the Doab's sensitive ecological system, particularly the part south of Delhi as far as Kanpur, was permanently damaged during the first three decades of the nineteenth century. The move from food crops and sustainable farming to soil-intensive cash crop production and the clearance of extensive forest and grass jungle areas to extend the crop area was decisive. Furthermore, ravaged agricultural areas, salinization and severe erosion have led to desertification in large parts of the Doab.

Thus, it can be argued that temporal climate change is the leading cause of natural calamities in north India. Mishaps that occurred in the past have disrupted the ecosystem, which has proven to be significant curse for living beings. At times, their frequent occurrence brought changes the relationships among humans, animals and plants. For instance, the change in landscape and habitat loss combine, often leading to questions about settlement and migration for living creatures. Moreover, the spread of diseases like plague, cholera and diarrhea has often led to a high mortality rate, affecting the country's demographical structure. Furthermore, natural, calamities have resulted in the loss of precious biodiversity. On the other hand, the British forest policy also contributed to changes in the natural landscape of northern India, particularly in the Doab region of the United Provinces. As a result, soil erosion and deforestation became significant environmental issues in the Doab region.

NOTES

1. The Maunder Minimum occurred during a period of colder weather, implying that the lack of magnetic activity was coupled with a substantial reduction in the Sun's overall radiative output. From around AD 1650 to 1715, MM was a period of deficient solar activity.
2. For more detail, see Geoffrey Parker, *Global Crisis, War Climate Change and Catastrophe in the Seventeenth Century*, New York: Yale University Press, 2012, p. 07.
3. Ibid., p. xxii.
4. Dagomar Degroot, *The Frigid Golden Age: Climate Change, the Little Ice Age and the Dutch Republic 1560-1720,* Cambridge: Cambridge University Press, 2018, pp. 1-8.
5. Stanley Wolpert, *A New History of India,* New York: Oxford University Press, 1989, p. 45.

6. Peter Mundy, *The Travels of Peter Mundy, In Europe and Asia 1608-1667,* vol. II, London: Hakluyt Society, 1913, p. 197.
7. Victor Lieberman, *Strange Parallels Southeast Asia in Global Context, c. 800-1830,* vol. I, Cambridge: Cambridge University Press, 2003, pp. 92-3.
8. Patrick K. O' Brien, ed., *Oxford Atlas of World History,* New York: Oxford University Press, 1999, Sh. No. 16.
9. Lt Col Sir Richard Carnac Temple, ed., *The Travels of Peter Mundy, in Europe and Asia, 1608-1667,* vol. II, London: Hakluyt Society, 1907, pp. 42-5.
10. This piece of information has been extracted from the English translation version of Abdul Hamid Lahori, *Padshahnama,* New York: Cornell University Library, pp. 7-16.
11. W.H. Moreland, *From Akbar to Aurangzeb: A Study in Indian Economic History,* London: MacMillan, 1923, pp. 205-20.
12. Aurangzeb's *farman* to Rasikdas puts the fall in prices among calamities (*afat-i-arzani*). Texts in the *Journal of Asiatic Society of Bengal* (*JASB*), vol. II, 1906, pp. 223-35.
13. Shireen Moosvi, *People, Taxation and Trade in Mughal India,* Aligarh: Aligarh Historians Society Series, 2008, pp. 229-40.
14. Ibid., pp. 229-40.
15. Alfre W. Crosby, *Ecological Imperialism: The Biological Expansion of Europe, 900-1900,* Cambridge: Cambridge University Press, 1986, p. 443. He argues from the American perspective. It should not be forgotten that the plague which broke out in Europe in the mid-fourteenth century had moved slowly from the South Asian region and that Europeans had no immunity against this disease. Within a hundred years, the population of Europe was halved.
16. K. Biermann, *Miscellanea Humboldtiana Beitraege zur Alexander von Humboldt Forchung,* Berlin, 1990, p. 73.
17. Niccola Manucci, *Storia do Mogor or Mogul India (1653-1708),* vol. II, tr. William Irvine, London, 1907, p. 428.
18. Shukra & Prajabhatta, *Rajavalipatrika,* tr. Y.C. Dutta under the cation *Kings of Kashmir,* vol. III, pp. 373-4.
19. Abul Fazl, *Akbarnama,* vol. II, *tr.* H. Beveridge, pp. 55-7; Nizamuddin Ahmad, *The Tabaqat-i-Akbari,* tr. B. De, vol. I, p. 365; S.S. Kulshreshtha, *The Development of Trade and Industry under the Mughals,* p. 32.
20. *Akbarnama,* vol. II, op. cit., pp. 56-7.
21. Abul Fazl, *Ain-i-Akbari,* vol. III, tr. Jarrett & Sarkar, Chap. XIV, p. 489.
22. V.A. Smith, *Akbar: The Great Mughal,* Chapter X, Oxford: Oxford Clarendo Press, 1917, p. 259.
23. Ibid., p. 476.
24. Jahangir, *Tuzuk-i-Jahangiri,* vol. I, tr. Rogers and Beveridge, p. 49.
25. Edwards and Carrett, *Mughal Rule in India,* vol. II, Chapter II, Oxford: Oxford University Press, 1930, pp. 240-1.

26. Abdul Hamid Lahori, *Padshahnama,* vol. I, pp. 362-4.
27. William Foster, *Factory Records (1642-55),* p. 137.
28. Col. Tod, *Annals and Antiquities of Rajasthan,* II, p. 455.
29. John Marshal, *Notes and Observation in Bengal (1668-72),* pp. 149, 150 and 252.
30. Thomas Bowry, *A Geographical Account of the Countries Round the Bay of Bengal (1669-79),* p. 226.
31. Marshal, op. cit., p. 150.
32. Ibid., p. 125.
33. *District Gazetteer Uttar Pradesh,* ed. Balwant Singh, Allahabad, 1987, pp. 88-89; Report of the Indian Famine Commission (hereafter IFC), 1901, p. 1.
34. C.E.R. Girdlestone's Report on the Past Famines in North West Provinces, Allahabad, Government Press (Provincial) 1868, para 109.
35. Indian Famine Commission Report: 1880-85, New Delhi: Agricole Publication Academy, 1989, para 47.
36. R.C. Dutta, *Land Revenue & Famine in India,* New Delhi, 1985, p. 6-7.
37. Colonel Bird Smith's Report on the North-West Provinces Famine of 1860-61, dated 14 August 1861, paras 32 & 38.
38. Girdlestone's Report, op. cit., p. 47.
39. IFC Report 1880-85, op. *cit.,* pt. I, para 47.
40. Ranjan Chakrabarti, ed., *Critical Themes Environmental History of India,* Sage (ICHR), 2020, p. 378.
41. C.M. Agrawala, *Nature Calamities and the Great Mughals,* Bodh Gaya: Kanchan Publication, 1987, p. 22.
42. Chakrabarti, op. cit., p. 389.
43. Gulbadan Begum, *Humayun Nama,* tr. Mrs. Beveridge, pp. 104-5.
44. Sir Richard Burn, *The Cambridge History of India,* vol. IV, Cambridge: Cambridge University Press, 1937, p. 69, 112.
45. Edwards & Garrett, *Mughal Rule in India,* pp. 191-3; Motamid Khan, *Iqbalnama-i-Jahangiri,* pp. 88-9.
46. Jahangir, *Tuzuk-i-Jahangiri,* tr. Rogers, vol. I, p. 330; Elliot and Dowson, *The History of India as Told by its Own Historians,* vol. IV, pp. 405-6.
47. Sir Thomas Roe's Journal, *'Travels in India in the seventeenth Century',* London, 1873, pp. 307-8.
48. William Foster, *English Factories in India (1618-1621),* p. 479.
49. *Ain-i-Akbari,* vol. I, op. cit., pp. 334-6.
50. Edward and Garret, op. cit., pp. 191-3.
51. Haig and Burn, *The Cambridge History of India,* vol. IV, p. 166.
52. Foster, op. cit., p. 49.
53. Ira Klein, 'Imperialism, Ecology and Disease: Cholera in India, 1850-1950'. *The Indian Economic and Social History Review,* 31, 4 (1994), p. 496.

54. *Ain-i-Akbari,* vol. II, op. cit., p. 44.
55. Muhammad Akbar, *The Punjab Under the Mughals,* Lahore: Ripon Printing Press, 1945, p. 104.
56. Jahangir, *Tuzuk-i-Jahangiri,* vol I, tr. Rogers, p. 118.
57. W.H. Moreland, *From Akbar to Aurangzeb,* pp. 205-10.
58. Abdul Hamid Lahori, *Padashahnama,* vol. II, pp. 289, 632.
59. Kulshreshtha, *The Development of Trade and Industry under the Mughals,* p. 183.
60. *Babarnama,* op. cit., pp. 384-6.
61. Kulshreshtha, op. cit., p. 183.
62. Jahangir, *Tuzuk-i-Jahangiri,* tr. Rogers, vol. I, p. 66.
63. *Akbarnama,* op. cit., pp. 308-9.
64. Mustad Khan. *Maasir-i-Alamgiri* (*A History of the Emperor Aurangzeb,* 1658-1707), tr. J.N. Sarkar, Calcutta: Royal Asiatic Society, 1947, p. 215.
65. Abul Fazl, *Ain-i-Akbari,* vol. III, tr. Jarrett and J.N. Sarkar, Chapter XIV, p. 489.
66. Edward and Garrett, op. cit., pp. 240-1.
67. Moreland, op. cit., pp. 211-12.
68. Edward and Garrett, op. cit., p. 74.
69. Abdul Hamid Lahori, *Padashahnama,* vol. I, pp. 362-4.
70. Ibid., vol. II, p. 282.
71. Elizabeth Whitcombe, *Agrarian Conditions in Northern India: The United Provinces Under British Rule, 1860-1900,* vol. I, New Delhi: University of California Press, 1971, p. 4.
72. R. Baird Smith, 'Report', p. 301
73. H.B. Webster, Officiating Collector, Aligarh, to Government, NWP, 19 November 1861, in NWP, 'Revenue Proceedings', 14 December 1861, Index No. 22, Proceeding No. 19.

CHAPTER 6

Conclusion

In the last part of this book, a few basic questions need to be addressed. First, when did environmental issues begin to gain importance in historical writings? Second, when and where did environmental history emerge as a discipline? Third, why should we discuss the details of India's environmental history during the medieval and early modern periods particularly given that north India is considered as the most critical area?

Scholars who write on environmental issues have noted that Fernand Braudel, a historian from the Annales School, was possibly the first to begin his 1939 history of the Mediterranean world with a chapter on 'The Role of the Environment'. Another historian, Emmanuel Le Roy Ladurie, explored 'climate history' and 'changing meteorological patterns'. According to them, environmental issues eventually appeared in the discourses of historical writings over time.'[1] However, scholars should know Sir Sayyid Ahmad Khan (1817-89) begins the fourth chapter of the first edition[2] of his magnum opus *Asar-us-Sanadid* with a comment on 'The Climate and Ecology of Delhi.' Sir Sayyid would notice how increasing urbanization in cities had wreaked havoc on the natural scenery and ecology. How did the water bodies of cities once believed clean, become polluted? How did the water in the bodies become indigestible? How have diseases, including liver ailments, indigestion, colds and coughs, become a continual source of pain for individuals because of the city's over-population? In modern terminology, the process that Sir Sayyid refers to what is known as 'population ecology'. As a result, one could reasonably argue that Sir Sayyid's statement on Delhi's climate and environment should be considered a starting point for adequately incorporating environmental themes into historical works.

According to our understanding, the study of environmental history as a discipline began in 1978 at the University of California, Santa Barbara, in America West. Later, scholars, including E.P. Thomson, Raymond Williams, Paul Sweezy, Baran, Magdoff, Braverman and John Bellamy Foster worked to address the relevance of relating Marxian concepts to the broader natural physical realm through their work, each contributing in their own manner to ecological issues.

In South Asian environmental history, particularly Mughal north India, only a few writers from ancient to the early modern period have addressed past ecological issues. Most of their writings seemed to be more concerned with regional issues than north India specifically. Meena Bhargava draws our attention to the environmental history of medieval India, providing an in-depth analysis of the medieval and early modern periods. She writes, 'The complexity and diversity of ecological and environmental history, intense and contentious debates on themes and issues, primarily related to modern and contemporary times, led to introspection and venture into understanding the ecological and environmental problem in medieval and early modern Indian history'. This analysis is necessary to renew the historical relevance of the medieval period in assessing the environmental process more accurately. To maintain this sense of understanding, it would be reasonable to apply Bhargava's explanation to Mughal north Indian history. Most aspects of northern India have remained unexplored regarding environmental issues until now, which provides both reason and opportunity for emerging scholars to delve into the nuances of this period north Indian of history.

According to a few exceptional writers from ancient to early modern times, Mughal north India appears to have had a holistic view of the ecology and environment. These writings examine not only the relationship between people and land but also complex encounters between humans with animals, helping us understand attitudes toward animals and study the fauna in their natural habitat. Mughal chronicles, particularly the memoirs of Babur and Jahangir, provide a rich repository of information for this type of historical research, enabling us to understand better human-animal interactions.

It is worth noting that Jahangir had a distinct approach to depicting nature among the emperors. To use Alvi and Rahman's terms, his description is precise enough to allow for accurate scientific identification of the objects described. His fascination with Biology (Zoology and Botany) emerges from a persuasive aesthetic bent of mind. His observations of animal and bird behaviour, temperament, cunning, fidelity, memory and devotion are frequently astonishing in Zoology, including Ornithology.

The agrarian environment is also a part of environmental history. As a result, civilization has changed the environment to make agriculture possible in many dimensions, especially in north India throughout the Mughal and post-Mughal periods. However, with Rajasthan, it is interesting to note that agriculture is a mix of pastoral production, especially by members of the specialist Raika herding caste community and farming carried out by various traditional agricultural castes. Inputs into rural and agricultural production draw heavily on the forest. Forest species are the primary source of grazing and browsing resources for the large regional herd of cattle, camels, sheep and goats. Forest fruits, fodder coppice, construction wood, medicinal plants and grasses supplement farm household production and reproduction. Forest nutrients—as sheep and goat dung cycled through daily grazing in the forested hills—are the primary sources of agricultural fertilizers.

Besides, there were two fairs of Ramdeoji held in *Magh* (January-February) and *Bhadav* (August-Septempber) throughout Thar but the main fair taking place in Pokhran during *Bhadav*, attended by cattle traders throughout the region. The essential contribution of this cattle fair was the manure from livestock and silt from ponds, as reservoirs were concentrated on the irrigated lands to enhance the fertility and composition of soils. The beneficial effects of such nitrogen-fixing trees and shrubs as the indigenous *Prospis, cineraria* and the recently introduced *Prosopis julifora* were recognized. Grain fields with ploughed land usually have these trees protected.

Questions about growing sense of compassion Mughal emperors showed for animal life and historians' view on hunting during the

Mughal period are important. The Mughals saw hunting grounds as transitional zones between cultivated land and uncultivated forests. A distinctive feature of the Indian subcontinent was the proximity of forested areas and wildlife to the edges of cultivated land. Many Mughal miniature paintings depict this relationship. For instance, in a Bodleian manuscript (*c.* 1660), a Mughal prince is shown hunting blackbucks in a chariot near an irrigation tank. In Punjab, the provinces of Lahore were watered by the five tributaries of the Indus, known for their 'unequalled agricultural fertility'. Key *shikargah-i-mugarrars,* like Hasanabad, Rohtas, Girjhak, Bhera and Bhimbar, were well-connected with cultivated areas, famous for high-quality rice production, as noted by Emperor Jahangir in the *Tuzuk*. These areas attracted wildlife from the nearby wastelands, providing ample opportunities for hunting. In the area between Pattan and Baroda in Gujarat, Abul Fazl recorded a fertile belt with orchards producing mango, muskmelon, fig and other fruits and flowers. He also noted that *cheetahs* in nearby forests, though dense forest growth was often cleared by woodcutters before hunts. That clearing led to increased conflict between human and wild animals, steadily reducing animal populations, particularly in the Agra and Awadh regions because of the degradation of forests.

Moreover, Awadh is endowed with a rich natural geography, with rivers, tributaries, varied soil types and forest belts at the edges of agricultural fields. While the Mughal Empire used its abundant natural resources, the landscape of Awadh changed significantly because of the East India Company's growing involvement in its politics. Before 1857, when Awadh was under nawab rule, the British criticized the region's agriculture especially its revenue administration, for the depletion of forests. However, the British presence significantly altered Awadh's natural landscape. In 1807, Francis Buchanan estimated that 1,450 sq. miles of Awadh's 7,438 sq. miles were covered in forest. By 1833, Donald Butter noted that only 888 sq. miles of forest remained, meaning, 563 sq. miles had been lost within twenty-three years.

The ongoing destruction of forest cover in Awadh had an adverse effect on the region's climate. Donald Butter noted that the annual average rainfall declined and the water table dropped, causing irrigation difficulties. Despite this, forest reclamation continued unchecked. Agricultural statistics from 1885 to 1886 show no forest area in that district, whereas Sleeman estimates forest area as 8,821/8,822 sq. miles. By 1885-6, vast tracts of forest comparing around half a million acres, had been cleared for cultivation, leading to the destruction of wildlife. For instance, the *terai* forest of Gorakhpur *sarkar*, once known for its large elephant herds that threatened agriculture, saw a dramatic reduction in wildlife. Tigers, previously abundant between Gorakhpur and the mountains, were hunted extensively by. English residents and military officers hunted after 1801 owing, to as forest-clearing intensified. Herbivorous animals, which were crucial for sustaining tigers, suffered during the 1769 famine, resulting in widespread tiger starvation.

The study of north India's ecological history, especially in climate change, reveals that monsoon failures primarily caused natural disasters like famines, floods, and droughts. Following these events, diseases such as cholera, plague, smallpox, malaria, fever and asthma become prevalent. Importing food and medical supplies from other provinces and state-sponsored rehabilitation were common relief measures. Rulers often responded to these challenges. Abul Fazl records Akbar was particularly concerned for the welfare of the distressed, regardless of the caste and creed. In 1583, Akbar established three free kitchens—one for Hindus, another for Muslims and a third for ascetics.

Natural calamities also significantly impacted administration. The imperial treasury often depleted due to falling revenue and the high cost of relief measures. Losing key officers and the shifting of the population created administrative challenges.

To sum up, studying the records left by rulers has enriched our understanding of north India's ecological and environmental history during the medieval and early modern periods. Historians such as Alvi and Rahman, Salim Ali, Ebba Koch and more recently Michael H. Fisher have given significant attention to imperial records. Mayank Kumar, in particular, is well-recognized for his work on the environmental history of Rajasthan, where he investigated the region's ecological past through vernacular literature like *Nainsi-ri Khayat.*

In conclusion, the historical records left by rulers include both positive and negative insights into their environmental and ecological efforts. This current analysis seeks to present these diverse approaches and their impacts.

NOTES

1. For more details see, Mahua Sarkar, ed., *Environment and History: Recent Dialogues,* New Delhi: Kalpaz Publication, 2008, p. 16.
2. See, Sayyid Ahmad Khan, *Asar-us-Sanadid,* tr. Rana Safvi, *The Remnants of Ancient Heroes,* New Delhi: Tulika, 2018, pp. 207-8.

APPENDICES

APPENDIX I

List of the Trees in the Punjab Plain

Common Name (Local Name)	*Scientific Name*
Amrud	Prunus communis
Babul	Acacia eburnean
Bamboo	Dendrocalamus strictus
Ber (dier)	Zizyphus jujuba
Ber	Ficus indica
Charind	Xylosma longifolium
Dhak (chichera)	Butea frondosa
Dhrek (drek)	Azadirachta melia
Guler	Ficus cunia
Gum	Premna latifolia
Hingo	Balanites aegyptiaca
Jal	Salvadora
Kamela (raini)	Mallotus
Kasumbh	Carthamus tinctorrus
Khair	Acacia katechu
Khajur	Longi folium
Mango (am)	Mangifera indica
Mulberry (nut)	Morus indica/laevigata
Nimbar (reru/raunjh)	Acacia/eucophlora
Nimbu	Citrus acida

Palak	Ficus infectoria
Pansara	Wenlandia excreta
Persian iliac (bokain)	Melia sempervirens
Rambal (gular)	Ficus glomerta
Shisham (tali/tahli)	Dalbergia sissu
Sufeda	Populus alba
Tamarisk (jhao/tuhla)	Tamarix orientalis

APPENDIX II

List of the Shrubs, Plants and Weeds in the Punjab Plain

Common Name	*Scientific Name*
Plants	
Akk	Calatropic procera
Akoi	Nithania coagulans
Banna	Tamarix gullica
Bansa/bansuti	Adhatoda vesica
Barari	Diploca aphylla
Garanda	Adhatoda vassica
Harmal	Peganum hurmala
Kair	Salvadora deciduas
Lai	Tamarix dioica
Madar	Calatropis gigantean
Phog	Calligonum polygonoides
Shrubs	
Anjan	-
Benku	-
Bhurat	Cenchrum echinatum

Chemmbar	Eleosine plagellifera
Chimbal	-
Chimbal	-
Dab	Eragrostis cynosuroides
Dhaman	-
Dhub/Dhubra/Dubra	Cynodon dactylon

Weeds

Bughat/leek weed/wild leek	-
Convovlulus	-
Jowasa	-
Kandiari/thistle	-
Maina	-

APPENDIX III

Chronology of Extinction of *Cheetahs*

Date	*Location*	*Remarks*	*Sources*
1825	Farukhabad, UP	Coursing with cheetahs	Johnson, 1827
1829	Rajkot	One cheetah spread	T.U. 1829
1835	Agra, UP	Coursing with cheetahs	Park, 1580
1837	Lucknow, UP	Two cheetahs Accompany Lord Auckland	Dunbar, 1955
1840	Agra, UP	Coursing with cheetahs	Vigne, 1844
1840	Lucknow, UP	Coursing with cheetahs	Hoffmeister 1858
1857	Banda, UP	Coursing with cheetahs	Halliday, 1857
1860	Jaipur, Rajasthan	Photograph of two cheetahs	Fabb, 1986
1880	Punjab, Rajputana	Cheetahs central India	Blandford, 1888
1880	Sind, Rajputana	Cheetahs	Murray, 1884

1890	Deogarh, Bihar	Two cheetahs shot	Braddon, 1895
1894-1919	Mirzapur, UP	Five cheetahs shot	Allen, 1919

Source: The above information is taken from Divyabhanusinh's book, *The End of a Trail: The Cheetah in India,* New Delhi: Oxford University Press, pp. 215-17.

APPENDIX IV

Fauna Found in the Awadh

District	*Species*	*Habitat*
Lucknow	Jackals, Hog (common), Antelope and Nilgai	
Pratapgarh	Wolves, Wild Hog, Nilgai, Jackals, Forees	
Faizabad	Nilgai, Antelope	*Dhak* Jungle
Barabanki	Hog, Nilgai, Jackals	
Sultanpur	Wolves, Jackals, Nilgai and Wild Hog	
Rai Bareli	Wolves, Jackals, Nilgai and Antelope	
Kheri	Tigers, Bears, Wolves, Leopard, Wild Dogs, Jungle Cats, Five Species of Dear, Antelope	
Unao	Wolves, Jackals, Wild Hogs, Nilgai	
Gorakhpur (Div.)	Wolf, Jackal and Fox (common), Wild Hog, and Nilgai (occasionally)	
Basti	Wild Hog, Nilgai, Wolves, and Jackals (spotted) Spotted Dear (occasionally)	

Gorakhpur	Tiger and Leopard (common) Wild Buffaloes, Rhinoceros (common). The Spotted Deer and Sloth dear (occasionally), Wild Hog, Nilgai	Short within the few years

Source: Imperial Gazetteer of India, Provincial Series of the United Provinces of Agra and Awadh, vols. I & II.

Bibliography

Persian Works

Ahmad, Khwaja Nizamuddin, 1936, *The Tabaqat-i-Akbari*, vol. III, Eng. tr. Brajendranath De, rpt. 1996, Calcutta: Asiatic Society, Calcutta.

Allami, Abul Fazl, 1927/1977, *Ain-i-Akbari,* vol. I, Eng. tr. H. Blochmann, 2nd edn., revd. and ed., Colonel D.P. Phillott, New Delhi: P.L. Printers.

———, 1949/2006, *Ain-i-Akbari,* vol. II, Eng. tr. Colonel H.S. Jarrett, corrected and annotated, Jadunath Sarkar, 2nd edn., Calcutta: The Asiatic Society.

———, 1977, *Akbarnama*, Eng. tr. H. Beveridge, vol. III, rpt., New Delhi: The Asiatic Society.

Babur, Zahiruddin Muhammad 1979, *Baburnama* or *Memoires of Babur,* English tr. from the original text by Beveridge, vol. II, New Delhi: Penguin India.

Badauni, Abdul Qadir, 1973, *Muntakhbut-Tawarik*, vol. II, W.H. Lowe, New Delhi: Low Price Publication.

Battuta, Ibn, 1953, *Rehala*, Eng. tr. Mahdi Husain, Baroda: Oriental Institute.

Begum, Gulbadan, 1902, *Humayunama*, tr. A.S. Beveridge, London: The Royal Asiatic Society.

Bernier, Francois, 1983, *Travels in the Mogul Empire AD 1656-1668,* revd. edn., Vincent A. Smith, rpt.: New Delhi: Asian Educational Services.

Butter, Donald, 1839, *Outline of the Topography and Statistics of the Southern District of Oudh, and the Cantonment of Sultanpur-Oudh*, G.H. Huttman, Calcutta: W.H. Allen & Co.

Firishta, Muhammad Qasim, 1829, *Tarikh-i-Firishta*, *History of the Rise of Mohamedan Power in India*, Eng. tr. J. Briggs, vol. IV, rpt. 1881, New Delhi: Oriental Reprint Corporation.

Foreign Traveller Accounts & British Official Works.

Foster, Sir William, 1900, *The Embassy of Sir Thomas Roe in India, 1615-1619*, New Delhi: Munshiram Manoharlal.

———, 1910, *The English Frontiers in India 1630-1633*, vol. XIII, trans. William Irvine, Cambridge: Cambridge University Press.

Jahangir, 1624, *Tuzuk-i-Jahangiri,* ed. Syed Ahmad Khan 1863-4, Aligarh: Sir Syed Academy, rpt. 2007; Eng. tr. Alexander Rogers, ed. Henry Beveridge, London, 1904-14: rpt.; New Delhi: The Asiatic Society, 2006; Thackston Wheeler M., 1999 *Jahangirnama: Memoirs of Jahangir, Emperor of India*, trans. ed. and annotated edn., New York: The Aga Khan Programme for Islamic Architecture.

Khan, Inayat, 1990, *Shahjahanama,* ed. W.E. Begley and Z.A. Desai, New Delhi: Oxford: Oxford University Press.

Khan, Mustad, 1947, *Maasir-Alamgiri: A History of the Emperor Aurangzeb, 1658-1707*, Eng. tr. J.N. Sarkar, London: The Royal Asiatic Society.

Lahori, Abdul Hamid, 1868, *Badshahnama*, vols. I & II, Calcutta: Asiatic Society.

Latif, Abdul, 1919, *Travel in Bihar 1680 A.D.*, vol. V, tr. J.N. Sarkar, Calcutta: Journal of the Bihar and Orissa Research Society (JBORS).

Manucci, Niccolao, 1907, *Storia do Mogor or Mogul India, 1653-1708*, vol. II, Eng. tr. William Irvine, London: Curzon Press.

Marshal, John, 1927, *John Marshall in India: Notes Observation in Bengal* 1668-72, ed. S.A. Khan, London: Oxford University Press.

Moreland, W.H., 1962, *India at the Death of Akbar: An Economic Study*, New Delhi: Print and Publication.

Mundy, Peter, 2014, *The Travels of Peter Mundi in Europe and Asia 1680-1677*, vol. II, London: Hakluyt Society.

Pelsaert, Francisco, 1925, *Jahangir's India*, tr. W.H. Moreland and O. Geye, Cambridge: Cambridge University Press.

Rai, Sujan, 1918, *Khulasat-ut-Tawarik*, ed. Zafar Hasan and Maulana Abrar Hasan, Delhi: J. & Sons Press.

Roe, Sir Thomas, 1926, *The Embassy of Sir Thomas Roe to the Court of the Great Mughal, 1615-1619*, vol. II, ed. William Foster, London: The Hakluyt Society.

Sleeman, W.H., 1971, *Sleeman in Oudh: An Abridgement of W.H. Sleeman's A Journey through the Kingdom of Oude in 1849-50*, ed. P.D. Reeves, Cambridge: Cambridge University Press.

Tavernier, J.B., 1889, *Travels in India*, vol. I, London: Ball.

Twining, Thomas, 1893, *Travels in India a Hundred Years Ago, with a Visit to the United States,* London: John Murray.

Official Publications

District Gazetteer Azamgarh, Lucknow: Government of Uttar Pradesh, 1988.

District Gazetteer of Allahabad, vol. XXIII, Allahabad: Government of Uttar Pradesh, 1911.

District Gazetteer of Ambala, vol. XIII, pt. A, Lahore: Government Press, 1926.

District Gazetteer of Amritsar, vol. XIV, part A, *Civil and Military Gazetteer,* Lahore: Government Press, 1914.

District Gazetteer of Benaras, vol. XXVI, Allahabad: Government of Uttar Pradesh, 1910.

District Gazetteer of Bikaner, Powlett P.W: Calcutta: Government Press, 1874.

District Gazetteer of Chanab Colony; Civil and Military Gazetteer, Lahore: Government Press, 1905.

District Gazetteer of Delhi, vol. V, pt. A, *Civil and Military Gazetteer,* Lahore: Government Press, 1913.

District Gazetteer of Dujana, vol. VII, pt. A, *Civil and Military Gazetteer,* Lahore: Government Press, 1908.

District Gazetteer of Gujranwala, Lahore: Government Press, 1905.

District Gazetteer of Gurudaspur, vol. XXI-A, Lahore: Government Press, 1905.

District Gazetteer of Hoshiarpur, vol. XIII, pt. A, Lahore: Government Press, 1905.

District Gazetteer of Kapurthala, vol. XIV, part A, *Civil and Military Gazetteer,* Lahore: Government Press, 1914.

District Gazetteer of Muzaffargarh, vol. XIV, pt. A, *Civil and Military Gazetteer,* Lahore: Government Press, 1914.

District Gazetteer of Shahpur, Lahore: Government Press, 1908.

District Gazetteer of Sialkot, vol. XXIII, pt. A, Lahore: Government Press, 1921.

District Gazetteer of United Province; Agra, Government Press, 1905.

District Gazetteer of United Provinces, Agra and Oudh Division, vol. III, Allahabad: Government Press, 1905.

District Gazetteer of United Provinces, vol. A, *Allahabad District,* Allahabad: Government Press, 1928.

Gazetteer of Rajasthan State, vol. I, *Land and People,* Jaipur: State Government of Rajasthan Press, 1995.

Imperial Gazetteer of India, Provincial Series Punjab: The Province; Mountain, Rivers and Historical Area, vol. I, Calcutta, 1908.

Rajputana District Gazetteer, Ajmer-Mewar, vol. 1A, Scottish Mission Industries, Ajmer: C.C. Watson, 1904.

Rewa State Gazetteer, vol. IV, Lucknow: Nawal Kishore Steam Printing Press, 1907.

Unpublished Thesis/Dissertations

Jafari, S.Z.H., 1985, 'Agrarian Condition of Awadh under the Mughal and Nawab Wazir', Ph.D. thesis, Aligarh Muslim University, Aligarh.

Khan, Mohd Kamran, 2018, 'Environment in European Traveller Accounts during the 17th Century Mughal India', M.Phil. dissertation, Lucknow: Babasaheb Bhimrao Ambedkar University,.

Government Reports

Agricultural Statistics of British India, 1885-6, Calcutta.

Bird-Smith, Colonel, 1861, *Report on the North-West Provinces Famines of 1860-61*, Para 32 & 38.

Buchanan, Francis, 1838, *The History, Antiquities, Topography and Statistics of Eastern India: District Report, 1807-11*, ed. and abridge by Montgomery Martin.

Girdlestone, C.E.R. 1868, *Report on the Past Famines in the North-West Provinces*, Allahabad: Government Press.

Indian Famine Commission Report, 1989, 1880-85, New Delhi: Agricole Publication Academy.

Indian State of Forest Report, 2019, *Forest Survey of India*, vol. II, Ministry of Environment, Forest and Climate Change: Government of India, Dehradun.

Ramsar Sites of India-Factsheets, 2019, Wetlands Division, Ministry of Environment, Forest and Climate Change, Government of India, Dehradun.

The Red Data Book on Indian Animals, 1993, Vertebrate, Part-I, Zoological Survey of India: Government of India, Calcutta.

Webster, H.B., 1861, Officiating Collector, Aligarh, to Government of North-West Provinces, 'Revenue Proceeding,' 14 December 1961, Index No. 22, Proceeding No. 19.

Government Archival Records

Foreign Department, Political Branch 'C' Consultation, 17 December 1858, File Nos. 247, 249, New Delhi: National Archives of India.

Foreign Department, Political Proceeding, 10 June 1859, File No. 252, New Delhi: National Archives of India.

Foreign Department, Political Proceeding, 21-26 January 1859, File No. 104, New Delhi: National Archives of India.

Foreign Department, Political Proceeding, 30 December 1859, File No. 498, New Delhi: National Archives of India.

Oude Forest Report for 1861-2, Public Work Department, Revenue and Forest Branch, New Delhi: National Archives of India.

Modern Works

Agnihotri, Indu, 1996, 'Ecology, Land Use and Colonization: The Canal Colonies of Punjab', *Indian Economic and Social History Review*, 33/1: 37–58.

Agrawal, Arun, 2005, *Environmentality: Technologies of Government and the Making of Subjects*, Durham: Duke University Press.

Agrawal, Arun and K. Sivaramakrishnan, eds., 2000, *Agrarian Environments: Resources, Representations, and Rule in India*, Durham: Duke University Press.

Agrawal, C.M., 1987, *Nature Calamities and the Great Mughals*, Bodh Gaya: Kanchan Publication.

Agrawal, D.P., 1971, *The Copper Bronze Age in India*, New Delhi: Munshiram Manoharlal.

Ali, Daud and Emma J. Flatt, eds., 2012, *Garden and Landscape Practices in Pre-Colonial India: Histories from the Deccan*, London: Routledge.

Ali, Salim A., 1927, 'The Mughal Emperors of India as Naturalists and Sportsmen', vol. XXXI, *Journal of the Bombay Natural History Society*.

Ali, Tanvir, 2007, 'Impact of Participatory Forest Management on Financial Assets of Rural Communities in Northwest Pakistan', *Ecological Economics* 6/3: 588–93.264

Allchin, F.R., 1995, *The Archaeology of Early Historic South Asia: The Emergence of Cities and State*, Cambridge: Cambridge University Press.

Alley, Kelly, 2002, *On the Banks of the Ganga: When Wastewater Meets a Sacred River*, Ann Arbor: University of Michigan Press.

Arnold, David, 1988, *Famine: Social Crisis and Historical Change*, Oxford: Basil Blackwell.

———, 1996, *The Problem of Nature: Environment, Culture and European Expansion*, Oxford: Basil Blackwell.

———, 2000, *Science, Technology and Medicine in Colonial India*, Cambridge: Cambridge University Press.

———, 2008. 'Plant Capitalism and Company Science', *Modern Asian Studies* 42/5: 899-928.

———, 2013, 'Pollution, Toxicity and Public Health in Metropolitan India, 1850–1939,' *Journal of Historical Geography* 42:124-33.

———, 2016, *Toxic Histories: Poison and Pollution in Modern India*, Cambridge: Cambridge University Press.

Arnold, David and Ramachandra Guha, eds., 1995, *Nature, Culture and Imperialism: Essays on the Environmental History of South Asia*, New Delhi: Oxford University Press.

Asher, Catherine, 1992, *Architecture of Mughal India*, Cambridge: Cambridge University Press.

Asthana, Vandana, 2009, *Water Policy Processes in India: Discourses of Power and Resistance*, New York: Routledge.

Badhwar, Inderjit, 1988, 'The Tiger Widows', *India Today*, New Delhi: Living Media India Ltd.

Baker, A., ed., 2003, *Geography and History: Bridging the Divide*, Cambridge: Cambridge University Press.

Baker, Kathleen and Sarah Jewitt, 2007, 'Evaluating 35 Years of Green Revolution Technology in Villages of Bulandshahr District, Western UP, North India', Journal of Development Studies 43/2: 312-39.

Banga, Indu, 1967, 'Ahmad Shah Abdali's Design over the Punjab', *PIHC.*

Baron, Hugel Charles, 1970, *Travels in Kashmir and the Punjab*, Patiala: Punjab Language Department.

Barton, Gregory, 2002, *Empire Forestry and the Origins of Environmentalism* Cambridge: Cambridge University Press.

Barton, Gregory A., and B.M. Bennett, 2008, 'Environmental Conservation and Deforestation in British India 1855–1947: A Reinterpretation', *Itinerario* 32: 83-104.

Bayly, Susan, 1999, *Caste, Society and Politics in India from the Eighteenth Century to the Modern Age,* Cambridge: Cambridge University Press.

Beattie, James, 2012, *Recent Themes in the Environmental History of the British*, London: Routledge.

Bhattacharya, Neeladri, 2018, *The Great Agrarian Conquest: The Colonial Reshaping of a Rural World*, Hyderabad: Orient BlackSwan.

Bhola, M.P. and S. Hussain, 1940, 'Taungyas in the Gorakhpur Forest Division', Bulletin No. 4, United Provinces, Indian Forestry.

Boyle, J.A., 1968, *The Cambridge History of Iran: The Seljuq and Mangol Period,* vol. V, Cambridge: Cambridge University Press.

Burn, Sir Richard, 1937, *The Cambridge History of India*, vol. IV, Cambridge: Cambridge University Press.

Chakrabarti, Ranjan, ed., 2009, *Situating Environmental History*, New Delhi: Manohar.

Chakrabarty, Dipesh, 2009, 'The Climate of History: Four Theses', *Critical Inquiry* 35:197-222.

Chakravarti, Ranbir, ed., 1988, *The Creation and Expansion of Settlements in Ancient India, as well as the Management of Hydraulic Resources*, New Delhi: Oxford University Press.

Chakravorty, Ranes, 1993, 'Diseases of Antiquity in South Asia', in Kenneth F. Kiple, ed., *Cambridge World History of Human Disease,* Cambridge: Cambridge University Press.

Charda, Divyabhanusinh, 1995, *The End of the Trail: The Cheetah in India,* New Delhi: Banyan Books.

———, 2005, *The Story of Asia's Lions,* Mumbai: Marg Publication.

Chaturvedi, M.D., 1938, *Land Management in the United Provinces,* Allahabad: Government Press.

———, 1938, 'Roadside Avenue and Compounds, Bulletin No. 12, United Provinces', Forest Department, Allahabad: Government Press.

Cohen, Benjamin, 2011, 'Modernizing the Urban Environment: The Musi River Flood of 1908 in Hyderabad, India,' *Environment and History* 17: 409-32.

Crosby, Alfre W., 1986, *Ecological Imperialism: The Biological Expansion of Europe, 900-1900,* Cambridge: Cambridge University Press.

Crumle, C., 1994, *Historical Ecological: Cultural Knowledge and Changing Landscape*, Santa Fe: School of American Press.

Dalrymple, William, 2006, *The Last Mughal, the Fall of Dynasty*, 1857, New Delhi: Penguin, India.

Damodaran, A., 2010, *Encircling the Seamless: India, Climate Change and the Global Commons*, New Delhi: Oxford University Press.

Damodaran, Vinita, V. Winterbottom and A. Lester, eds., 2015, *The East India Company and the Natural World*, London: Palgrave Macmillan.

Dangwal, Dhirendra, 2009, *Himalayan Degradation: Colonial Forestry and Environmental Change in India*, Cambridge: Cambridge University Press.

Das, Ashok Kumar, 1999, 'The Elephant in Mughal Painting', in *Flora and Fauna in Mughal Art*, ed., Mumbai: Marg Publication.

Das, Pallavi, 2015, *Colonialism, Development, and the Environment: Railways and Deforestation in British India, 1860-1884*, London: Palgrave Macmillan.

Degroot, Dagomar, 2018, *The Frigid Golden Age: Climate Change, the Little Ice Age and the Dutch Republic 1560-1720*, Cambridge: Cambridge University Press.

Devra, G.S.L., ed. 1999, *Problem in the Delimitation of the Rajasthan Desert during the Medieval Period*, Jaipur: Rawat Publication.

Dhavalikar, M.K., 2001, 'Green Imperialism: Monsoon in Antiquity and Human Response', *Man and Environment*, vol. 36, 2001, p. 18-28.

Digby, Simon, 1971, *Warhorse and Elephant in the Delhi Sultanate: A Study of Military Supplies*, New Delhi: Orient Monographs.

Donges, J.F., et. al. 2015, 'Non-linear Regime Shifts in Holocene Asian Monsoon Variability: Potential Impacts on Cultural Change and Migratory Patterns', *Climate of the Past* 11: 709-41.

Douie, James, 1994, *The Punjab North-West Frontier Province and Kashmir,* New Delhi: Low Price Publication.

Duara, Prasenjit, 2014, *The Crisis of Global Modernity: Asian Traditions and a Sustainable Future,* Cambridge: Cambridge University Press.

Dubash, Navroz, ed., 2012, *Handbook of Climate Change in India: Development, Politics and Governance,* London: Routledge.

D'Souza, Rohan, 2006b, 'Water in British India: The Making of a "Colonial Hydrology",' *History Compass,* 4/4: 621-8.

Eaton, Richard, 1993, *Rise of Islam and the Bengal Frontier, 1204–1760,* Berkeley: University of California Press.

Eaton, Richard and Philip Wagoner, 2014, *Power, Memory, Architecture: Contested Sites on India's Deccan Plateau, 1300–1600,* Oxford: Oxford University Press.

Edney, Matthew, 1987, *Mapping an Empire: The Geographical Construction of British India, 1765–1843,* Chicago: University of Chicago Press.

Edwardes, S.M. & H.L.O. Garrett, 1930, *Mughal Rule in India,* vol. II, London: Oxford University Press.

Ellerman, J.R., 1961, *The Fauna of India, Mammalia,* vol. III, New Delhi: Manohar.

Falk, Tobay and Mildred Archer, 1981, *Indian Miniatures in India Office Library,* Oxford: Oxford University Press.

Feldhaus, Anne, 2003, *Region, Pilgrimage and Geographical Imagination,* London: Palgrave MacMillan.

Fisher, Michael H., 1987, *A Clash of Culture: Awadh, the British and the Mughals,* New Delhi: Manohar.

———, 2007, *Visions of Mughal India*, London: I.B. Tauris.

———, 2015, *A Short History of the Mughal Empire*, London: I.B. Tauris.

Foltz, Richard, Frederick Denny, and Azizan Baharuddin, 2003, *Islam and Ecology: A Bestowed Trust,* Cambridge, MA: Harvard University Press.

Forsyth, James, 1999, 'Game Animals and Birds of the Plains', *The Oxford Anthology of Indian Wildlife*, vol. I, ed. Mahesh Rangarajan, New Delhi: Oxford University Press.

Francklin, William, 1803, *Military of George Thomas,* London: John Stockdale.

Fraser, James, 1742, *The History of Nadir Shah*, London: A. Millar.

Gadgil, Madhav and Ramachandra Guha, 1992, *This Fissured Land: An Ecological History of India,* Oxford: Oxford University Press.

———, 1995, *Ecology and Equity: The Use and Abuse of Nature in Contemporary India*, London: Routledge.

———, 1990, 'Human Ecology in India: Some Historical Perspectives', *Interdisciplinary Science Reviews* 15/3: 209-23.

Gadgil, Madhav and V.D. Vartak, 1975, 'Sacred Groves of India: A Plea for Continued Conservation', *Journal of the Bombay Natural History Society* 72/2: 313-20.

Gee, E.P., 1964, *The Wildlife of India*, Collins: London.

Gold, Ann Grodzins and B.R. Gujjar, 2001, *In the Time of Trees and Sorrows: Natural, Power and Memory in Rajasthan*, Durham: Duke University Press.

Government of India, 2010, *Report of the Elephant Task Force: Gajah: Securing the Future for Elephants in India*, ed. Mahesh Rangarajan et. al, Ministry of Environment and Forests.

Greenough, Paul, 2001, 'Nature Ferae: Wild Animals in South Asia and the Standard Ecological Narrative', in James C. Scott, and Nina Bhatt, eds., *Agrarian Studies: Synthetic Work at the Cutting Edge*, New Haven: Yale University Press.

Grimmett, Richard, 2003, *Birds of Northern India*, Oxford: Oxford University Press.

Grove, Richard, 1993, 'Conserving Eden: The European East India Companies and their Environmental Policies on St. Helena, Mauritius and in Western

India, 1660 to 1854', *Comparative Studies in Society and History* 35/2: 318-51.

———, 1995, *Green Imperialism: Colonial Expansion, Tropical Island Edens and the Origins of Environmentalism, 1600-1860,* Cambridge: Cambridge University Press.

Grove, Richard, Vinita Damodaran and Satpal Sangwan, eds., 1998, *Nature and the Orient: The Environmental History of South and Southeast Asia,* Oxford: Oxford University Press.

Guha, Ramachandra, 1995, 'Radical American Environmentalism and Wilderness Preservation: A Third World Critique', in J. Baird Callicot and Michael P. Nelson, eds., *The Great New Wilderness Debate,* Athens: University of Georgia Press.

———, 1997, 'Mahatma Gandhi and the Environmental Movement', in Ramachandra Guha and Juan Martinez-Alier, eds., *Varieties of Environmentalism: Essays North and South,* London: Earthscan.

———, 1999, *Savaging the Civilized: Verrier Elwin, His Tribals, and India,* Chicago: University of Chicago Press.

———, 2000a, *Environmentalism: A Global History,* Oxford: Oxford University Press.

———, 2000b, *The Unquiet Woods: Ecological Change and Peasant Resistance in the Himalayas,* 2nd edn., Oxford: Oxford University Press.

———, 2006, *How Much Should a Person Consume? Environmentalism in India and the United States,* Berkeley: University of California Press.

Guha, Ranajit, 1996, *Rule of Property for Bengal,* rpt., Durham: Duke University Press.

——— et. al, eds., 1982–2012, *Subaltern Studies,* 12 vols., Oxford: Oxford University Press and New Delhi: Permanent Black.

Guha, Sumit, 1999, *Environment and Ethnicity in India, 1200-1991,* Cambridge: Cambridge University Press.

Gupta, Hari Ram, 1944, *Studies in Later Mughal History,* New Delhi: The Minerva Book Shop.

Haberman, David, 2013, *People Trees: Worship of Trees in Northern India,* Oxford: Oxford University Press.

Habib, Bilal, 2014, *Ecology of Leopard: In Relation to Prey Abundance & Land use Pattern in Kashmir,* Dehradun: Wildlife Institute of India.

Habib, Irfan, 1982, *Atlas of the Mughal Empire,* Oxford: Oxford University Press.

———, 1999, *Agrarian System of Mughal India,* Oxford: Oxford University Press.

———, 2010, *Man and Environment: The Ecological History of India, A People's History of India,* Aligarh: Aligarh Historians Society.

Hardiman, David, 1995, 'Small-Dam Systems of the Sahyadris', in David Arnold and Ramachandra Guha, eds., *Nature, Culture and Imperialism*, Oxford: Oxford University Press.

Hari Bias, Sardar, 1911, *Ajmer Historical and Descriptive*, Ajmer: Scottish Mission Industries Company.

Hunt, John Dixon, 2000, *Greater Perfection: The Practice of Garden Theory*, London: Thames & Hudson.

Hussain, Yusuf, 1957, *Glimpses of Medieval Indian Culture*, Bombay: Asian Publication House.

Jafri, Saiyid Zaheer Husain, 2016, *Awadh from Mughal to Colonial Rule: Studies in the Anatomy of a Transformation*, New Delhi: Gyan Publishing House.

Jeffery, Roger, 1998, *The Social Construction of Indian Forest*, New Delhi: Manohar.

Jodha, N.S., 2001, *Life on the Edge: Sustaining Agriculture and Community Resources in Fragile Environments*, Oxford: Oxford University Press.

Kapur, Nandini Sinha, 2002, *State Formation in Rajasthan: Mewar during the Seventeenth Fifteenth Centuries*, New Delhi: Manohar.

Kautilya, 2013, *Arthashastra*, trans. Patrick Olivelle as King, Governance.

———, 2014, *Law in Ancient India: Kautilya's Arthashastra*, Oxford: Oxford University Press.

Kavoori, P.S., 1999, *Pastoralism in Expansion: The Transhuming Herders of Western Rajasthan*, Oxford: Oxford University Press.

Kazmi, Sabina, 2013, 'Colonial Intervention in Awadh: Indigenous Political Structures and Indirect Rule in Eighteenth-Century', 74th Session, Proceeding Indian History Congress.

Kenoyer, Jonathan Mark, 2000, 'Wealth and Socioeconomic Hierarchies of the Indus Valley Civilization', in Janet Richards and Mary Van Buren, eds., *Order, Legitimacy, and Wealth in the Ancient States*, Cambridge: Cambridge University Press.

Khan, Mohd Kamran, 2022, 'Exploring Pre-Colonial Rajasthan from Ecological Perspective: A Study of Mughal Suba of Ajmer', *Quarterly Journal of Pakistan Historical Society*, vol. LXX, Karachi.

Klein, Ira, 1984, 'When the Rains Failed', *Indian Economic and Social History Review* 21/2: 185-214.

———, 1994, 'Imperialism, Ecology and Disease: Cholera in India, 1850-1950', *The Indian Economic and Social History Review*, vol. 31, Issue 4.

———, 1988, 'Plague, Policy and Popular Unrest in British India', *Modern Asian Studies* 22/4: 723–55.

Koch, Ebba, 1988, *Shah Jahan and Orpheus: The Pietre Dure Decoration and the Programme of the Throne of the Mughals*, Graz: Akademische Druck.

Kolff, Dirk H.A., 1990, *Naukars, Rajput and Sepoy: The Ethnohistory of the Military Lahore Market of Hindustan 1450-1850*, Cambridge: Cambridge University Press.

Kothari, Ashish, 2007, *Birds in Our Lives*, Hyderabad: Universities Press.

Kothiya, Tanuja, 2016, *Nomadic Narratives: A History of Mobility and Identity in the Great Indian Desert*, Cambridge: Cambridge University Press.

Kumar, Deepak, Vinita Damodaran and Rohan D'Souza, eds., 2011, *The British Empire and the Natural World: Environmental Encounters in South Asia* Oxford: Oxford University Press.

Kumar, Mayank, 2005, 'Claims on Natural Resources: Exploring the Role of Political Power in Pre-Colonial Rajasthan', *Conservation and Society* 3, no. 1.

———, 2013, *Monsoon Ecologies: Irrigation, Agriculture and Settlement Patterns in Rajasthan during the Pre-colonial Period*, New Delhi: Manohar.

Lal, Makhan, 1986, 'Iron Tools, Forest Clearance and Urbanization in the Gangetic Plain', *Man and Environment.*

Lieberman, Victor, 2003, *Strange Paralles South Asia in Global Context, c. 800-1830,* vol. I, Cambridge: Cambridge University Press.

Ludden, David, 1999, *An Agrarian History of South Asia*, Cambridge: Cambridge University Press.

MacKenzie, John M., 1988, *The Empire of Nature: Hunting, Conservation and British Imperialism,* Manchester: Manchester University Press.

———, 2004, 'Introduction to Special 10th Anniversary Issue', *Environment and History*, UK: White House Press Cambridgeshire, vol. 10, pp. 1-7.

Mann, Michael, 2007, 'Delhi's Belly: On the Management of Water, Sewage and Excreta in a Changing Urban Environment during the Nineteenth Century', *Studies in History* 23/1 n.s.:1-31.

———, 2013, 'Environmental History and Historiography on South Asia: Context and Some Recent Publications', *Südasien-Chronik-South Asia Chronicle* 3: 324-57.

McNeill, J.R., 2003, 'Observations on the Nature and Culture of Environmental History', *History and Theory* 42:5-43.

McNeill, John, Jose Augusto Padua and Mahesh Rangarajan, eds., 2010, *Environmental History: As if Nature Existed,* Oxford: Oxford University Press.

Meena, Bhargava, 1999, *State Society and Ecology: Gorakhpur in Transition,* 1750-1830, New Delhi: Manohar.

———, ed., 2017, *Frontiers of Environment: Issues in Medieval and Early Modern India,* New Delhi: Orient BlackSwan.

———, 2007, 'Changing River Courses in North India: Calamities, Bounties, Strategies-Sixteenth to Early Nineteenth Centuries', *The Medieval History Journal* 10, nos. 1 & 2.

Misra, V.C., 1967, *Geography of Rajasthan*, New Delhi: National Book Trust.

Misra, V.M., 1984, *Climate, a Factory in the Rise and Fall of the Indus Civilization: Evidence from Rajasthan and Beyond*, ed. S.P. Gupta, New Delhi: Books and Books.

Moorcroft, William and George Trebeck, 1837, *Travels in the Himalayan Provinces and Punjab*, London: Longman, Rees, Orme, Brown and Green.

Moosvi, Shireen, 2008, *People, Taxation, and Trade in Mughal India*, Oxford: Oxford University Press.

Morrison, Kathleen, 2014, 'Conceiving Ecology and Stopping the Clock: Narratives of Balance, Loss, and Degradation', in Mahesh Rangarajan and K. Sivaramakrishnan, eds., *Shifting Ground,* Oxford: Oxford University Press.

Morrison, Kathleen D., ed., 2005, *Production and Landscape in the Vijayanagar Metropolitan Region: Contribution of the Vijayanagara*, New Delhi: Manohar.

Mosse, David, 2003, *The Rule of Water: Statecraft, Ecology, and Collective Action in South India,* Oxford: Oxford University Press.

Mosse, David, 2003, *The Rule of Water: Statecraft Ecology and Collective Action in South India*, Oxford: Oxford University Press.

Mukhia, Harbans and Maurice Aymard, 1988, *French Studies in History*, vol. I, New Delhi: Sage.

Murty, M.K.L., 2002, 'Sheep/Goat Pastoral Cultures in the Southern Deccan: The Narrative as a Metaphor', in S. Settar & R. Korisetta (eds.), *Archaeology and Historiography, Indian Archaeological in Retrospect IV*, pp. 296-307.

Nath, Prataya, 2019, *Climate of Conquest: War Environment and Empire in Mughal North India*, Oxford: Oxford University Press.

Negi, S.S., 1940, *Forest Development in the United Provinces*, Indian Forestry, vol. 66, no. 7, pp. 398-709.

O'Brien, Patrick, ed., 1999, *Oxford Atlas of World History*, Oxford: Oxford University Press.

Pandey, Mithila Sharan, 1963, *The Historical Geographical and Topography of Bihar,* Department of Ancient Indian and Archaeology, Patna: Patna University.

Powell, Baden H., 1868, *Handbook of Economic Products in the Punjab,* vol. I, Roorkee: Thomson Civil Engineering College Press.

Prasad, Archana, 2003, *Against Ecological Romanticism: Verrier Elwin and the Making of an Anti-Modern Tribal Identity,* Oxford: Oxford University Press.

Rangarajan, Mahesh, 1996a, 'Environmental Histories of South Asia: A Review Essay', *Environment and History* 2/2: 129-43.

———, 1996b, *Fencing the Forests: Conservation and Ecological Change in India's Central Provinces, 1860–1914,* Oxford: Oxford University Press.

———, 2013, 'Animals with Rich Histories: The Case of the Lions of the Gir Forest, Gujarat, India', *History and Theory* 52: 109-27.

Rangarajan, Mahesh, ed., 2007, *Environmental Issues in India*, Noida: Pearson.

Rangarajan, Mahesh and G. Shahabuddin, 2006, 'Debate: Displacement and

Relocation from Protected Areas: Towards Biological and Historical Synthesis', Conservation and Society, 4/3:359-78.

Rangarajan, Mahesh and K. Sivaramakrishnan, eds., 2012, *India's Environmental History,* 2 vols., New Delhi: Permanent Black.

———, 2014, *Shifting Ground: People, Animals, and Mobility in India's Environmental History*, Oxford: Oxford University Press.

Ratnagar, Shereen, 1991, 'Pastoralism as an Issue in Historical Research', *Studies in History*, vol. 7, Issue 2, New Delhi: Sage Publications, pp. 181-193.

Ravi, Rajan S., 1988, 'Foresters and the Politics of Colonial Agro-Ecology', *Studies in History*, vol. 14, no. 2.

Raychaudhari, Tapan and Irfan Habib, eds., 1982, *The Cambridge Economic History of India 1200-1750,* vol. I, Cambridge: Cambridge University Press.

Ribbentrop, B., 1900, *Forestry in British India,* Government of India.

Richards, John, 1993, *Mughal Empire*, Cambridge: Cambridge University Press.

———, 2003, *The Unending Frontier: Environmental History in the Early Modern Centuries,* Berkeley: University of California Press.

Richards, John, James R. Hagen and Edward Haynes, 1985, 'Changing Land Use in Bihar, Punjab and Haryana, 1850-1970,' *Modern Asian Studies* 19/3: 699-732.

Rosin, R. Thomas, 1993, *The Tradition of Ground Irrigation in Northwestern India*, New Delhi: Springer.

Saberwal, Vasant and Mahesh Rangarajan, 2005, *Battles over Nature: Science and the Politics of Conservation,* New Delhi: Orient BlackSwan.

Saikia, Arupjyoti, 2011, *Forests and Ecological History of Assam*, Oxford: Oxford University Press.

Sankalia, S.D., 1962, *Indian Archaeology Today*, Bombay: Government of India Press.

Seetal, Jit Singh, 1995, *Shah Husain: Jiwan te Rachna*, Patiala: Punjabi University, Publication Bureau.

Sen, Aloka Parasher, 1998, 'Of Tribes, Hunters and Barbarians: Forest Dwellers in the Mauryan Period', *Studies in History*, vol. 14, Issue 2, pp. 173-191.

Shahabuddin, Ghazala, 2010, *Conservation at the Crossroads: Science, Society and the Future of India's Wildlife,* New Delhi: Permanent Black.

Shahabuddin, Ghazala and Mahesh Rangarajan, eds., 2007, *Making Conservation Work: Securing Biodiversity in this New Century*, New Delhi: Permanent Black.

Sharma, Dashrath, 1966, *Rajasthan through the Ages*, Jaipur: Rajasthan State Archives.

Sharma, Yogesh, 2009, 'The Circuit of Life: Water and Water Reservoirs in Pre-modern India', *Studies in History*, vol. 26, Issue 1, pp. 69-108.

Singh, Chetan, 1995, 'Forests, Pastoralist and Agrarian Society in Mughal India', in David Arnold and Ramachandra Guha, eds., *Nature, Culture, Imperialism* Oxford: Oxford University Press.

Singh, Gurdeep, 1971, *The Indus Valley Culture, Archaeology and Physical Anthology in Oceania*, 6, no. 2, pp. 177-89.

Singh, R.L., ed., 1971, *India: A Regional Geography, National Geography Society of India*, vol. 12, Varanasi: NGSI.

Singh, Satyajit, 2016, *The Local in Governance: Politics, Decentralization, and Environment*, New Delhi: Oxford University Press.

Sivaramakrishnan, K., 2000, 'State Sciences and Development Histories: Encoding Local Forestry Knowledge in Bengal',' in Martin Doornbos, Ashwani Saith and Ben White, eds., *Forests: Nature, People, Power*, Oxford: Blackwell.

———, 2008, 'Science, Environment and Empire History: Comparative Perspectives from Forests in Colonial India', *Environment and History*, 14/1: 41-65.

———, 2011, 'Environment, Law and Democracy in India', *Journal of Asian Studies*, 70/4: 905-28.

———, 2015, 'Ethics of Nature in Indian Environmental History', *Modern Asian Studies* 49/4: 1261-310.

Sivaramakrishnan, K. and Arun Agrawal, eds., 2003, *Regional Modernities: The Cultural Politics of Development in India,* Oxford: Oxford University Press.

Skaria, Ajay, 1998, 'Being Jangal: The Politics of Wildness', *Studies in History*, vol. 14, Issue 2, pp. 193-215.

Skariya, Ajay, 1999, *Hybrid Histories: Forests, Frontiers, and Wildness in Western India*, Oxford: Oxford University Press.

Smith, A.M., 1904, *Sports and Adventure in the India Jungle*, London: Hurst and Blackett.

Sorlin, S. and Paul Warde, 2005, 'The Problem of Environment History: A Reading of the Field and its Purpose', *Environmental History*.

Spate, O.H.K., 1964, *India and Pakistan: A General and Regional Geography*, London: Methun & Co. Ltd.

Stebbing, E.P., 1926, *The Forests of India*, 3 vols., London: John Lane.

Stein, Burton, 1989, *Vijayanagara*, Cambridge: Cambridge University Press.

Sukumar, R., 1994, *Elephant Days and Nights: Ten years with the Indian Elephant*, Oxford: Oxford University Press.

Talbot, Lee Merrian, 1965, 'A Look at Threatened Species', vol. V, *Fauna Preservation Society*, London.

Talib, Gurubachan Singh, 2001, *Sri Guru Granth Sahib*, Eng. tr., Patiala: Punjabi University.

Thapar, Romila, 2001, 'Perceiving the Forest: Early India', *Studies in History* 17/1 n.s.: 1-6.

Thapar, Valmik, ed., 2001, *Saving Wild Tigers, 1900-2000*, New Delhi: Permanent Black.

Tomalin, Emma, 2009, *Biodiversity and Biodiversity: The Limits to Religious Environmentalism,* Farnham: Ashgate.

———, 2014, *Wild Fire: The Splendours of India's Animal Kingdom*, New Delhi: Aleph Book Company.

Trautmann, Thomas, 2015, *Elephants and Kings: An Environmental History,* Chicago: University of Chicago Press.

Trivedi, K.K., 1981, 'Historical Geography of Ganga-Yamuna Doab', Proceedings of Indian History Congress, vol. 42, pp. 303-9.

———, 1993, 'Estimating Forests, Wastes and Field', *c.* 1600, *Studies in History,* no. 14, New Delhi: Sage.

Trivedi, Madhu, 2010, *The Making of the Awadh Culture*, New Delhi: Primus Book.

Tucker, Richard, 2012, *A Forest History of India,* New Delhi: Sage.

Urfi, Abdul Jamil, 2008, Birds of India: A Literary Anthology, ed. Oxford: Oxford University Press.

Wahi, Tripti, 1997, *Water Resources and Agricultural landscape: Pre-colonial Punjab*, New Delhi: Manohar.

Welch, Anthony, 1996, 'Garden that Babur did not Like: Landscape, Water and Architecture for the Sultans of Delhi', in *Mughal Gardens: Sources, Places, Representation and Prospect,* Philadelphia: Wescoat & J. Wolschke.

Whitcombe, Elizabeth, 1972, *Agrarian Conditions in Northern India: The United Provinces under British Rule, 1860-1900*, Berkeley: University of California Press.

William, M., 1994, 'The Relations of Environmental History and Historical Geography', *Journal of Historical Geography,* vol. 20, Issue 3, pp. 3-21.

Wink, Andre, 1997, *Al-Hind: The Making of the Indo-Islamic World*, vol. II, Leiden: E.J. Brill.

Wolpert, Stanley, 1989, *A New History of India*, Oxford: Oxford University Press.

Wroughton, R.C., 1929, 'Bombay Natural History Society's Mammal Survey of India', Report 1-45, *Journal of Bombay Natural History Society*, vol. 21, no.2.

Zaidi, Syed Inayat Ali, ed., 2011, 'Akbar and the Rajput Principalities: Integration into Empire', *Akbar and His Age*, Oxford: Oxford University Press.

Zimmermann, Francis, 1987, *The Jungle and the Aroma of Meats: An Ecological Theme in Hindu Medicine*, Berkeley: University of California Press.

Zvelebil, Kamil, 1975, *Tamil Literature,* Leiden: E.J. Brill.

Index